The
Cosby
Show

The Cosby Show—Top: Sabrina LeBeauf, Tempestt Bledsoe, Malcolm Jamal-Warner (l. to r.); Bottom: Lisa Bonet, Bill Cosby, Keshia Knight Pulliam, Phylicia Rashad (l. to r.)

THE COSBY SHOW

Audiences, Impact, and Implications

LINDA K. FULLER

Contributions to the Study of Popular Culture, Number 32

GREENWOOD PRESS
WESTPORT, CONNECTICUT · LONDON

Library of Congress Cataloging-in-Publication Data

Fuller, Linda K.
    The Cosby show : audiences, impact, and implications / Linda K.
Fuller.
      p. cm.—(Contributions to the study of popular culture,
ISSN 0198-9871 ; no. 32)
    Includes bibliographical references and index.
    ISBN 0-313-26407-4 (alk. paper)
    1. Cosby show (Television program).   2. Cosby, Bill.
3. Television viewers—Attitudes.   4. Television programs—Social
aspects.   I. Title.   II. Series.
PN1992.77.C68F84   1992
791.45'72—dc20   92-884

British Library Cataloguing in Publication Data is available.

Library of Congress Catalog Card Number: 92-884
ISBN: 0-313-26407-4
ISSN: 0198-9871

First published in 1992

Greenwood Press, 88 Post Road West, Westport, CT 06881
An imprint of Greenwood Publishing Group, Inc.

Printed in the United States of America

The paper used in this book complies with the
Permanent Paper Standard issued by the National
Information Standards Organization (Z39.48-1984).

10 9 8 7 6 5 4 3 2 1

Bill Cosby may be considered the quintessential husband/father of the United States, but Eric Fuller fits that description for me and our sons—William, Keith, and Alex. And the wider Fuller family, including parents, brothers, and their families, plus other relatives, make for a life full of love, laughter, and learning. The Huxtables would be our friends.

Contents

Illustrations

Acknowledgments

The number of quality people who participated in this book was remarkable. From the start, Cosby-related personnel were helpful within their legal limitations; several people from NBC, Viacom, and Bill Cosby's own personal staff lent their assistance. In addition, academic colleagues from around the world contributed both ideas and data. Media chiefs are also represented, as are a number of mass communication publications and personnel. I want to express my deepest appreciation to the following in particular:

Ellen M. Almaas, Norsk Rikskringkasting, Oslo, Norway

Joanne Alsano, former press representative to *The Cosby Show*

Macu Alvarez, Bilbao, Spain

Josef Andorfer, Osterreichischer Rundfunk, Vienna, Austria

Erica Weintraub Austin, Edward R. Murrow School of Communication, Washington State University

Cora E. Bain, Women's Affairs Unit, Ministry of Youth, Sports and Community Affairs, Nassau, Bahamas

Dr. Venise T. Berry, department head, Department of Mass Communication, Huston-Tillotson College, Austin, Texas

Brajesh Bhatia, consultant, Asia-Pacific Institute for Broadcasting Development, Kuala Lumpur, Malaysia

Laura Black, assistant to executive producers, Carsey-Werner Company

Barbara Blinn, Williams Middle School, Longmeadow, Massachusetts

Professor Betsy J. Blosser, Department of Communication and Theatre, University of Illinois at Chicago

Carolyne Blount, editor, *about...time magazine*

William R. Boles, Research Department, *Boston Globe*

Elirea Bornman, Human Sciences Research Council, Pretoria, South Africa

David Brokaw, The Brokaw Company (Bill Cosby's publicist)

Norman Brokaw, William Morris Agency (Bill Cosby's agent)

Kathy Butler, research manager, CTV Network, Ltd., Toronto

Pablo Casares, Departamento de Comunicación, Universidad Iberoamericana, Lomas de Santa Fe, Mexico

Jennie Celona, Literature and Languages Department, Worcester State College, Massachusetts

Dr. Dianne Cherry, Department of Communication Studies, University of Massachusetts at Amherst

Lance Davis, Script City, Hollywood, California

Marieke deBruyne, Oudenhoorn, Holland

Sandra Dickerson, Cambridge, Massachusetts

Joanne Dix-Wisdom, director of P/R, WGGB-TV, Springfield, Massachusetts

Dr. Aliza Duby, South African Broadcasting Corporation, Johannesburg, South Africa

Hedvig Ekerwalk, Informationsvetenskap, University of Uppsala, Sweden

A.J. Ellul, chief executive, Malta Broadcasting Authority

Shehina Fazal, Independent Broadcasting Authority (IBA), London

Lynn Fero, Office of Business Affairs, Viacom International

Robert K. Gahan, assistant director general, Radio Telefis Eireann, Dublin, Ireland

Tim Gallimore, Journalism Department, University of Missouri

George Gerbner, Communications Department, Annenberg School for Communications, University of Pennsylvania

Dr. Morton Giersing, chief, Section of Free Flow of Information and Communication Research, Unesco, Paris

Todd Gitlin, Sociology Department, University of California at Berkeley

Anna Giza, Audience Services, Channel 22-TV, Springfield, Massachusetts

Eva Goldwater, Statistical Consulting Center, University of Massachusetts

Dr. Andrew Griffin, Georgia Association of Educators

Dr. Barrie Gunter, head of research, Independent Broadcasting Authority (IBA), London

Paige Harrigan, Sherman Oaks, California

Markku Henriksson, co-director for North American Studies, University of Helsinki, Finland

Anneliese Hodovanec—for German translation

Charly Hulten, Audience and Programme Research, Sveriges Radio AB, Stockholm, Sweden

International Radio and Television Society, Inc., New York

Youichi Ito, Institute for Communications Research, Keio University, Tokyo

Klaus Bruhn Jensen, Center for Mass Communication, University of Copenhagen, Denmark

Arthur Kananack, president, International Theatrical & Video Sales, Viacom Pictures

Miriam K. Keating, Boynton Beach, Florida

D. O. Kellman, director, Bureau of Women's Affairs, Ministry of Employment, Labour Relations and Community Development, St. Michael, West Indies

Dr. Hans Mathias Kepplinger, Institut für Publizistik, Mainz, Germany

Kazuto Kojima, Institute of Journalism and Communication Studies, University of Tokyo

Howard Krosnick, managing director of policy, research, and planning, TV Ontario

Claire LaVigna, Rome, Italy

John A. Loftus, vice president of communications, Nielsen Media Research

Tommy Lott, Philosophy Department, University of Massachusetts, Boston

Marie Louden-Hanes, Bowling Green State University, Bowling Green, Ohio

William R. May, sports writer, Kyoto News Service, Tokyo

Jeanie McDonald, St. Vincent, West Indies

Bishetta Merritt, associate professor, Department of Communications, Howard University

Sergiusz Mikulicz, director, Polskie Radio I Telewizja, Warsaw, Poland

Musa Mohammed, a Nigerian student at the University of Leicester, United Kingdom

Joy Morrison, a South African student at the University of Iowa

Alex Muns, Barcelona, Spain, who lived with our family under the auspices of the Spanish Heritage program

Graham Mytton, head of International Broadcasting and Audience Research, British Broadcasting Corporation, London

Mary Neagoy, former press representative to *The Cosby Show*

Niels-Aage Nielsen, Danmarks Radio, Seboug, Denmark

Rosemary O'Brien, press representative to *The Cosby Show*

Larry Pace, A. O. White, Inc., Springfield, Massachusetts

Kitt Paikera, an Indian student at the Centre for Communication, Culture and Society, Carlton University, Ottawa

Kim Palansky, Media Communications, Nielsen Media Research

George Papamitrou and Andy Haidis—for Greek data

Rev. Msgr. Pierfranco Pastore, Pontificio Consiglio, Delle Comunicazioni Sociali, Città del Vaticano

Julie Phillips, SAH Enterprises—secretary to Bill Cosby

Luc Picot, Baden-Baden, Germany

Professor Dr. Walery Pisarek, director, Osrodek Badan Prasoznawczych, Press Research Centre, Krakow, Poland

Annette Posell, marketing manager, The Caption Center, Boston

James B. Poteat, Television Information Office

Alvin F. Poussaint, M.D.—psychological consultant to *The Cosby Show*

Francisco Prieto, Departamento de Comunicación, Universidad Ibero American, Mexico

R. Reddock, Institute of Social and Economic Research, University of the West Indies, Trinidad

Gloria Rella, former director of public relations, Viacom International

Professor Donald F. Roberts, Institute for Communications Research, Stanford, California

Santiago Cavazos Roel, Monterrey, Mexico, who lived with our family under the auspices of the Experiment in International Living

Ursula Rommerskirchen, vice consul, Generalkonsulat der Bundesrepublik Deutschland

Laura Siegel, Public Relations Department, Viacom International

John Sinclair, senior lecturer in Sociology Cultural Studies Unit, Footscray Institute of Technology, Victoria, Australia

Gail Speer, French Department, Minnechaug Regional High School, Wilbraham, Massachusetts

Tina M. Spiro, Kingston, Jamaica, West Indies

Horst Stipp, director, Social and Development Research, NBC

Dr. Stuart H. Surlin, Department of Communication Studies, University of Windsor, Ontario

Kim Tinsley, director of public affairs, *The Cosby Show*

Oya Tokgoz, Ankara University, Turkey

Keyan Tomaselli, Contemporary Cultural Studies Unit, University of Natal, Durban, South Africa

Lim Heng Tow, head of public relations, Singapore Broadcasting Corporation

Kostas Valetas, program director, Hellenic Radio-TV, Athens, Greece

Dr. D. P. Van Vuuren, South African Broadcasting Corporation, Johannesburg, South Africa

Sal Venturini—for Italian translation

Betsy Vorce, Public Relations, Entertainment Division, Viacom International

Anna Wahlgren, Swedish freelance writer

Tom Wehner, Photo Department, Springfield (Massachusetts) Newspapers

Vera Wells, director of corporate relations and audience services, NBC

Joella West, counsel for the Carsey-Werner Company

Joan Williams, director, Bureau of Women's Affairs, Ministry of Employment, Labour Relations and Community Development, St. Michael, West Indies

Dr. Peter Winterhoff-Spurk, Fachrichtung Psychologie, Universitat de Saarlandes, Saarbrucken, Germany

Haji Ilias Haji Zaidi, head, School of Mass Communication, Institut Teknologi Mara, Selangor, Malaysia

Thanks also go to the many libraries that were helpful to me—notably, the Worcester State Library, Western New England Library, University of Massachusetts Library, Emerson College Library, Springfield (Massachusetts) Public Library, and many others for interlibrary loan resources.

Particular thanks go to Dr. Robert G. Picard, professor of communications at California State University at Fullerton for reading an earlier draft of this manuscript and making important, insightful comments; Professor Muriel G. Cantor of the Department of Sociology at the American University for sharing some of her research on domestic comedies; Bob Galvin, former technical director of *The Cosby Show*, for reading the chapter on production; and David Baker of Yale University, who helped me cut enormous amounts of data for this manuscript into palatable portions. Thanks, of course, also go to my own family and friends for their continuing input into this project.

It is with great warmth and sincerity that I acknowledge how pleasant it has been working with Marilyn Brownstein of Greenwood Press. My original notion was to present the topic of *The Cosby Show* phenomenon in terms of its massive press; it was Marilyn's idea to have me write this book in narrative rather than edited form, and she was absolutely right.

Maureen Melino of Greenwood's Editorial Department has maintained a much-needed persistence, along with a much-appreciated sense of humor, throughout the many details of clearing copy. Lynn Taylor took on the editorship for this manuscript near the end of its tenure and cheerfully helped speed up the process toward publication.

And finally, there are hundreds of people who participated in my survey—nearly two hundred in the United States and more than six hundred worldwide. Many of their extra comments are recorded in these pages. Acknowledgment goes to all people who contributed, directly or indirectly, to *The Cosby Show: Audiences, Impact, and Implications*.

Preface

Instead of using the words "impact" and "implications," the subtitle of this book could just as easily have suggested the images and illusions of *The Cosby Show* in addition to its immense audience. In its chronicling of a television program that has dominated the ratings since its premiere in 1984, this work systematically describes how both the show's star and staff have been instrumental in determining its phenomenal success.

This project was initiated from a marketing perspective as an investigation of how *The Cosby Show* was originally sold to the networks and how it has since become NBC's principal marketing tool. From the start, the working thesis has been that, through both television programming and advertising, Bill Cosby has simultaneously used and been used by the media. For that original study,[1] a content analysis was performed on media coverage of *The Cosby Show* (see Appendix), demonstrating the show's widespread popularity. Nearly every major newspaper and magazine in the United States has featured articles dealing with the show; many magazines have used the famous Cosby face on their covers to sell issues.

Bill Cosby appeared on the cover of the Black magazines *about…time* (Adolph Dupree) and *Ebony* (Lynn Norment) in, respectively, January and June 1985. *Jet,* another Black publication, has frequent articles on Cosby, but its last cover story predates the show: May 31, 1982. *Ladies' Home Journal* (Alex Haley) and *Life* (Brad Darrach) both featured the star for their June 1985 covers. *Newsweek* ran "Cosby: He's No. 1" (Harry F. Waters) on September 2, 1985, whereas *Time* (Richard Zoglin) waited nearly two years to produce "Cosby, Inc." on September 28, 1987; *Time* included a secondary article (Dan Goodgame) crediting Cosby's help, entitled "I Do Believe in Control." Both the *Saturday Evening Post* (Todd Klein) and *US* (James

McBride) interviewed the star. Cosby appeared on the covers of *TV Guide* on October 13–19, 1984, August 17–23, 1985, March 22–28, 1986, July 26–August 1, 1986, September 24–30, 1988, and, in animation form, February 18–24, 1989. *USA Today* ran articles on Cosby on its front page in the December 23, 1986, and August 31, 1987, editions. In addition, *The Cosby Show* has received major, continued attention from prestigious newspapers like the *New York Times*, *Christian Science Monitor*, and *Wall Street Journal*, as well as industry publications like *Broadcasting* and *Variety*.

Andy Rooney, the crusty commentator on CBS's *60 Minutes*, has commented that NBC would like to have dollar bills printed with Cosby's face on them.[2] My own suspicion is that NBC must often be tempted to change its peacock logo to that of *The Cosby Show*.

The phenomenon of *The Cosby Show* as the number 1 rated show since it premiered in the fall 1984 season is compelling, and yet it raises a number of questions:

- How is it that a Black family has become the quintessential role model for families both in the United States and abroad?
- How is it that unprecedented audiences have loyally stayed tuned through these eight seasons every Thursday night?
- How is it that *The Cosby Show* is credited with giving new life to the sitcom genre?
- How is it that one show has been responsible for lifting a network from last place to domination over the ratings?
- How is it that *Cosby* spinoffs, clones, spillovers, and successors have all been successful?
- How is it that syndication for *The Cosby Show* has broken new ground for future bartering?

These six issues are the focus of this book.

I also wanted to know: Who are the more than 60 million people in the United States who have structured their lives around consistent viewership? Furthermore, why has *The Cosby Show* also been ranked first in South Africa and the Middle East, in addition to enjoying great popularity wherever it has aired worldwide? It turns out that the show cuts across boundaries of age, sex, race, religion, occupation, and television viewership.[3]

In order to obtain demographic and psychographic information on that global audience, I constructed a survey instrument (see Appendix 2), which has now been translated into more than half a dozen languages. Networking with communications colleagues around the world has yielded information on *The Cosby Show* from more than 800 survey respondents in twenty-five countries (see Appendix 3). Three target audiences were chosen from the United States: affluent New England sixth graders, Florida retirees, and members of California healthclubs, for a total of 192 survey respondents. In addition, the audience data obtained from Australia to the West Indies are also

reported here. Of particular importance are the various idiosyncratic comments a number of participants added to the survey; these comments are
presented later in this book.

THEORETICAL CONSIDERATIONS

The next step after constructing the survey was to question theoretical
constructs related to the phenomenon of *The Cosby Show*.

I considered a number of prospective approaches to the phenomenon of
The Cosby Show. Todd Gitlin of the University of California at Berkeley began
his study of prime time "(w)ith a question—or rather a curiosity—about how
much a show's commercial success depended on its 'fit' with social trends
abroad in the land" (1985, p. 12). Concerned about hegemonic issues of social
control and power, Gitlin claims: "Therefore television bears special watching.
It needs criticism and understanding which cut beneath annoyance or apol-
ogia. To be seen properly, it has to be seen as the place where force-fields
intersect: economic imperatives, cultural traditions, political impositions"
(1986, p. 4). His economic emphasis, along with that of Muriel G. Cantor,
forms a critical element of this study.

Horace Newcomb, Professor of Radio, Television, and Film at the University
of Texas at Austin, calls for a critique of that medium that so predominates
our lives—or, as he calls it, *TV: The Most Popular Art* (1974)—whose aesthetic
consists of intimacy, continuity, and history. As he contends, because of their
tightly knit structure, situation comedies in particular can often be directed
toward social commentary, and our knowledge of and attitudes toward their
characters go beyond formulaic responses. "Whatever the messages and
meanings of television," claims Newcomb, "we, the viewers may read them
in our own ways, receive them only as raw material for our own uses, bend
them to our purposes, subvert, parody, distort, and otherwise appropriate
them at will" (1986, p. 223). His usage of literary analysis to look at the
messages, myths, and symbols of television content constitutes another valuable part of television research.

John E. O'Connor has posited four approaches to television as "historical
artifact":

1. Television news and documentary as primary evidence for historical events.

2. Television as social and cultural history.

3. The history of television as industry and as art form.

4. Television as interpreter of history (1983, pp. xxii–xxxvi).

Although *The Cosby Show* fits these categories neatly, the show might more
appropriately be labeled as a cultural rather than simply an historical artifact.

Sociologist Herbert Gans, in his examination of "(m)ass media as institutions which deliver symbolic content to an audience," wrote: "there are three major and interrelated areas of study: the institutions themselves, the content, and the audience" (1972, p. 697). The present book seeks, among other things, to incorporate these topics. Furthermore, Jay Blumler (1985, p. 185) has pointed out differences in European and American approaches to communication research. This book pays serious heed to his suggestion that attention be given to media context, and in audience data from countries other than the United States that context is given full attention.

Semiologist Jack Solomon has analyzed the runaway success of *The Cosby Show* as "a representation of our desires for a world that is practically the inverse of the one in which we actually live."[4] Numerous symbols are associated with the show: designer sweaters, paintings by Black artists, the omnipresent sofa (used by the whole family, as opposed to Archie Bunker's armchair that was reserved just for him), the smooth introduction of various celebrities (see Appendix 4), and the whole spaciously furnished brownstone at #10 St. Luke's Place. The conspicuous prosperity of the Huxtable family has not gone unnoticed.

Considering an economic perspective, Mark Crispin Miller of Johns Hopkins University claims that "(l)ike its star, *The Cosby Show* must owe much of its immense success to advertising, for this sitcom is especially well attuned to the commercials, offering a full-scale confirmation of their vision." He adds: "On the face of it, the Huxtables' milieu is as upbeat and well stocked as a window display at Bloomingdale's, or any of those visions of domestic happiness that graced the billboards during the Great Depression" (1986, pp. 207–8).

Marxist interpretations of the show would dwell on its emphasis on materialism, false consciousness, and the role of advertising in creating consumer anxieties. Its goal of demythologizing ideology becomes evident in my discussion of racial considerations of *The Cosby Show*'s ramifications by and for Blacks.

Feminists would zero in on Bill Cosby's patriarchal role as Dr. Huxtable and would question the superwoman ability of his lawyer-wife, as she balances her personal and professional roles. Another perspective that merits consideration is the equality with which the various Cosby children are treated, regardless of skin color variation.

From yet another perspective, John D. H. Downing (1988) of Hunter College has performed a discourse analysis of *The Cosby Show* in terms of its treatment of social class, the family, sexism, racism, and humor. In the tradition of Fiske and Hartley (1978) and Breen and Corcoran (1982), narrative analysis is gaining in popularity as a means of communication research. David Thorburn's *Story Machine* (1990), for example, discusses television as consensus narrative. Examples of the language of *The Cosby Show* are also included in this study.

RITUALISTIC TELEVISION VIEWING

Focusing on the notion of television viewing as myth and ritual, a number of media researchers have become interested in the storytelling functions of television in various cultures. Concerned with what television is saying and how it conveys its messages, Roger Silverstone argues that "(t)elevision, supremely among the other media of mass communication, is coherently, systematically and centrally at work in the articulation of culture and in the mediation of alien bodies of knowledge and experience" (1984, p. 4). Silverstone discussed his theory at the May 1986 meeting of the International Communication Association's annual conference in Chicago. The Round Table Seminar on "Current Research on Television as Myth, Ritual and Storytelling," organized and chaired by Robert A. White of London's Centre for the Study of Communication and Culture and by Stewart Hoover of Temple University, was organized into a book, edited by James W. Carey; see *Media, Myths, and Narratives: Television and the Press* (1988).[5] Inverting politics and culture, it is an important volume for helping to explain ritualistic television viewing of *The Cosby Show*'s loyal audience worldwide.[6]

In his introduction to *Television Mythologies: Stars, Shows & Signs*, Len Masterman credits Roland Barthes's pretelevision *Mythologies*[7] as the pioneering effort in this area of study. "Yet television," Masterson contends, "constantly denying its own mode of production, continually manufacturing for its audiences a seamless, plausible and authentic flow of 'natural' images, easily outdoes all other media in its effortless production of cultural myths, 'realities' which go-without-saying. Uncovering such myths ought to be an important objective for any television criticism" (1984, p. 5).

Television, Michael Marsden would add, "(p)rovides a series of common, shared experiences and images which have become part of the collective, shared traditions of our society" (1980, p. 124).

In addition to the current popularity of Joseph Campbell in this country and Leszek Kołakowski's recent translation from Polish of work on myth, researchers interested in television mythologies include Michael Real (*Mass-Mediated Culture*, 1977; *Supermedia: A Cultural Studies Approach*, 1989), who focuses on the communal celebrations and collective experiences that television provides; Frank McConnell (*Storytelling and Mythmaking Images from Film and Literature*, 1979), who writes: "Stories matter, and matter deeply, because they are the best way to save our lives" (p. 3); Douglas Kellner ("TV, Ideology, and Emancipatory Popular Culture," 1979), who sees television as the dominant producer of cultural symbolism; and William G. Doty (*Mythology: The Study of Myth and Rituals,* 1986), who writes on sociofunctionalism, with myth as "cement" and "charter."

George Gerbner has long been fascinated by the cultivation effects of television's pervasive messages to a heterogeneous audience. Concerned about minority groups having their images formed by the dominant interests of the larger culture, he gives a rationale for cultivation analysis: "The message systems of a culture not only inform but form common images. They not only entertain but create publics. They not only satisfy but shape a range of attitudes, tastes, and preferences. They provide the boundary conditions and overall patterns within which the processes of personal and group-mediated selection, interpretation, and image-formation go on" (1973, p. 567).

Gerbner, in his keynote address at the Conference on Communication in Terrorist Events that took place in March 1988 at Emerson College, entitled "Symbolic Functions of Violence and Terror," said that "Most of what we know, or think we know, we do not personally experience. Perhaps the most distinguishing characteristic of our species is that for all practical purposes we live in a world we erect through the stories we tell." He expands on this storytelling theme in his 1987 article "Telling Stories in the Information Age."

In his co-authorship with Kathleen Connolly of "Television as New Religion," (1978), Gerbner draws on an analogy on the power of television, presenting "a total world of meaning to the state... not unlike that of the Church in an earlier time." That religious, ritualistic theme for television is also echoed in Gregor T. Goethals's *The TV Ritual: Worship at the Video Altar* (1981) and Andrew Greeley's "Today's Morality Play: The Sitcom" (1987).

"To understand the myth life of our television culture," argues Brooklyn College's Hal Himmelstein

we must first consider the construction of the television message and the social, political, and economic nature of the processes of construction as they are reflected in the powerful visual and verbal symbols produced and perpetuated by the "diversified entertainment companies" of advanced capitalism—financial institutions masquerading as culture producers. We must then consider the status of the message receiver—the well-trained viewer—in the process. (1984, p. 2)

These factors are all considered in this study.

Rolling Stone has called *The Cosby Show* "a national drug—everybody takes it once a week and feels better about livin' in the U.S.A."[8] This notion is also worth exploring.

APPROACH OF THIS BOOK

First, let me say a word about terms. Concerned about using nonsexist, nonracist language,[9] I consulted Dr. Alvin F. Poussaint, psychological production consultant to *The Cosby Show*[10]; his choice of the term "Black," capitalized, guided my terminology usage.

Because the phenomenon of *The Cosby Show* is interrelated with so many aspects of the wider popular culture, a systems-theoretical approach has been taken in this book (see Figure 1). Elsewhere it is argued that systems theory

Figure 1
Systems-Theoretical Approach to Researching *The Cosby Show*

THE COSBY SHOW phenomenon
Context
THE COSBY SHOW statistics
Socio-cultural implications   Role within television criticism
  Universality of Bill Cosby and
    the show's appeal
  Transcendancy across demographics   History/background
  Ramifications by and for Blacks   Description
  Effect on sitcom genre   Origins
  Evaluation of this case study   Bill Cosby: persona, parent
                    Theories on show's success

Kudos and criticism
Accolades and accomplishments
Reactions by people and press   Economics of THE COSBY SHOW
                Marketing/media
                Advertising
  Audiences   Ratings
  United States   Promotions
  Worldwide   Syndication

    Production   Politics and legalities
    Cast and crew   Lawsuit over idea for THE COSBY SHOW
    Bill Cosby's role   THE COSBY SHOW and Writers Guild Strike
    Production process   'Cosby' captioning
    Case study   Bill Cosby's personal legal problems
                Legalities of syndication

is a valuable means of taking overviews of various phenomena, especially as they relate to mass communication, in an effort to understand their many configurations and implications.[11]

Chapter 1 examines the background of *The Cosby Show* phenomenon, introducing a number of impressive statistics about the show and then reviewing the literature on television genre studies in general and *Cosby* in particular. It also describes the show's content, philosophy, issues and non-issues, origins, and the role of Bill Cosby as persona and parent. Some theories as to the success of *The Cosby Show* are also included. Chapter 2, on the economics of the show, is the real story: the relationship between its marketing and the media, advertising, promotions, ratings, and syndication. Politics and legalities are dealt with in chapter 3, including who had the original idea for the show, *The Cosby Show* and the Writers Guild strike, the closed-captioning battle, Bill Cosby's own legal problems, and the legalities of the show in syndication. Next, chapter 4 outlines the production of the show: cast and crew are introduced, especially vis-à-vis Cosby's role, the production process is described, and a case study of one episode, "Gone Fishing," is detailed. Chapter 5 talks about global audiences for the show, including the most valuable data of all in terms of idiosyncratic responses to it—those 192 survey respondents from the United States, as well as another 617 from more than twenty-five countries around the world. Their responses, both kudos and criticisms, are elaborated in chapter 6. This section includes comments on escapist/unrealistic complaints about the show, the "Black" issue, Cosby himself, the show's storyline and style, and both favorable and unfavorable critical perspectives. Finally, chapter 7 discusses the sociocultural implications, concentrating on the show's universal appeal and transcendency across audience boundaries. The universality of Bill Cosby, the show's broad appeal, and positive, prosocial ramifications by and for Blacks are included, demonstrating the show's uniqueness. Of particular importance here is the show's effect on the sitcom genre.

Finally, this case study of a media phenomenon is examined. Media scholars continue to call for future research on the acculturation effects of television viewing, particularly with respect to the "active audience" perspective. Media critics continue to call for future research on complete, contextual studies of specific television genres; this work attempts to fill those gaps. As the first scholarship to emerge on a prime time phenomenon, historically, economically, politically-legally, production-wise, audience-wise, critically, and socio-culturally, it aims at being a benchmark study.

The
Cosby
Show

1

Background of *The Cosby Show* Phenomenon

Few shows in the history of television programming have been as universally loved and applauded as *The Cosby Show*, which revived the situation comedy...(and) has been hailed as a breakthrough in the portrayal of black families.

> Jarice Hanson and Alison Alexander,
> *Taking Sides*

The Cosby Show is the biggest thing to happen to TV...it has now reached icon status.

> Mary Neagoy,
> former press representative to *The Cosby Show*

The Cosby Show started off simply enough when it premiered in the fall of 1984: It was a family sitcom, featuring a Black nuclear family. No one—not Bill Cosby; not the producers, Carsey-Werner; not NBC; not the viewing public—could have predicted the record-breaking-ratings hit it would become. With its wide-ranging impact, *The Cosby Show* has become a demarcation point for describing and judging television history.

INTRODUCTION

The Cosby Show can be described simply as the weekly adventures of a closely knit, upper-middle-class family who "just happen" to be Black. It stars Bill Cosby as Cliff Huxtable, an ob/gyn father; Phylicia Rashad as his lawyer-wife Clair; four daughters, Sondra, Denise, Vanessa, and Rudy, played by Sabrina LeBeauf, Lisa Bonet, Tempestt Bledsoe, and Keshia Knight Pulliam, respectively; and a son, Theo, played by Malcolm-Jamal Warner. In addition, there is the extended family of grandparents and, as the show developed, two sons-in-law and grandchildren, including fraternal twins from daughter Sondra and a precocious daughter who came with Denise's previously married husband. The show presents a traditional family with the typical problems of children in a typical age group.

It is particularly intriguing that the trials and tribulations of a Black family should top the ratings charts, drawing one out of every four American homes into its weekly storytelling. Hosts of critics and commentators have attempted to solve the riddle of the widespread fascination with the Huxtable household. Before exploring some of the reasons that have been proposed, and before positing my own theories, it makes sense to focus first on just what the show is. One of the best ways is by example.

"First Day of School": A Typical Episode

Written by John Markus and Elliot Shoenman, this episode provides a good case study for examining some of the characterizations of *The Cosby Show*, for it captures the show's peculiar blending of character and plot. Aired in 1985, it features most of the cast except Sondra, who is away at college.

The first scene takes place in the master bedroom, where a clock shows it to be 6:55 A.M. and both parents are sleeping soundly. Rudy, the youngest child, enters and stands in front of her mother so that she will wake up, but instead it is her father who does:

Cliff: Rudy, you're supposed to knock before you come in here.
Rudy: I didn't want to wake you.

A rule has been broken. It is actually quite an interesting rule and one that inevitably affects every household with children: whether or not children should be allowed free access to their parents' bedroom. It has all sorts of hidden connotations about the parents' privacy, encompassing, among other things, their sexuality. It brings up questions of what the lines of communication between parent and child should be. The door isn't locked, there doesn't appear to be a stance on whether children can or should climb into bed with the parents, and the likely response to a knock is not known. All these thoughts are diffused by Rudy's simple response.

When Clair does open her eyes, she looks at Cliff, kisses him, and delightedly states that since it is the first day of school, they will get the house back. We see them as a distinct twosome and they convince us that these are two people who love each other. Later in the episode Clair announces that after she drops Rudy off at school, she will pick up some fresh pastries and cappucino for their "First Day of School" celebration. Cliff sorrowfully says he can't join Clair later because he has a new patient coming in early that day.

But it turns out that Clair herself has made the appointment under a fictitious name, anticipating their free time together.

The house is in chaos on this first day, with everyone having to get up at the same time, sharing the bathroom, getting breakfast, checking all the clothing and hairstyles, all the while yelling to one another throughout the house. Rudy is excited, Vanessa anxious, Denise groggy, and Theo tired, claiming he needs adjustment time to come off vacation. Cliff gives his definition of a vacation as something earned from a job and declares: "As far as I'm concerned, what you had the last three months was time in between vacations."

One example of humor occurs when Cliff notices that Vanessa's bra strap is showing. They carry on what appears to be a normal conversation, but the real issue is the bra strap with Cliff continually trying to cover it up and Vanessa trying to expose it stylishly under her boat-necked top. The audience gets more caught up in the action than in the dialogue.

Rudy gets complimented on how pretty she looks for the first day of school, and Clair is amazed at how well she wrote her name: "Very good. I was married to your father fifteen years before I could spell Huxtable." It turns out that Rudy also has already made her own lunch. The problem is that she made it—a tunafish sandwich—on the day she got her new lunch box—two weeks ago! Cliff arrives, hears this, and opens the lunch box: "It's bubbling. Did she put seltzer in it?" The audience is roaring, but the parents don't laugh; instead, they explain how tuna sandwiches need to be eaten the same day, help her make another one, and clean out the lunch box.

Rudy also has trouble with her new shoes, which she claims she has no control over; therefore, she "can't help" sliding in the house. Denise arrives for breakfast announcing what a big day this will be for her—not just beginning senior year, but also being without braces for the first time in all her high school years. Vanessa has been in front of the mirror since 5 A.M. Theo is wearing a new sweatshirt cut off at the sleeves, about which Cliff remarks:

You know, son, when we were in the store and you first saw the shirt, you picked it up in your hands, looked at me with those beautiful eyes of yours, and said, "Dad, I gotta have this." It was $30, and I thought, "That's a little expensive for a sweatshirt, but for my son's first day of school nothing's too good." If fashion dictates you make a few alterations to it, fine. However, sometime, and somewhere, you're going to wear those sleeves.

Cliff makes another comment to the kids before they head off for school. They are teasing him about wanting them out, when Clair defends him by saying he's just excited about their resuming their educations. "No, Clair," Cliff deadpans, as only Cosby could carry off the next part: "I want them out. We've put up with them for three months." He then turns to their offspring, as they put on their jackets, "And none of this coming home right after school stuff. This year I want everybody to take on extracurricular activities. And even if you can't find anything after school, wander around the neighborhood, knock on doors, ask people if there's anything you can do for them up until six o'clock. Just sit around their living rooms perhaps. Watch TV with them."

After school, Denise gets picked up by her girlfriends. Before she leaves, Cliff says, "Have a good time." Denise waits for more: "And . . . ? Whenever I go out, you always say, 'Have a good time.' Then you say, 'Where are you going?' I tell you, and then you say, 'Don't do anything stupid.' " Cliff responds with a caring comment about how much maturity and sense of responsibility she has shown lately, then adds: "So I figure wherever you're going and whatever you're doing, you'll be fine." It would be difficult to find a better lesson in supportive parenting.

Later, Theo describes his first day of school as a "nightmare." "Let me guess," teases his father, "You got to school and everybody else had sleeves." No, Theo has the dreaded Mrs. Westlake for math: "She's the worst teacher in the school. All the kids hate her. Anybody's who's ever had her says she's ruined the whole year for them." Why? How? It turns out she loves to call on kids who don't have their hands up, she makes you stay until she's finished saying something even though the bell has rung, she's been known to correct kids' grammar, and she even gave homework on the first day. To each of these accusations Cosby's face shows an incomparable mix of horrified in-credulity and joy.

Vanessa was relieved to have found all her rooms, and all her teachers seemed "pretty smart," but she was worried about her sweater, which she put in her locker and now she has forgotten the combination. Her father asks her why she didn't write down the number for the combination. She would have, she replies, "but the other kids said it wasn't cool."

Rudy's first day of school was more dramatic. Her response to inquiries about the school, the lunch, the teacher, and the kids was simply "Fine." Then, "I don't want to go back. I hate it." A kid named Paul Smith, it turns out, called her a name. The audience holds its collective breath. No, it was not a racial slur but simply a funny pronunciation of her last name—he called her "Rudy Huckleberry." Dr. Huxtable turns what could have been a very harmful situation around:

In every grade there's a namecaller. He spends all day trying to think up names to call people. When it was your turn, he walked up to you and checked you out for material. He looked at your ears and said to himself, they're not big enough to call you "Trophyhead." Then he looked at your feet, your beautiful little feet, and he knew he couldn't call you "The Forklift." Your clothes checked out okay, your hair looked good, and everyone knows how smart you are. So, all that was left was your name. And our name is the kind of name that's easy to make fun of. When I was a kid, they made fun of my name all the time.

Each child, then, has been treated individually, the parents' rapport is established, and the cross between education and humor is well depicted by this single episode.

The universal themes of families and child-raising are the underpinning of most episodes of *The Cosby Show*. The basic message is a familiar one to domestic sitcoms: that together, the family's love for one another can help solve whatever problems might loom. But this particular series has several other unique characterizations.

First and foremost, the show centers on Bill Cosby. The capers presented on the show come from Bill Cosby's own experiences as a father, just as his *Fat Albert* series was an extension of his childhood. One of the classic lines from the show is symbolic in many ways: "I am your father . . . I brought you into this world and I'll take you out." Plotted on an axis, Bill Cosby's role on *The Cosby Show* is not only located smack in the center, but it also permeates throughout. As Cantor has pointed out about Cosby, "Not only is the father in charge, but most episodes revolve around him and his escapades and the children, although talented and entertaining, are secondary to him" (1991, p. 213).

Each season has featured different musical introductions, but they all begin by orienting the viewer to the star. Cosby usually appears first and last in these opening numbers, dancing with each individual cast member, and makes it very clear who is at the center of it all. Credits of his contributions to each episode are flashed on the screen; they might include any of these combinations: "Story idea: Bill Cosby," "Created by Ed. Weinberger, Michael Leeson, and William H. Cosby, Jr." "Bill Cosby, (Co)-Producer," or perhaps "Bill Cosby: (Co)-Director," "Theme music by Stu Gardner and Bill Cosby," and so forth. "Dr. William H. Cosby, Jr., Ed.D.," in all its redundancy, inevitably appears at the end.

As will be noted in more detail in chapter 4, most of the scripts not only originate with Cosby's own ideas, but they contain plot lines and devices that showcase the star's talents. The central father figure has its early roots in sitcoms like *Life of Riley, Make Room for Daddy, The Honeymooners, Father Knows Best,* and *Ozzie and Harriet*. Just as David Barker (1985) makes the case for how members of Archie Bunker's family were defined not necessarily by their own individuality and idiosyncrasies but by their relationship with the father figure, so, too, can it be argued about the various characters on *The Cosby Show*. Although some critics might object to Cosby's control over the show, others applaud it as the first time all the details lay in a Black person's hands. It is no accident, you can be sure, that the show is titled *The Cosby Show*, and not *The Huxtables*.

The Huxtables represent a very different kind of sitcom family. In some ways they are reminiscent of earlier sitcom families on "warmedies" like the Cleavers (of *Leave It to Beaver*), the Andersons (of *Father Knows Best*), the

Stones (of *The Donna Reed Show*), or the Douglas family (of *My Three Sons*)—
focusing on typical adolescent concerns like dating, schoolwork, and general
coping. Yet, unlike many other later sitcom families, the Huxtables don't
shout insults to one another or to their neighbors or don't shout across the
yard; in fact, they don't shout at all. Compromises and family teamwork are
in order. For example, in one episode Clair has a day off with her sister and
some other women friends, while Cliff takes Rudy and her playmates out to
a riotous lunch. Still, individuality is sacrosanct, with another episode cen-
tering around seeking privacy in the busy household.

Although Cosby is clearly the head of the household—a particularly poignant role for a contemporary Black family—stress is given to equality of the
sexes. Cliff gets his due when he botches the job of being sent out in the
rain to buy those last-minute extras for the Thanksgiving dinner. Yet, he's
quite comfortable in the kitchen, always brewing up some specialty or other
of his—again, quite in contrast to the many commercial advertisements that
show most men as wimps in that department, as if cooking should be exclusively a woman's province. Cliff is on the hot seat another time at Clair's
literature-discussion group, where he allows himself to confess ignorance of
their topics. Cosby as Cliff is today's archetypical "sensitive guy." Another
touch of the times is the fact that the children's opinions in this sitcom family,
like their parents', are all given their due.

The Cosby Show has become well engrained in our popular culture as
synonymous with the ideal family, the one we all wish we were part of. It
even appeared, for example, in this sentence from John Updike's 1990 "Rabbit
at Rest":

On the *Cosby Show* rerun, the Huxtables are having one of those child-rearing crises
bound to dissolve like a lump of sugar in their warm good humor, their mutual
lovingness: Vanessa and her friends get all excited about entering a local dance contest,
with lip synching, and get instruction from an old black nightclub pianist and when
the time comes to demonstrate for their parents in their living room they bump and
grind with a sexuality so startling and premature that Mrs. Huxtable, Clair, in real life
the terrific Phylicia Rashad, married to the frog-eyed black sports commentator, re-
stores decency, stopping the record and sending the girls back upstairs, yet with that
smile of hers, that wide white slightly lippy black woman's smile, implying that in-
decency is all right, in its place, its wise time, as in one of those mutually ogling
Huxtable snuggles that end many a *Cosby Show*. (pp. 336–37)

Focus is on the family—a particularly tight one, made deliberately multigenerational. Why deliberately include an extended family? For one thing, of
course, it helps advance the plot(s); more importantly, however, it advances
the wide-ranging demographics of the show, which is television programming's greatest goal. It is no accident that Cliff's parents appear so frequently;
Clair's are there less often but fairly regularly. As will be seen in chapter 5,
a substantial number of senior citizens are among the loyal viewers. Many

children's favorite episode, it is noted, was the grandparents' forty-ninth anniversary celebration. (The producers took care to have a fiftieth!) For the
teenage-viewing population, there are plenty of fashionable antics, clothing,
and language. Cliff and Clair themselves are depicted as a modern, if middle-
aged, couple: stylish and sharp, even sexy.

Nor is it an accident that at the other end of the spectrum new, younger
characters are being introduced. Sondra's twins, symbolically named Winnie
and Nelson (for the Mandelas), were worth a rare two episodes for their
labor and delivery, and they continue to delight audiences. Also, as Rudy
grew from age five in the first season to become an adolescent, her previous
role has been taken over by Denise's stepdaughter, Olivia; it helped—the
September 21, 1989, show introducing Olivia had a 26.1 rating and a 44 share.
(For a discussion of ratings, see Chapter 2.)

Everywhere on the show, we see material symbols of a family that is living
the American dream. The Huxtables appear to have moved easily into an
upper-middle-class status. Not only are both parents professionals, but also
their forebears appear to have been monied. Tidbits from family stories and
old friends' reminiscences let us know that this Black family has been up-
wardly mobile for a long time. They aren't "nouveau" but are cultured: they
appreciate the theater, enjoy a range of musical types, and take trips abroad.

The Cosby Show also has moments of multiracialism/multiethnicism, even
though Blacks make up the major cast ensemble. Both the parents and the
children typically have friends who are Caucasian, Hispanic, and even Asian;
one episode featured the fact that Clair can speak Portuguese. At one point
Olivia, curious about Santa Claus, asks, "Is he white, Black, Chinese, what?"
Deeper racial issues, however, like interracial dating, housing discrimination,
or ethnic media stereotyping, remained taboo throughout the show's eight-
year run.

One of the most obvious differences between this sitcom family and its
predecessors has to do with the subject of race. Yet *The Cosby Show* has
deliberately chosen not to use race as a subject. Philosophically, Cosby prefers
a colorblind approach to comedy: "I don't think you can bring the races
together by joking about the differences between them. I'd rather talk about
the similarities, about what's universal in their experiences."[1] Refusing to
stereotype is "the guiding principle of *The Cosby Show*—to show a family
that doesn't dwell on its own particular 'club.' "[2] Ralph Ellison, author of the
classic *Invisible Man,* says the show " 'cuts across race and class' in its comic
appeal and does the country a favor by showing that blacks can be cultured
and well-off."[3] Some critics have claimed that with *The Cosby Show*, Blacks
get their own *Father Knows Best,* more than twenty years after the prototype
was last aired.[4]

Running a tightrope between critics who dismiss the show as *Leave it to
Beaver* in blackface and those who decry it for not being "Black enough,"
Cosby, in an interview with *Ebony* magazine, responded: "I'm here because

I am a human being and I want to have fun. I want to show the happiness within our people. I want to show that we have the same kinds of wants and needs as other American families. I'm going to take this show and make it last as long as I can to show Black people that they have something to be proud of" (Norment, 1985, p. 34). A *New York Times* article entitled "Cosby Puts His Stamp on a TV Hit" states: "Indeed, part of Mr. Cosby's goal is to transcend questions of race, to concentrate on family life per se" (Smith, 1985, p. B27). Cosby's overriding sense is that white Americans are largely ignorant about Black people, and he wants to educate them.

When discussing *The Cosby Show,* we are tempted to think back to another media phenomenon a half-century ago that also happened to feature a Black family. Yet, differences between this television program and radio's *Amos 'n' Andy* are noticeably marked by means of positive versus negative images and approaches.[5]

A program with its roots reaching back to the blackface minstrel days of the late nineteenth century, *Amos 'n' Andy* made its debut on NBC radio on August 19, 1929. Sponsored by Pepsodent toothpaste, the show apparently enjoyed phenomenal popularity with both white and Black listeners who could identify with its characters and their money-hungry schemes during the Depression era. Although some of the statistics from that era are rather unreliable, it is thought that the 7:00–7:15 P.M. nightly program drew audiences of more than 40 million listeners at its peak. Anecdotal evidence of its popularity abounds. For more than a quarter century, this white rendition of Black folk humor remained a national institution—until the national temperament changed after World War II. With the advent of television and a growing Black protest against *Amos 'n' Andy's* negative stereotyping, the show enjoyed only a brief transition to television, from 1951 to 1953.

Although the extent of the similarities and differences between *Amos 'n' Andy* and *The Cosby Show* is beyond the scope of this book, it is a comparison that would be worth exploring, especially in terms of how far Black entertainers have come in our society, both professionally and in terms of audience appreciation. The contrast can also provide an instructive lesson in the roles of historical and societal context on broadcast programming's ratings responsiveness.

The educational mission is yet another aspect of the underlying philosophy of *The Cosby Show*. The idea is to teach through humor. When he was awarded an honorary degree of fine arts from the University of Massachusetts in 1986, the same institution from which he received his doctorate of education (Ed.D.) ten years earlier, Bill Cosby's acceptance speech mentioned how everything he does has to do with some form of educating people about their options. The title of his dissertation is "An Integration of the Visual Media Via 'Fat Albert and the Cosby Kids' into the Elementary School Curriculum as a Teaching Aid and Vehicle to Achieve Increased Learning"; it is reported on in

Daniel Okrent's (1987) discussion of Cosby's "Early Years." "In a word, he teaches—and he teaches with magical ingenuity," writes Brad Darrach.

He teaches little children how to tie their shoes, young boys how to pole-vault, total strangers how to dig jazz. And as Dr. Cliff Huxtable, he is teaching America that all people really are created equal, that humanity is truly more than skin-deep, that it is time to abandon the cult of me and get back to the world of us, that the dream of Martin Luther King actually can come true. (1985, p. 42)

A good example is the story of Malcolm-Jamal Warner's being cast in the part of son Theo. During the interview "young Warner, himself a child of the middle class, automatically adopted the jive-talking manner that he assumed TV producers wanted from black actors trying out for sitcoms."[6] Cosby asked him if he spoke that way to his parents in real life, to which Warner responded negatively—that, in fact, his parents would kill him if he did. Cosby instructed him to use that comment as his guide.

Evidence of the emphasis on education in the Huxtable household abounds. Both parents are professionals, and although they are rarely seen working or even discussing their work, their status as such is frequently mentioned. They discuss their former college experiences and their college friends, and the subject of college for the Huxtable children is another common topic. Homework assignments and teachers have made up entire episodes, such as when Theo and Cockroach were studying *Macbeth* or when Sonia Braga, the "witch lady"/math teacher, came to dinner.

Beyond school education, there is also evidence of Cosby's humorous attempts to discuss some of "life's lessons." One storyline focused on the problems of getting lost/losing someone in a crowd; another centered on what Vanessa and her friends learned about drinking from playing the "Alphabet Game"; and yet another focused on when Vanessa and her friends went to Baltimore after they had told their parents they would be spending the night at a local friend's house—which was then in the news, as the friend's apartment block had a fire.

Transcending race and educational notions on *The Cosby Show* is the universal theme of parenting. Earl Pomerantz, co-executive producer and head writer, explains that the point of the show is to show a real family, in a real way: "We think there's humor in just showing what parents go through with children, and what children go through with parents."[7] At a benefit for the National Council of Negro Women in Washington, D.C., Cosby himself pointed out that "(p)eople are starved to see the love of husband and wife. They're starved to see genuine respect children have for their parents and parents for their children."[8]

Writing "For Parents Particularly," educator Shirley J. O'Brien cites how numerous family life educators and counselors use various episodes from

The Cosby Show as problem-solving training for both themselves and others. Here is a brief summary of some of the strong family guidelines that she sees consistently at work in the program:

1. Self-esteem building—The Huxtable children are supported in their problems and triumphs, and when the time comes to learn responsibility, everyone in the family becomes part of the teaching.

2. Independence—Expectations are neither too high and thus unattainable, nor too low and thus limiting.

3. Trust—The Huxtables develop trust in their children and show them, in turn, how to trust them.

4. Values—The show emphasizes support for family members, respect for grandparents, responsibility for actions, consideration of others' feelings, and honesty in all endeavors.

5. Humor—The ability to laugh at oneself is seen as an important child-rearing guideline. (1989, p. 308)

The truth of some of these observations is evident in the Huxtable children's developing characters. C. J. Blair has used *The Cosby Show* as a vehicle for teaching students to write descriptions of the various cast members and episodes. Over the years, as the characters have matured, some changes have occurred in them both physically and mentally:

Rudy has developed from being a totally dependent pre-schooler to a more self-asserting grade-schooler. Vanessa has changed from an annoying, quirky pre-teen to a charming, generally thoughtful teenager. Theo has shifted from being boyishly irresponsible to being more self-reliant. Denise has grown from an overtly funky high schooler to a busy, self-directed college freshman. Saundra (*sic*), who appeared very seldom originally, has matured from a predictably moody college student to a more resilient adult. Clair remains a staunch, beguiling feminist; Cliff just grows older. (1988, p. 61)

The Cosby Show makes an effort to monitor the children's growth. Donald Bogle, considered one of the country's leading experts on Blacks in American popular culture, cites examples of the touching delicacy with which Cliff treated his oldest daughter, Sondra, on her return home for the Thanksgiving holidays from Princeton, who is in the midst of her passage to adulthood. There is also the incident when Theo decides to get his ear pierced to please a girl—just as Cosby himself had once conked his hair to woo Clair, and his father in turn had once tattooed himself to impress Cosby's mother:

Each Huxtable male is embarrassed by his exploits in the name of love. And each sees that time alters a lover's style but not his great desire to impress or please, even in the corniest way, a loved one. The episode ended with the three Huxtable males sitting together on the sofa, eyeing one another furtively, then affectionately wrapping their arms around each other. What appeared perhaps to be a tame episode really was something quite new to TV: a rare glimpse of black fathers and sons relating with warmth and regard for one another. (1988, pp. 263–64)

Family rules are both implicit and explicit. We see Rudy get into a terribly messy situation when she uses the new electronic juicer without permission; dicta about how old you have to be wear makeup, go out on dates, or change your curfew are very clear. Parental consent is both sought and freely given— whether it be to attend a class field trip, take flying lessons, learn what to wear, or be able to deal with a current flame.

Bill Cosby, author of *Fatherhood*, explained in an interview with fellow comedian Milton Berle: "My show came at a time when the kids on sitcoms— or what was left of the sitcoms—seemed to be running their parents. When my show came on, the parents took over. The Huxtables began parenting, sometimes giving answers to questions that many parents didn't have answers to" (1987, p. 76). The psychologist Dr. Joyce Brothers gives high marks to Clair and Cliff Huxtable for their teaching the "fine art of effective discipline. The rules in this family have been carefully explained, so the youngsters know exactly what's expected of them... the Huxtables set rules, explain them, and enforce them—usually with humor" (1989, p. 24).

Humor is a hallmark of *The Cosby Show*. Using Elihu Katz's (1977) advice "to take entertainment seriously," it behooves us to consider the effects of the program's very funny overlay.[9] Bill Cosby is primarily a comic. Michael Real labels him a comic genius: "His nonverbal skills are marvelous. The bell rings, he lifts his eyes, and he does a very subtle dance move across the room to 'charmingly' open the door. Nothing has been said, but the live audience responds with genuine laughter. As Cosby does it, it is funny!" (1989, pp. 118– 19). Unlike most other contemporary comedians, Cosby deliberately goes for the laugh based on our common experience—the rigors of dieting, the home-owner as plumber, the impractical gifts of Father's Day, getting the flu, and so on. We laugh because we've been there. We laugh, too, at Cosby's won-derfully rubber face, which seemingly can move around in all directions. It is no accident that we laugh: between the best creative writers, the best classically conceived schemes, and the best comedic actor(s), how can we resist?

The Huxtables delight in playing jokes on one another. These escapades can range from using funny little purchased practical jokes to concocting elaborate schemes for a surprise party, or to deliberately setting someone up. Then, too, there's another kind of humor that underlies narrative, such as when Cliff tries to steal a portion of someone else's dessert while their backs are turned. Although some people will argue that there is a difference between Black humor and white humor, the former being thought as more attitudinal than strictly verbal, humor in this series crosses racial boundaries; it is universal.

Humorous issues and topics on the show focus on events that occur in everyone's household, regardless of complexion. Instead of going for the "big gag," the show prefers the "series of 'small moments' in the characters' lives, seemingly 'little' events that alter their consciousness" (Bogle, 1988, p. 262). Typical episodes might focus on roughhousing, a boy's first shave, using the family car, boyfriends and girlfriends, grades, Theo getting his ear pierced, snakes, holidays, eating and dieting, homework, a slumber party, report cards, curfews, and other everyday trivialities. What makes the show different is that humor and lessons in caring are injected into the story.

Eisenach claims that the show is based on four equal operating principles.

1. First, the show looks at problems from a fresh perspective. Cosby's loose style inspires a refreshing break from crusted formulas in scripting.

2. Second, the family faces their various situations in a loving and supportive fashion. Audiences especially react to the playful affection between the parents, and that love is extended to the children by means of letting them be themselves. The "slice of life" approach is used—a goldfish dying, a son's first shave, a fight over a hairbrush, a pimple.

3. That real-life approach is the third underlying principle of the show. It simply must be real and honest—reality is never sacrificed for a joke. Cosby's philosophy: "In true situation comedy, you can put the characters in a funny situation and let the humor evolve naturally."

4. And lastly, comedy must be funny! "If it's comedy," says co-executive producer/ head writer of *The Cosby Show* John Markus, "it's funny and real, human, intelligent and compassionate." Producer/writer Carmen Finestra adds, "The people who are watching us all have interesting families of their own and are quite smart enough to learn *with* us, not from us." (1986, pp. 10–11)

Some atypical episodes on *The Cosby Show* also merit some discussion here. When Theo has a brush with the law, the parents openly turn their anger on one another and later discuss their multiple feelings about all that occurred. When a marijuana joint is found among his belongings, an important parental exercise in listening is enacted. When Rudy writes a story about "The Nasty People vs. the Happy People," the whole family gets in the act of performing it. When Cliff eats a huge late-night sausage sandwich, he is visited by the Muppets in a hilarious dream.

The episode featuring the funeral for Rudy's goldfish is a classic, standing out in television history as one of the few times that death is dealt with.

As part of the program's intent to educate and introduce viewers to an appreciation of Blacks and their culture, the Huxtable brownstone not only features paintings by Black artists, but it has also become a "celebrity show-case" for a number of well-known Black personalities, among others.

Typically, television programs use celebrities to boost their ratings. That incentive has not been necessary on *The Cosby Show*, for it has always been consistently popular. It is a testament to good scriptwriting that so many Black musical personalities including Stevie Wonder, Lena Horne, Max Roach, Dizzy Gillespie, Sammy Davis, Jr., B. B. King, and Ray Charles have been easily incorporated into various shows. Nor does it discriminate against white celebrities: singers Placido Domingo and Tony Orlando fit in just as easily, as do any number of actors and actresses. The episode with Danny Kaye as a dentist, for example, was a classic; he showed Rudy's friend how to overcome his fears, and he made going to the dentist fun. Armand Hammer appeared as himself on yet another program dealing with overcoming fears. In this episode, when Theo has to come to terms with visiting a friend who has cancer, the approach is more instructive in tone, but just the right amount of humor is inserted to make it palatable.

As a means of showcasing Cosby's interest in sports and fitness, a number of athletes have also appeared on the show. One whole episode centered on former professional basketball players Dave DeBusschere, Senator Bill Bradley, Walt Hazzard, and Wali Jones, who were cast in competition against a women's team headed by Nancy Lieberman. Josh Culbreath, a 1956 Olympic medalist, is featured in another episode.

Robin Givens, Robert Culp, Ann Reinking, Rita Moreno, Sonia Braga, Sheldon Leonard, Meg Foster, Vanessa Williams, Wallace Shawn, and even the Muppets have been among the guest celebrities. For a complete list, see Appendix 4.

Bill Cosby: Persona and Parent

> As a complex, multifaceted phenomenon with social, textual, and institutional dimensions, stardom occupies a central position in all of America's information and entertainment industries.
>
> Jimmie L. Reeves, 1988, p. 148

It is a well-known fact that "Bill Cosby is one of today's most popular entertainment personalities. His reputation as a comedian and actor and his status as a family man and father figure to fans of all ages attest to the remarkable career of a remarkable man" (Kettelkamp, 1987, p. 1). Cosby's "genius at tapping the popular sensibility" places him, according to Michael Real (1989, p. 106), "in the tradition of Charlie Chaplin, Walt Disney, Lucille Ball, Steven Spielberg, Monty Python, and precious few others. As both performer and producer, [he has] achieved the stature of an institution." His humor and "magical sense of the ridiculous" (Griffin and Hill, 1986, p. 97) have long appealed to people of all ages, all ethnicities. Bill Cosby is a star.

Most news sources report that Cosby earns over $95 million a year. This makes him the world's third highest paid entertainer (after Michael Jackson and Steven Spielberg). From *The Cosby Show* alone, he reportedly earns $250,000 per episode, or just about $8,000 per minute, $7 million annually; estimates are that by 1992 he will have earned at least $180 million from its syndication.

Bill Cosby's historic accomplishments both within and outside the entertainment field are most impressive:

- He was the first Black to guest host Johnny Carson's *Tonight* show regularly.

- He was the first Black to co-star on a regular weekly television series—with Robert Culp in *I Spy* (1965–1968). An early biographer wrote that Cosby was particularly excited about "the opportunity to pioneer a major breakthrough for Negroes in television. Another thing that appealed to him was the fact that Alexander Scott [Cosby's role in *I Spy*] was definitely 'not a Tonto,' not an obedient man-of-one-syllable serving his master" (Cohen, 1972, p. 76). J. Fred MacDonald, author of *Black and White TV*, has assessed Cosby's role on *I Spy*: "Cosby proved uniquely qualified for the part. His talent for subtle comedy was matched by a dramatic skill which allowed him to range with apparent ease between emotions of patriotism and self-doubt, romance and intrigue" (1983, p. 110). The role has been billed as a Jackie Robinson-type breakthrough.

- He was the first Black to become an on-camera spokesperson for Fortune 500 corporations—General Foods (Jell-o), Ford Motor Company, and Coca-Cola, and later also Texas Instruments, Kodak, and E. F. Hutton.

Recently, Cosby was also voted "most believable" celebrity endorser in a survey by Video Storyboard Tests, Inc. One of its respondents added, "Bill Cosby really knows how to sell a product. I'd buy mud if he advertised it."[10]

Cosby has also been an extremely successful author, producing four best-sellers:

1. *Fatherhood* (Dolphin/Doubleday, 1986). It sold 2.6 million hardcover copies and 2.5 million trade paperbacks and edged past *Iacocca* to set a modern-day record. *Fatherhood* is the fastest-selling hardcover book ever documented, staying on the *New York Times* best-seller list for fifty-five weeks. Serial rights went to *Good Housekeeping* and the *National Enquirer*, and paperback rights alone sold for $1.6 million.

   As documented by Gayle Feldman, *Fatherhood* was a book for the times. People at Doubleday wanted a timely celebrity book, and "attention was directed to Bill Cosby, whose television show, offering a Reagan-era vision of unbridled optimism and traditional family values, was beaming its way into homes all across America" (1990, p. 11). Quite obviously, the match worked. Doubleday made about $15 million on sales of the book, and Cosby about $4 million. Cosby's live concert album, "Those of You With or Without Children," which contained several routines from the parenting book, coincided with the book's release.

2. *Time Flies* (Doubleday, 1987). This work, based on the notion that Cosby was turning fifty years old, had a record-breaking first printing of 1.75 million copies and was the number 1 nonfiction best-seller of the year. Although sales were far

down from the previous book, the author was able to secure an incredible advance of $3 million.

3. *Love and Marriage* (Doubleday, 1989). This celebration of Cosby's twenty-fifth anniversary came with a $3.5 million advance. Although not listed among the fifty best-selling books of the 1980s, like Cosby's previous two, this book also commanded space for over twenty weeks on the best-seller list.

4. *Childhood* (G. P. Putnam's Sons, 1991). The author did a major media blitz for this book, giving an extra push to *The Cosby Show* at every opportunity. For example, on NBC's *Today Show* Cosby talked about its right timing, and on National Public Radio's "Fresh Air" program he told interviewer Terry Gross that his foremost concern was not the color issue but getting control of the family back in the hands of parents.

USA Today has billed Cosby as "Father of our nation, every Thursday night . . . the USA's ideal dad" (Britt-Gibson, 1986, p. D1). A book reviewer for the *Christian Science Monitor* starts his review of *Time Flies* with this appropriate comment: "If you don't know this by now, pay attention: In America today when things happen to Bill Cosby, everybody doubles over" (Danziger, 1986, p. 18).

In "real life," Cosby has been married to Camille Cosby since 1964, a woman who has earned great respect in her own right. Apparently, she pushed her husband to portray an educated, upper-class character on *The Cosby Show*. And so Dr. Cliff Huxtable, obstetrician/gynecologist, was created. Cosby adds his claim: "I wanted to be able to talk to women who were about to give birth and make them feel comfortable. I also wanted to talk to their husbands and put a few messages out every now and then."

Cosby is a father to four daughters (Erika, born in 1965, Erinn in 1966, Ensa in 1973, and Evin in 1976) and one son (Ennis, born in 1969). Especially since his book *Fatherhood* came out in 1986, "Cosby the father is Everyman— a cross between the old-fashioned patriarch and a modern liberated parent" (McGuigan, 1986, p. 70). Even athlete-turned-sportscaster Ahmad Rashad (1988) tells of wanting and even needing his friend Bill's approval before marrying the show's co-star, Phylicia Ayers-Allen.

In an article on the Black presence on television, television critic John J. O'Connor assesses it as being "less separate, more equal." In this regard Bill Cosby's role in the phenomenon is credited:

In addition to being an employer of black performing talent, Mr. Cosby oversees a bustling environment for the development of black writers, producers, and directors. The subsidiary ripple effects are widespread. Mr. Cosby can personally persuade NBC to carry a special prime-time tribute to the late modern-dance choreographer Alvin Ailey. Keshia Knight Pulliam, who portrays the youngest Huxtable daughter, gets the leading roles in recent television remakes of "Pollyanna" and "A Connecticut Yankee in King Arthur's Court." The Cosby influence extends far beyond Cliff Huxtable's living room. (1990, p. 35)

The wide popularity of *The Cosby Show* might be symptomatic of a world-wide concern about the status of family life. Television-wise, Americans simply appear to be tired of domineering and/or out-of-it fathers, and Cosby allows "a return to patriarchal dignity" (Rapping, 1987, p. 53). Mark Crispin Miller describes Cosby as "today's quintessential TV Dad . . . the cuddliest and most beloved of TV Dads: Bill Cosby, who, as Dr. Heathcliff Huxtable, lives in perfect peace, and in a perfect brownstone, with his big happy family, and never has to raise his hand or fist, but retains the absolute devotion of his wife and kids just by making lots of goofy faces." (1986, pp. 207–8).

Cosby's wide appeal is undisputed. In Roper polls he has placed well ahead of Ronald Reagan, Pope John Paul II, Jacques Cousteau, Lee Iacocca, Billy Graham, and many others as the man Americans most admire. He continues to top the TVQ Index, an annual survey of performer popularity. And according to Roz Starr, who operates a New York City celebrity service, Cosby receives more calls from agents, producers, directors, ad agencies, and fellow stars than any other celebrity. Celebrity testimonials uniformly praise him lavishly. For example:

Joan Collins: He's the kind of father/husband/uncle we would all like to have. His natural humor and dignity, his attitude toward his family, and people in general, are what make him so attractive.

Jane Seymour: He's just unbelievably talented and real and funny and warm.

Shari Belafonte-Harper: He's got that humorous, warm, huggable, teddy-bear look. Yet, I know him as the intellectual that he is. (Warren, 1986, p. 6)

Alex Karras, writing on "The Real Men on TV—and the Wimps" in *TV Guide*, puts Cosby in the category of "real men," adding: "Cosby's show reflects the man, too. I've known Bill a long time. He's a believer in principle, in morality, in equal rights. Why do kids like him so much? Because he doesn't talk down to them. He talks *with* them—on equal terms. He's secure enough, strong enough, to do that" (1985, p. 6).

What are Cosby's personal credos? For one thing, there's his Uncle Jack Theory:

Well, I had an uncle Jack who owned a bicycle shop. The man knew that I loved bikes, and I'd go down to his shop on North Broad Street in Philadelphia and just salivate at the sight of all those bicycles. I was 12 years old and my uncle Jack knew how much I wanted a bike, but he'd never given me one. He let me ride bikes inside the shop, and one day I ran into his glass showcase and cracked it. Uncle Jack said to me, "Bill, I was going to give you a bike, but since you just broke my showcase, forget about it."

Well, at the age of 12, I just said to myself, "Uncle Jack wasn't going to give me a bike anyway." That was a valuable lesson to learn. (Linderman, 1985, p. 80)

Using life's lessons to build character is kept under control by Bill Cosby, a man who admittedly likes being in charge, sometimes to the point of perfectionism. That sense of control is manifest in his regular athletic regimes, his lifelong abstention from drugs and alcohol, his financial matters, and in *The Cosby Show*, which he sees as ultimately his: "I'm responsible for making it work. If I have to rewrite, redo it to make it work for me, then I do it" (Goodgame, 1987, pp. 63–64).

Theories on the Success of *The Cosby Show*

Why has *The Cosby Show* been so successful? A number of different theories have been posited. "The appeal of the program derives in large part from the strong baby-boomer orientation of the scripts," writes a media critic in *National Review* (Teachout, 1986, p. 59). Melbourne S. Cummings, a professor from Howard University, goes further, characterizing the show as the ultimate Black family television production to date, with

all the elements necessary for a successful production. It has excellent script writers, high priced and respected sponsors, a superb production crew—several members of which are black, seasoned directors, and a well educated, highly trained, experienced, attractive, "all-American" black cast, hand-picked by the star of the show, Bill Cosby. (1988, p. 82)

Tom Werner, executive producer of the show, thinks that "(p)eople respond to the love the Huxtables feel for each other. It doesn't feel artificial. They say they wish they were part of that family."[11] Former NBC Entertainment president, now chairman of Paramount Pictures, Brandon Tartikoff adds, "Bill Cosby makes us see the humor, joy and beauty of our everyday existence."[12]

"In 22 minutes of weekly magic, the Huxtables, and the universal ripples of recognition they've spread, have lifted Cos into that special realm where a face on a screen becomes part of our family—perhaps even, as he eerily seems at times, its most privy insider. It's as if America has fallen in love with someone who's been wiretapping its homes," wrote *Newsweek* media critic Harry F. Waters (1985, p. 52). In response, the magazine received a number of letters talking about the therapeutic quality of the show.

Attempting to explain why viewers are so attached to fantasy families like the Huxtables, Delia Ephron calls Cosby and his wife "perfect parent prototypes," and then explains the general attachment to them: "Wishful thinking, of course. But, also, there is something so comforting about a family in which the parents are always wise and the children only adorably bad. While we watch them, we feel secure" (1988, p. 10).

Adolph Dupree surmises that "(p)erhaps *The Cosby Show* works because it transcends the black category. The emphasis is more on family situations than blackness but the physical presence of the performers and the familiar family episodes are natural indicators of ethnic identity" (1985, p. 9). Picking up on part of that theme is Lewis Grossberger, who, pointing out that "*Cosby* cannot be successfully Xeroxed," says the show has succeeded because it's about family. He adds:

Yes, Americans must be crying out for warm *family* comedies, traditional *family* values, wise dads, sweet moms, adorable tots, wisecracking-but-vulnerable teens, heartwarming pets, crusty-on-the-outside-but-lovable-on-the-inside grandpas. America wants clean-cut clans of verbal, upscale, telegenic men, women and children who bicker comically for 19 minutes then fall into each other's arms for the big-hug-fadeout-following-the-solving-of-the-weekly-life-problem-that-triggers-the-vital-'aw'-response (the latter being that part of the show where the studio audience, en masse, its heartstrings atwang, goes "Awwwwwww"). (1986, p. 55)

Another word describing the show's mystique is "togetherness": "(it) is the coolest show on the air—but in its very sophisticated coolness, it somehow subtly projects old-fashioned familial values which used to be termed 'togetherness'" (Ungar, 1985, p. 29). Cosby himself has commented on this subject: "So many people identify with what goes on in the Huxtable household. They ask themselves, 'How did they find out what's happening in *our* house?' Other times a situation will click and a parent will use it as a teaching tool."[13]

And then there's the widespread notion that the show succeeds primarily because of its star. In a four-year retrospective on *The Cosby Show, New York Times* media critic John J. O'Connor wrote, "From the beginning, the source of its appeal has been rooted in the personality of Mr. Cosby himself" (1988, p. C26). That notion supports a finding reported fifteen years earlier in *Psychology Today* (Murphy and Pollio, 1973) about Cosby's humor transcending the individual. The researchers used fourteen groups of subjects made up of strangers or mutual friends who listened to excerpts of Bill Cosby and Don Rickles recordings. While both comics elicited more enjoyment when friends listened together, there was markedly less movement, laughing, or smiling when strangers listened to Don Rickles. It is suggested that Cosby's humor may transcend the individual, while the audience makeup is critical for Rickles' "here-and-now" humor. Viewers frequently cite the transcendency of Cosby's humor (Murphy and Pollio, 1973). Jannette L. Dates writes that Cosby "demonstrated the skills of a craftsman and artist who had polished his art through years of hard work and careful study. Cosby's comedy reflected an ability to generate a pace, a control of thought patterns, a control over other people, and the use of subtleties to make a point. His style embraced a kind of comedic humanism" (1990, p. 282).

Horst Stipp, director of Social and Development Research at NBC, claims that the show is a great success simply because it's so "funny."[14] He also maintains that it means different things to different people. Downing (1988) refs to the show's "frequently sparkling wit, which is an integral element of its style" (p. 63).... The humor in the show is never of the 'laughometer' variety, never cheap. Perhaps being taped before a live studio audience helps a great deal insofar as it obviates the wooden pauses for canned mirth that punctuate so many other comedies" (p. 66). David Marc is "convinced that American television has defined itself as a comic medium" (1984, p. xiv); *The Cosby Show* is clearly the exemplar.

David Lerner, vice president and broadcast supervisor for Foote, Cone & Belding, offers a detailed answer as to why *The Cosby Show* has flourished:

1. *Multigenerational appeal.* The show focuses on a widely ranging nuclear family that regularly interacts with one another.

However, the trenchant cause for the aggregate appeal of *The Cosby Show* is the ubiquity of Bill Cosby in the American popular culture of the past 25 years. Middle-aged Americans' attachment to Cosby stems from the early 1960's, when club appearances, record albums and Ed Sullivan injected the comedian into their psyches. Yuppies recall Alexander Scott of *I Spy* and Chet Kincaid of *The Bill Cosby Show*. Teenagers grew up with Fat Albert in the 1970's. Children are familiar with the genial comedy displayed in the numerous Cosby commercial endorsements of the early 1980's (1986, pp. 86–87).

2. *When in doubt, do shtick.* "Cosby's monologues and rubber-faced reactions emit the feeling of live television and create a direct relationship between the performer and his audience."

3. *The parents win.* Cosby has given us his own version of why the show has been successful. "On *The Cosby Show*, discipline is not offensively exercised to subjugate the children, but judiciously employed to aid the youngsters' maturation in an increasingly complex society. The results, reflected by Nielsen, represent broad-based national acceptance of 'The parents win,' cutting across all ideological and demographic lines."

For Michael Real, the show is successful because it has drawn a large viewership in its "[recoding of] Black ethnicity around the father figure and the strong nuclear family, an affirmation of the value of education, a sense of affluence and fiscal responsibility, and a population that is multigenerational and multiracial" (1989, p. 120).

"The show puts black images on the screen that people could admire," according to Dates (1990, p. 282).

The characters on *The Cosby Show* seemed authentic, representing a real African American upper-middle-class group rarely presented on American television. That the characters were good-looking, witty, charming, and conscientious about their love and respect for each other helps to explain why viewers enjoyed visiting with them each week.

"Perhaps the single most important factor of *Cosby*'s success," according to Edward Jay Whetmore, "has been the informality of the episodes. The show's family members are so lifelike, so realistic. Each Thursday night they would carry on the business of family life in an almost offhanded way. In the process, they have become an enduring and endearing aspect of the American psyche" (1992, pp. 134–135). Rebuttals to this evaluation of *The Cosby Show* as realistic can be found in chapter 6, but Whetmore speaks for many audience members who fell into a loyal ritual of Huxtable-monitoring.

"Demographics" is Ella Taylor's explanation for *The Cosby Show*'s success: it appeals to a wide mass audience. She argues that the formats for this show and *Family Ties* "develop discrete themes for small children, teenagers, and adults, for women and men as well as for the family as a whole" (1990, p. 157). The case study of "First Day of School" presented earlier would seem to bear out her theory, for it showed mini-themes designed to appeal to various interest groups.

This notion of format and/or formula reiterates this author's interest in myth and ritual in television viewing. Audiences come to *The Cosby Show* with certain expectations, and thus far they do not appear to have been disappointed. The various theories proposed to explain the show's success have ranged from its empowering capabilities to its social hyperbole to its representation of the ultimate fantasy theme.

Since no one theory predominates, the thesis of the present book is that individual viewer response to *The Cosby Show* and its ratings success should be explored and appreciated, whatever the frame of reference. And, "Wish fulfillment or role model, Cosby's TV family shows no sign of losing its appeal" (Zoglin, 1987, p. 60).

THE COSBY SHOW PHENOMENON

The Cosby Show may well be described as a phenomenal cultural artifact. Consider: Every Thursday evening at 8 P.M. EST more than 60 million people across the United States opt to stay at home and turn their television dials to NBC for *The Cosby Show*. Since it premiered in the fall of 1984, the show has become legend.

These two sentences require close analysis. First, "every Thursday evening at 8 P.M." is a unique television programming strategy that the network has decided to continue.[15] Typically, when a show does well in the ratings, it is positioned against another network's highly rated shows; *The Cosby Show*, however, has become the standard. In its own way, it has established its own ritualistic viewership. Although this time slot describes the Eastern Standard section of the United States, and although the show has already gone into syndication, that loyal audience remains tuned in, both here and abroad.

Second, "more than 60 million people" in America comprises an enormous audience, especially when we consider that by its second season *The Cosby Show* was drawing nearly half of the total television-viewing public. Put in perspective, that audience number is "more than the combined attendance

(46.8 million) of every major league baseball game that year, more than 8 times the combined attendance at all Broadway shows (7.4 million), more than the attendance for 1985's biggest movie, "Back to the Future" (50 million), and more than the number of voters it took to elect President Ronald Reagan in 1984 (53 million)" (Stewart, 1985, p. 1D).

Historically, *The Cosby Show* has coincided with the politically conservative Reagan–Bush era, characterized economically by continuing concern since the October 19, 1987, stock market plummet, the S&L scandals, and a widening gap between rich/Yuppies and the poor/homeless. Racially, it appears that we have not made much progress since the civil rights movement of the 1960s; many issues of justice and equality remain unsolved. Demographically, the population growth of Blacks, Hispanics, and other minority groups is outpacing that of whites in this country. Family-wise, we still have a six-out-of-ten divorce rate, and one in four children is being raised by a single parent; we are also facing increasing teenage pregnancies, an aging population, an increase of women in the workforce, and ever-changing conceptions of what family means at all. The idealized, traditional nuclear family is continually disappearing from both our real and television-imaged worlds. James Lull discusses the postmodern perspective regarding families: "People living in the more highly developed societies face a complex, confusing, and often debilitating world in which the impersonal industrial, technocratic, and bureaucratic hazards of life are normative" (1988, p. 15).

The current status of network television is yet another critical part of this equation. From its earliest days, the three major networks have been in constant competition with one another; their combined hold on television-viewing audiences has seriously eroded in recent years. Their struggle has been intensified by the introduction of yet other competition: the new Fox network, the catch-all capabilities of cable channels, and new communications technologies such as VCRs, teletext and videotext, video-on-demand, and the "zipping, zapping, and grazing" possibilities with remote-control devices. From an all-time high of 93 percent of all television viewers in 1978, the three networks have now been reduced to about 67 percent of the tuned-in audience. Against this backdrop, *The Cosby Show* has become legend. Specifically,

The Cosby Show was consistently at the top of the charts, drawing loyal audiences of approximately half of all American television-viewing households. Since 1984, and for all of its eight seasons it ranked number 1 in the Nielsen annual reports on television. This is an unprecedented cumulative accomplishment.

The Cosby Show, as the highest-rated program on television, brought General Electric's NBC an estimated $1.5 million in weekly advertising revenues. It commanded the highest prices ever for a television series.

The Cosby Show's 1986–1987 season made television history as the best for any series since *Bonanza* in 1964–1965. Both as a form of culture and as a marketable product, the "series"[16] is an important component peculiarly unique to the broadcast medium.

The Cosby Show is credited with "saving" and transforming the prime time family sitcom genre. In the fall of 1984, just as *The Cosby Show* was making its debut, an article written by Susan Horowitz appeared in *Channels of Communication*, entitled "Sitcom Domesticus: A Species Endangered by Social Change." It argued that "(t)he broad base for broad comedy has split asunder, along with the nuclear family" (p. 22). With the exception of the success of *Kate & Allie*, a sitcom about two single mothers, she declared the death of the sitcom, cautioning: "Today, with all the diverging life-styles, and the splintering of both the television audience and the nuclear family, the sitcom must adjust to the viewers' new realities" (p. 50). *The Cosby Show* turned Horowitz's prediction upside down. The next question one might ask is whether the sitcom was worthy of its "saving" and transformation.

The Cosby Show helped make NBC the top-rated network for the first time ever.[17] When the series began, NBC was in the cellar. Then, in the prime time rankings for 1986–1987, NBC overpowered the competition with a 17.8/28 (rating/share annual composite) whereas CBS posted a 15.8/25 and ABC's 14.1/22 was the lowest rating for any network in television history since the affiliates began to be recorded in the early 1960s. During the week of December 29, 1986, when NBC preempted *The Cosby Show* for the Rose Bowl and the Orange Bowl, the network lost its number 1 position for the first time in seventeen weeks. By the summer of 1987, NBC had been first in the Nielsens for the twenty-eighth week in a row, and in May 1988 *Broadcasting* (v. 116, p. 55) declared 47 the magic number for the network in prime time—a record for a consecutive weekly ratings win.

Television historian Rick Marschall considers the show "symbolic of its [NBC's] success and overall creative quality" (1986, p. 193). The case is just the reverse: *The Cosby Show* was single-handedly responsible for the network's climb to the top. Institutionally, although there may not seem to be many differences between the networks, NBC's rise to the top spot was important in ending CBS' hegemony as ratings leader. With *The Cosby Show*, NBC became the network kingpin.

The Cosby Show also helped the NBC affiliates. Citing "Nielsen Household Report, Prime Time, Primary Affiliates Only," Viacom International constructed the accompanying "Everybody loves a winner" chart:

NBC Affiliates	First Place	Second Place	Third Place
Before *Cosby*			
1984	37	46	95
With *Cosby*			
1985	72	67	39
1986	90	62	28
1987	118	39	25

The Cosby Show has helped advance the image of Blacks on television beyond stereotypical jive-talkers to upscale, positive role models. Mass communication history is replete with examples of negative stereotyping of minorities, particularly Blacks, that are beyond the scope of this book to document. From the days of *Amos 'n' Andy* on radio (actually they were whites acting the roles of Blacks) and Stepin Fetchit in film (Cripps, 1990), these depictions have been biased and belittling.

To its credit, NBC has historically included Black performers in its schedule. As early as the mid–1950s it tried to introduce a variety show featuring Nat King Cole, and in the late 1960s it finally got advertising support for *Julia* featuring Diahann Carroll as the widow of a Vietnam War soldier and mother of a young son. In the 1970s the network introduced *The Flip Wilson Show* and *Sanford and Son*, and in the 1980s, with the success of *The Cosby Show*, it introduced *Amen, Diff'rent Strokes, Gimme a Break, 227*, and the Cosby spinoff, *A Different World*.

According to John D. H. Downing, the Huxtable family

presents in microcosm the importance of black unity—between genders and generations—without any sloganizing about the necessity of holding together for survival in a hostile environment. Nor is any child in the family favored for his or her lighter skin shade, historically one of the most insidious penetrations of the majority's racism into the minority's everyday life. (1988, p. 70)

This important topic of the ramifications of *The Cosby Show* for Blacks is discussed in depth in chapter 7.

The Cosby Show, under the "coat-tail effect,"guaranteed high ratings to its succeeding shows on Thursday nights. Network affiliates counted on *The Cosby Show* as a lead-in to local news programs and as an aid in broadening demographic profiles. Viacom International's promotional brochure, "The Cosby Factor" (1988, p. 11), calls the show "(a) winner that makes winners," stating that before *Cosby, Family Ties* ranked seventy-third, but then it moved to second place with *Cosby* as a lead-in; also, *Cheers* moved from fifty-fourth to third place.

The Cosby Show's audience, according to a Nielsen Duplication Study of February 1987, consisted heavily of news watchers. Yet, its once-a-week viewership outnumbers that of the three networks' morning broadcasts combined.

With regard to the percentages of viewers who watch both news and sitcoms, "The Cosby Factor" (1988, p. 16) cites Nielsen findings that 58.3 percent of *Cosby* viewers watch local news and 54.6 percent network news— higher numbers than were found for news viewers who watched other prime time sitcoms: *Family Ties* (56.7% local, 53.3% network), *Cheers* (48.9%, 46.6%), *Golden Girls* (46.5%, 43.6%), *Night Court* (43.4%, 41.1%), *Who's the Boss?* (41.3%, 38.0%), *Kate & Allie* (41.2%, 38.4%), *Newhart* (39.4%, 37.6%), *Growing Pains* (36.7%, 33.7%), or *Webster* (31.6%, 28.9%).

Since the name of the game in television audience studies is determining demographics and psychographics, presenting loyal television viewers for potential advertisers is invaluable. The audience for *The Cosby Show,* as will be discussed in depth in chapter 5, includes both men and women, young and old and in between, occupations ranging from preschoolers to professionals, and light (less than one hour a day), medium (one to three hours a day), or heavy (over three hours a day) watchers.

The Cosby Show's production studio was said to have improved the quality of life in its Brooklyn, New York, neighborhood. In its first three seasons the show was produced out of NBC's Brooklyn studios at 1268 East 14th Street.[18] It was then produced out of the Kaufman-Astoria Studios at 34–12 36th Street, in Astoria, New York. The Museum of the Moving Image, which opened in 1989, is also housed in the building.

The Cosby Show was said to be the "competition killer." When it began in 1984, pitted against the popular, sixth-place *Magnum, P.I.*, that show plunged to fifty-first place the next season. Tom Selleck, in an interview with *The Honolulu Advertiser,* was quoted as saying the show had made rigorous behind-the-scenes efforts to upgrade scripts and production values and was spending $1.5 million per episode in Hawaii. Some twenty shows have failed against *The Cosby Show* during its network run.

The show also fought other programs to retain its top spot in the ratings. Interestingly, its key competition at one point came from another Carsey-Werner production about a very different family: *Roseanne*, on ABC. The Fox network made some interesting bids with yet other families: the Bundys of *Married . . . With Children*, which portrays the family as jaded, something to escape, and the animated *Simpsons*, which Fox opted to air head-on against *Cosby*. (Some critics have dubbed these new family shows "slob-coms.") In addition, over this time period came *America's Funniest Home Videos* on ABC, in which we get to see families watching families. It has been a simple but surprising ratings success.

The Cosby Show was the object of the biggest American television programming barter deal ever, with Viacom International's advertising time sale of

$365,000 per episode in syndication, plus $60 million for the barter minute. Total sales of *The Cosby Show* in syndication are over $600 million for the initial three-and-a-half years of its run, a record-shatterer for off-network sales.

It is estimated that Bill Cosby personally will eventually earn $1 billion from the show.[19] *The Cosby Show* is now available five times per week in syndication to 96 percent of American television households; some 28 million households have been tuning in to the show each week, as they did to its usual Thursday slot.

The Cosby Show was marketed for syndication by Viacom International, which promoted the show's rerun potential by citing National Television Index (NTI) 1985–1986 statistics comparing it to other repeats (see "The Cosby Factor," 1988, p. 19). With original telecast shares of 50 and repeat shares of 48, it was promoted as demonstrating how it outdelivers the competition. The household shares of the top ten programs are as follows:

The Cosby Show (in repeats)	48
Original telecasts	
Family Ties	45
60 Minutes	37
Murder, She Wrote	37
Miami Vice	37
Golden Girls	36
Cheers	36
Dallas	35
Dynasty	33
Who's the Boss?	32

Since going into syndication in 1986, *The Cosby Show* has earned over $750 million and is, to date, the richest syndication deal ever constructed. Beyond that, it has completely altered the entire off-network game.

The Cosby Show's star, Bill Cosby, continues to balance many other successes: four books, multimillion dollar movies, albums and videos, lucrative commercial advertisements, and sellout concerts. Bringing many years of entertainment experience and marketing expertise, in addition to a wide and sizable group of devoted fans, as noted earlier Cosby has had unqualified successes in many areas. According to TVQ Index, the showbiz industry's annual nationwide survey of performer popularity, he scored its highest ever rating. In April 1986 Radio City Music Hall announced that Cosby set a record-breaker at the fifty-four-year-old concert hall, grossing $2.8 million for a fifteen-show run.

The Cosby Show wielded such ratings power that the first pitch in the fifth game of the 1988 World Series (the Oakland Athletics versus the Los Angeles

Dodgers) was delayed by a half-hour. Thursdays at 8 P.M. EST on NBC became sacrosanct, and the network determined a policy neither to change the show's schedule nor to cancel, postpone, or delay the program except in dire straits. The only time it was preempted was during the outbreak of the Persian Gulf War in January 1991.

The Cosby Show has also influenced the fashion world. Fashion psychologist Michael Solomon of New York University gives particular credit to Bill Cosby for the sweater phenomenon.[20] In addition, clothing styles, expressions, hairstyles, and names, originally from *The Cosby Show*, have become a part of our lives.

The Cosby Show's family, the Huxtables, were influential both in reviving nostalgia for earlier sitcom families and for creating current versions of different family types. In terms of parental guidance through love and humor, we have come a long way from the days of *Ozzie and Harriet, Leave it to Beaver, I Love Lucy, The Goldbergs, My Three Sons, The Danny Thomas Show, The Honeymooners, Donna Reed*, and *Father Knows Best*.

Yet, some observers are loath to say that *The Cosby Show* is merely a reversion to television's earliest family sitcoms. Ella Taylor (1990, pp. 26–27) has examined the earlier family comedies and has observed that

The family comedies of the 1950s articulated not so much the realities of postwar affluence as the received wisdom of post–New Deal capitalism: the end of ideology, a liberal conservative dream of a harmonious society in which the conditions for social conflict would disappear because there would be plenty of everything to go round. It did not matter much if Ralph Kramden's money-making schemes collapsed; and the small mishaps of Beaver Cleaver and Ricky Nelson played themselves out unclouded by financial troubles, street violence, drug abuse, or marital discord. The television children of the 1950s and 1960s inhabited a universe in which mild sibling quarrels were quickly but fairly adjudicated by sage, kindly parents equipped with endless reserves of time and patience—marital teams offering clearcut rules for moral guidance. Taken together, these shows proposed family life as a charming excursion into modernity, but resting on the unshakeable stability of tradition. Parents would love and respect each other and their children forever. The children would grow up, go to college, and take up lives identical in most respects to those of their parents.

If we go by this description, *The Cosby Show* neatly fits the earlier mold. Is the show simply reverting back to the escapist "feel-good" fare of the period that is now known as the Golden Age of Television?

There are a number of differences, however, between *The Cosby Show* and the earlier comedies. Himmelstein (1984, p. 95) reminds us that in earlier series "the inferior role of women and the status of adults as the agents of social control in this mythic world were continually represented." In *The Cosby Show* there is no doubt about the pecking order: It begins with Cosby's character as Cliff Huxtable, then comes his wife, and finally, perhaps, his parents. Yet, the children are encouraged to express their opinions, and most of their opinions are considered.

In their recent study of families in prime time, Skill, Robinson, and Wallace (1987) report that from 1979 to 1985, 36 percent of the network fare used the family as a primary story vehicle and 51 percent of the sitcoms used the family as the story focus. In these portrayals, the traditional nuclear family accounted for 65.7 percent of the conventions.

Think of all the men you know who still want to come home to June Cleaver, in pearls and apron, or who long for a Donna Reed companion who will smilingly, lovingly listen to all their woes. Think of all your friends who still think their problems can be solved in a half-hour. Think of battered women, lacking self-esteem, who still believe in patriarchal decision making for them. Think, too, of future generations who will quest for the perfect equal-partner marriage with the perfect work/career situation and perfect fun-but-faithful children. We have long been influenced by sitcoms.

The Cosby Show phenomenon is especially evident from the various anecdotes that surround it: Philadelphians who want to change the name of their city to "Billadelphia" in honor of its famous native son; the baby whose first word was "Cosby"; a teacher whose Special Needs second-grader was so excited that he "got" a riddle aired in a Cosby episode; clubs that have had to re-schedule events on Thursday nights; and so on.

According to Gitlin "anecdote is the style of industry speech, dialogue its body, and narrative its structure" (1983, p. 14). In studying *The Cosby Show*, as with many other social scientific endeavors, it is idiosyncratic, anecdotal evidence that often prevails over the "factual."

LITERATURE REVIEW

Before launching into an in-depth analysis of the findings of this study, it is appropriate to discuss similar genre studies, books related to Bill Cosby himself, and treatments of the show in scholarly studies.

In their Preface to *Interpreting Television: Current Research Perspectives*, editors Willard D. Rowland, Jr., and Bruce Watkins state that, "Over the past decade the quantity and quality of published literature on the role and meaning of television content has increased notably" (1984, p. 7). There are ever-increasing numbers of articles and conference papers, but to date only five scholarly books have been written about specific television programs:

1. In 1979 Richard P. Adler edited *All in the Family: A Critical Appraisal*, a collection of essays related to critical reaction to the show. Published as part of Praeger Special Studies, it discussed the milieu of the 1970's within which the program appeared, the role of its network (CBS), director Norman Lear, and the varied ratings and responses.
2. From the United Kingdom came Dorothy Hobson's *Crossroads: The Drama of a*

Soap Opera, published by Methuen in 1982. Hobson maintains that "soap operas have become part of contemporary popular culture, and what we should be asking is, 'Why does the series warrant such support from its audience and remain so popular?' " Her focus was on the work process behind production of a soap, and how various audience members translated those efforts.

3. Focus is also on audience in Ien Ang's 1985 *Watching Dallas: Soap Opera and the Melodramatic Imagination.* That audience was made up of forty-two respondents who answered the author's advertisement in a Dutch woman's magazine, inviting *Dallas* viewers to write about their likes and/or dislikes of the serial.

4. Another study of soaps that has been made into a book is Michael James Intintoli's *Taking Soaps Seriously: The World of "Guiding Light"* (1984), which views soaps as industrialized cultural production. It concentrates on the results of the work process on the viewer's experience.

5. The most recent entry into the television-show book field is Robert S. Alley and Irby B. Brown's *Murphy Brown: Anatomy of a Sitcom* (1990). The volume is loaded with appreciation to CBS for all kinds of permissions, and one wonders if, in fact, it was commissioned by the network itself. It deals mainly with the story of writer Diane English and her pivotal role in the series.

By way of review, then, the only full-length scholarly studies of television programs, with the exception of those on *All in the Family* and *Murphy Brown,* have been of soaps. True, too, there are guidebooks to *The Andy Griffith Show, Gilligan's Island,* and *The Honeymooners*—but they hardly advance our knowledge about popular television fare. Clearly, empirical limitations, data collection methods, and theoretical perspectives have made the study of program phenomena difficult, if not daunting.

A number of biographies have been written about Bill Cosby: Joel H. Cohen, *Cool Cos: The Story of Bill Cosby* (Scholastic Books, 1972); Harold and Geraldine Woods, *Bill Cosby: Making America Laugh and Learn* (Dillon Press, 1983); Caroline Latham, *Bill Cosby—For Real* (Tor Books, 1985); Barbara Johnson Adams, *The Picture Life of Bill Cosby* (Watts, 1986); Bill Adler, *The Cosby Wit: His Life and Humor* (Corevan, 1986); Robert Johnson, *Bill Cosby: In Words and Pictures* (Johnson Chi, 1986); Ronald L. Smith, *Cosby* (St. Martin's Press, 1986); Larry Kettelkamp, *Bill Cosby: Family Funny Man* (Wanderer Books, 1987); and Jim Haskins, *Bill Cosby: America's Most Famous Father* (Walker and Co., 1988).

Bibliographic, computer, and general networking searches show that a limited amount of academic research has been done on *The Cosby Show.*

Robert Staples and Terry Jones' "Culture, Ideology and Black Television Images" (1985) discusses the positive effect of the show, as does Herman Gray's "Television and the New Black Man: Black Male Images in Prime Time Situation Comedy" (1986).

David A. England (1985) cites episodes that suggest humanizing potential. Betsy J. Blosser and Donald F. Roberts have collaborated in a study of *Fat*

Albert and The Cosby Kids (1986), and determined that the show was a good example of positive television programs for children.

A comparison between *The Cosby Show* and *Family Ties* is the chief purpose of Lynn H. Turner's attempt in 1987 to define "family themes." Taylor concludes that, although the two shows deal with similar subject matter, they appear to be very different. Specifically, the Huxtables have a family theme placing their family's values ahead of those encountered outside the family, whereas the Keatons' family theme undergoes testing in the outside world.

As mentioned previously, John D.H. Downing (1988, p. 51) has performed a discourse analysis of *The Cosby Show*, demonstrating that its treatment of sexism, the family, social class, racism, and humor has enabled it to convey positive messages to multiple audiences.

In 1988 Dianne Lynne Cherry performed a pseudoexperiment on 550 undergraduate students to determine what effects *The Cosby Show* might have on social attitudes. She found that viewers and nonviewers of the show differed significantly in their assessments of real-world interracial relationships between African-Americans and Euro-Americans. Cherry underscores the societal importance of African-American character portrayals.

Marie Louden-Hanes has been working on "Theo's Role in *The Cosby Show*," and Bishetta Merritt on "Bill Cosby—T.V. Auteur." Stuart H. Surlin (1988) used a five-minute segment from the show in conjunction with a 30-second car commercial to determine cross-cultural perceptions.

With funding from the Cosby Foundation, Justin Lewis and Sut Jhally of the Communications Department at the University of Massachusetts at Amherst have been conducting interviews with fifty-two families or social groups to see what the show means to them. Their results have not yet been published.

Three current books deal with *The Cosby Show* in depth. First, David Marc's *Comic Visions: Television Comedy and American Culture* considers its historic role:

Surely the greatest hit of the 1980s, [it] is a kind of upside-down *Amos 'n' Andy*, offering a vision of a well-to-do inner-city black family living a life utterly compatible with the values and goals of the suburban middle class. The program achieves the family warmth, solidarity and love of *Father Knows Best*, while giving the lie to the ideal that such transcendental domesticity is the province of any one racial group. (1989, p. 217)

Second, Michael Real's *Super Media: A Cultural Studies Approach* devotes a chapter to "Bill Cosby and Recoding Ethnicity," based on structuralist analysis. Crediting Carroll Parrot Blue for coauthoring material on Black encoding and recoding, it argues that "Cosby's representation of ethnicity and gender, especially in his successful father role on prime-time television, occurs in a challenging context" (1989, p. 106), and that Cosby personally, and his mythical television family collectively, have become the "icons" of the super media.

Third, Ella Taylor's *Prime Time Families: Television Culture in Postwar America* (1989) focuses on the issues of the show's patriarchal dominance, conspicuous consumption, and seeming unconcern with the outside world— with Clair the lawyer/wife as "superwoman incarnate," learning experiences where nothing really happens, and family members self-regulated by "a benevolent dictatorship." She writes:

The show's endless rehearsal and efficient mopping up of mild domestic disorder stakes a claim for a perfect family that works, but its closure of all open endings, relative viewpoints, and ethical ambiguities and its energetic repression of the sources of suffering that afflict many families (especially black families) suggest a political retrenchment born of cultural exhaustion, a fearful inability to confront current reality and imagine new forms of community or new ways of living. (p. 164)

Diana C. Reep and Faye H. Dambrot in "Lasting Images of TV Parents" (in press), asked 210 television viewers, most of whom were white adults from nuclear families, to name television mothers and fathers who came to mind. *The Cosby Show* dominated the responses: 30 percent of the viewers named its mother and 46 percent its father.

Zhengkang Wu is doing his doctoral dissertation at the East-West Center in Hawaii on prime time sitcom fathers (1990). He calls *The Cosby Show* a reincarnation of *Father Knows Best* because of similarities in the family's social status and professional prestige, production attempts to present a successful middle-class family, emphasis on parental responsibility and domestic harmony, trivial domestic affairs, and a dodging and/or ignoring of social reality. Wu's work is particularly intriguing because, as a native of the People's Republic of China, he has only recently been exposed to the sitcom genre.

There actually is a book about *The Cosby Show* aimed at younger viewers. It is available through elementary school book fairs and in some Children's Books sections in bookstores. Edited by M.J. Edrei and published in 1986 by Sharon Publications, it is called "The Cosby Scrapbook: America's Favorite T.V. Family." Photo-profiles of the Huxtable Family are included, along with data on the performers such as when they were born, where they were raised, their talents, their hobbies, and their future plans.

As can be seen in the References section of this book, the bulk of information about *The Cosby Show* comes from popular and trade publications. Between wide media coverage in the popular press and frequent anecdotal citations of the show in people's daily conversations, agenda setting on the program's "importance" is quite evident.

Even though *The Cosby Show* has only now ended its eighth and final season at the time of this writing, the 1980s have already been called "the *Cosby* decade." That exact phrase is used in the 1986 film *Soul Man*, in which a Los Angeles preppie masquerades as a needy Black to gain entrance to Harvard Law School. The hero states: "This is the Cosby decade—America loves black people." In his *TV Guide* review of the decade, Neil Hickey points out that whereas *Dallas* dominated the networks in the first part of the 1980s, *The Cosby Show* has taken over that spot. As an example of its remarkable appeal, he states: "Of the 25 most-watched programs of 1986, *Cosby* segments accounted for 19 of them" (1989, p. 30).

This book aims to discuss this communications phenomenon in terms of its history, economics, politics and legalities, production, audiences, critical reaction, and sociocultural implications.

2

The Economics of
The Cosby Show

In the last four years, one program, "The Cosby Show," has essentially rearranged the network television business.

Peter J. Boyer,
New York Times (July 25, 1988), p. D8.

By any measure, *The Cosby Show* has changed the face of doing business in the business of television. This chapter examines the economic aspects of the show as a phenomenon—the bottom line. It also discusses how the series was sold in the first place, as well as the roles of marketing, advertising, ratings, promotions, and syndication.

As the Preface to this book states, this study was originally initiated from a marketing perspective; now, more than ever, economics remains a central aspect of *The Cosby Show* phenomenon. The most lucrative show in television history, having already earned more than a billion dollars in eight seasons, it has achieved new heights and set new records. It has managed to break old rules and write new ones into both the rulebooks and the record books.

The first economic marvel was that the show was even bought by NBC.

SELLING *THE COSBY SHOW* TO TELEVISION

Just when television seemed bleaker than ever, he appeared on prime time with his unique talents: the mastery of stand-up comedy, the passion of a parent, the wisdom of Solomon. Just when industry executives were prophesying the death of the half-hour comedy, he revived it with the healing powers of a fairground evangelist. Just when it seemed that television had become a hopeless abyss of tasteless jokes, violence, and sex, he rescued the idea of family entertainment. Just when television seemed most unfunny, he turned a half-hour each week into 30 minutes of laughter.

He is Bill Cosby.[1]

The year was 1984. Television was indeed bleak. CBS was the undisputed leader, followed by ABC, with NBC languishing in the cellar, as it had been for nearly a decade. *Channels of Communication* (Horowitz, 1984) had just written off the sitcom as an endangered species; not a single one was counted among the prime time ratings. Family shows were also "out," with advertisers instead favoring violent action-adventure programming. Hour-long dramas were the ruling leaders; shows like *Hill Street Blues* and *Miami Vice* topped the charts. Although marketers were just discovering that Blacks were not only a large portion of the television audience but were also willing consumers, programs featuring Black characters were mostly stereotypical, and programs featuring Black performers were almost nonexistent.

At this point, let us move to the home of former NBC television executive Brandon Tartikoff. It is midnight in Beverly Hills, and Tartikoff's baby daughter is being coaxed back to sleep in front of the *Tonight Show*. Bill Cosby is Johnny Carson's guest, and he is in his top form. Cosby has both the host and the audience roaring over his routine about parenting problems. Tartikoff, as the story goes, was not only laughing, he was also thinking.[2] Cosby seemed to have discovered fresh possibilities in a topic that was now close to the network programming genius: parenthood. Tartikoff began thinking about the topic's universal appeal. He also began thinking about NBC's slot at number 3, knowing there was relatively little risk in trying yet another family sitcom. After all, offending as few audience members as possible is the basic tenet of television programming strategy.

Also on the West Coast was the newly formed partnership of Marcy Carsey and Tom Werner, who were looking for shows to produce. They had worked together successfully at ABC and had decided to coordinate their skills in packaging talent. It is also important to know that they had struck a deal with Viacom long before this time.

It is also important to recall that NBC had run *The Bill Cosby Show* for two seasons (1969–1971), with the star as Chet Kincaid, a Los Angeles high school gym teacher. Bogle criticized the series as slow, anemic, lacking Cosby's "controlling sensibility and his remarkable sense of pacing.... Often [he], rather than playing a character, performs as if delivering a monologue in his nightclub act" (1988, p. 260). Some social issues emerged on the show, but they tended to be glossed over. Furthermore, *The Bill Cosby Show* was considered to be politically tame for the times, out of step. When we recall this program from more than a decade before, we find it all the more amazing that NBC was willing to try again.

Cosby had a number of demands for his new program. First, he wanted a network to commit to a firm series without filming a pilot episode. Second, he wanted to be able to tape the show on the East Coast, rather than the West, so that he could be near his family. Third, the television family was to be patterned after Cosby's own, so understandably he required that the show have dignity. Fourth, it was to have an all-Black cast. And finally, Cosby reputedly wanted a "huge, huge salary."

Since Carsey-Werner had established their careers at ABC, they were obligated to offer that network first option on *The Cosby Show*. ABC turned it down, as did CBS, both claiming that sitcoms were dead.

At this point Tartikoff reentered: He was receptive to the idea of Cosby's doing a family show, and he was willing to have NBC take a chance on it. His gamble went even further when he decided to pit *The Cosby Show* on Thursday nights in an 8 P.M. time slot against CBS's venerable *Magnum, P.I.*

Cosby handpicked his cast, and then set out to put together the six episodes NBC ordered; the network originally insisted on only six, so that if the show failed, the network would not lose too much money. At this point Cosby took a tough stance insisting on total control and at least thirteen weeks of shows, and won a number of concessions. The NBC studio in Brooklyn was remodeled to depict the Huxtable household, and production began for the first twenty-five episodes. The rest is history. Throughout the eight years of the show Cosby has maintained control over both internal concerns (such as scripts and personnel) and external concerns (such as public relations and image).

The network did little in the way of press buildup, for this was, after all, just another sitcom, and a gamble at that. Therefore, NBC's Press Department did little to publicly launch the show, although as part of its standard practice it did assign the show its own press representative.

Initial media reaction is interesting to review at this point. The day *The Cosby Show* premiered, the *New York Times* gave it a simple review: "In unadorned outline, this is just another family sitcom with lovable Mom and Pop struggling to raise their frisky but lovable children.... This particular family happens to be black but its lifestyle and problems are universal middle-class" (O'Connor, 1984, p. C30).

A month after the show began, a *TV Guide* interview with Bill Cosby (Fury, 1984, p. 36) compared *The Cosby Show* to its competition (*Magnum, P.I.*) as "Nice against Rowdy." The interviewer depicted Cosby as arrogant, defensive, and not very pleasant during the interview. That article confirmed the star's longstanding distrust of the press, and future interviews with him were reportedly difficult to secure.

But what a difference success can make. Within two months of the show's premiere, the *New York Times* labeled *The Cosby Show* "this season's prime-time phenomenon" (S. Smith, 1984, p. B1). Now the *Times* described the show as "(a) gently funny view of an upper middle-class couple ... [that] has achieved near-unanimous critical praise." *New York* (Leonard, 1984, p. 4) called *The Cosby Show* "a valentine to middle-class American family life, goodwill and domestic mess, vicissitude suborned by giggle." An editorial in the *Christian Science Monitor* stated: "It's funny. It's wholesome. And it's watched. It's 'The Cosby Show'...[and it] also is color-blind. Viewers of all races can relate to it; the family shown is black" (March 8, 1985).

That near-unanimity was also clouded by some sour reviews. The *Village Voice* declared that Bill Cosby no longer qualified as being black enough to be Uncle Tom.[3] Furthermore, referring to his role as Dr. Huxtable the gynecologist, it added: "If anything is going to awaken the well-buried racism of genteel America, it's the notion of black fingers messing with their womanhood's collective Down There."

A Cosby biographer, Ronald Smith, adds yet another early media attention-getter about the show: "A mark of success for a TV show is when it gets parodied in *Mad* magazine. But this time, some of the satire was sour. In true *Mad* tradition, *The Cosby Show* became 'The Clodsby Show,' and Cliff Huxtable 'Quippin Yockstable' " (1986, p. 182).

But in the business of television, the critics that matter are not necessarily found in the media. The critics that matter, for the bottom line, are counted in ratings numbers. So while the press quibbled about *The Cosby Show*, NBC was basking in winning ratings numbers and a flood of positive telephone calls and letters about the show. Vera Wells, director of corporate relations and audience services for the network, called it "one of the highest spontaneous reactions ever for a show"[4]—that is, for a show not in trouble, or not in fear of being canceled. Over and over viewers commented on how wonderful the show was and on how great it was to see a positive portrayal of a family. Comments like "(t)hey must have been eaves-dropping on our family" were typical.

Although the networks are always happy to get favorable calls and letters about a program, in the hardball game of television economics calls and letters are often as meaningless as newspaper reviews. The networks earn their money from sponsors, and sponsors count audience responses in the millions. To help them keep track of those millions of viewers, a whole industry has grown up: the ratings business.

RATINGS

According to the Television Information Office, as of summer 1988, over 98 percent of U.S. households had television sets.[5] (That is higher than the percentage of American households that have indoor plumbing!) The latest Nielsen figures found the average daily home use of those televisions to be 7 hours and 4 minutes per day, down slightly from a high of 7 hours, 10 minutes per day during 1985–1986.

A ratings point in television measures the percentage of the nation's population of 92.1 million television homes who are tuned to a particular broadcasting station during a given time period. Yielding a comparative estimate of television set tuning in specific and/or combinations of markets, ratings are determined by multistage area probability sampling, which tries to insure that the sample reflects actual population distribution. The formula for computing ratings is

$$\text{Rating} = \frac{\text{Number of households watching a certain channel}}{\text{Total number of households with television sets}}$$

The A. C. Nielsen Company, through its Nielsen Television Index (NTI), regularly collects, collates, and statistically interprets network television audience data in the form of so-called overnights. Because Nielsen has traditionally led the ratings field, viewing results are sometimes referred to simply as Nielsens.

A company of the Dun & Bradstreet Corporation, A. C. Nielsen is headquartered in Northbrook, Illinois, with offices in New York, Atlanta, Chicago, Dallas, San Francisco, Menlo Park, and Los Angeles.[6] In addition to the overnights, it supplies ratings on what viewers in the twelve largest urban markets were watching the previous night; two days later, Nielsen releases the national ratings for those same shows. Its television audiences are located in New York, Los Angeles, Chicago, San Francisco–Oakland, Philadelphia, Detroit, Washington, D.C., Boston, Dallas–Ft. Worth, Houston, Miami–Ft. Lauderdale, Denver, Atlanta, Seattle–Tacoma, Hartford–New Haven, Sacramento–Stockton, and Minneapolis–St. Paul. Each day, A. C. Nielsen processes information to produce national television ratings from the following: 4,068 household records, 11,066 persons-viewing records (diaries), 7,898 People Meter Units, and 2.4 million basic edits of data. Monthly, it depends on 17 million People Records and 74 million viewing minutes. Four times a year—November, February, May, and July—Nielsen conducts nationwide "sweeps" to determine local television reports to augment reports from regular ratings periods.

Since the most important goal in the business of television is getting a large audience to sell to advertisers, ratings have an enormous influence on the industry in terms of programming, revenues, stations, and certainly personnel. Although specific target niches are the aim for some programs and some advertisers, the networks predominantly seek to attract a large, heterogeneous audience such as that for *The Cosby Show*.

Another important element is reports on "shares"; these are estimates of the audience percentage from all television sets in use during a given time period. Although a program's rating is estimated on a percentage of the total possible households, its share is based only on households that use television at a particular time; this measurement is often referred to as HUT (Households Using Television). The formula for computing shares is as follows:

$$\text{Share} = \frac{\text{Number of households watching a certain channel}}{\text{Total number of households watching television}}$$

Since, as has been pointed out, more than 92.1 million households in the United States (98% of the total) have at least one television set, each Nielsen ratings point is equal to 1 percent of the nation's television households. A rating of 15, for example, means that an estimated 13.5 million television households have tuned into a particular program. A 20 share is considered quite acceptable in the ratings game, and anything over a 30 share is considered an absolute hit.

Thus, when *The Cosby Show* had an average rating of 34.0 during the 1985–1986 season (see Figure 2), that figure then represented 30.6 million homes. Its over 50 percent share means that it was consistently drawing more than half of all viewing households. When the series averaged a 47 share of the viewing public throughout the 1985 season and hit a peak of 51 at one point, NBC went wild.

In its third season, *The Cosby Show* garnered an overall 36.4 rating, as opposed to 15.4 for *Magnum, P.I.* and 6.8 for *Ripley's Believe It or Not*. It topped the ratings charts since its debut, was been first in its time period practically every week since. In February 1986 the show drew its largest rating ever: a 39.0 rating with a 56 share, the best performance for any regular series episode since *Dallas*'s episode "Who Shot J.R.?," a program that aired in 1980.

When *The Cosby Show* began in 1984, the Nielsen national probability sample was culled from 1,700 households throughout the United States. By 1988 that number had expanded to about 4,000 households, as measured by the introduction of Nielsen's People Meter. It continued to triumph at the number 1 spot.[7] In Nielsen households the small device is attached to each television set; each individual then uses an accompanying remote control unit to input information on his or her identity and program choice. People Meters have been criticized for incorrect operations that can be invalidated, difficulties in hardware installation, the perennial issue of sample composition, and a concern that the electronic devices are transforming passive viewers into active ones. Nevertheless Nielsen plans to stay with them, at least until their infrared audience scanning system is perfected. Despite continuing network concern about competition for television viewers, NBC's *The Cosby Show* continued to top the charts, even if toward the end those ratings were in the mid–20s range.

The show consistently appealed to a broad base of viewers, a fact that Viacom International capitalized on in its marketing plan (see Figure 3). *The Cosby Show* not only has the highest overall household ratings, but it also rates first with both men between the ages of eighteen and forty-nine and women between the ages of twenty-five and fifty-four; teens; and children (ages two to eleven). This aspect of the phenomenon is especially important to the programming concept of "lead-ins," which stresses the importance of

Figure 2
The Top-Rated Network Television Shows of 1985–1986

Viacom International's promotional advertisement asked the question, "Can you name the 15 top rated network television shows of 1985-6?"

Here are the answers:

Answers:

	Rating/Share
1.Super Bowl XX (1/26/86)	48.3/70
2.THE COSBY SHOW (2/27/86)	39.0/56
3.THE COSBY SHOW (1/16/86)	38.5/55
4.THE COSBY SHOW (1/9/86)	36.9/54
5.THE COSBY SHOW (3/6/86)	36.4/54
5.THE COSBY SHOW (3/20/86)	36.4/54
5.THE COSBY SHOW (2/20/86)	36.4/53
8.THE COSBY SHOW (12/5/85)	36.2/53
9.THE COSBY SHOW (1/30/86)	36.0/51
10.THE COSBY SHOW (12/12/85)	35.4/52
10.THE COSBY SHOW (2/6/86)	35.4/51
10.Super Bowl XX	
Post Game Show (1/26/86)	36.4/49
13.THE COSBY SHOW (11/21/85)	35.3/51
14.THE COSBY SHOW (2/13/86)	35.2/50
15.THE COSBY SHOW (1/2/86)	34.9/50

Figure 3
"TV's First Family"

Another Viacom International appeal relates to the demographic appeal of THE COSBY SHOW. Citing as its source "NTI, September-April network season, 1985-6. NTI, NAD, February 1986 ratings, prime time," the advertisement tries to demonstrate how THE COSBY SHOW outperforms the Top 10 prime time sit-coms:

Code:
HH: household
W: women
M: men

Rating	HH	W18-49	W25-54	M18-49	M25-54	Teens	2-11 Children
THE COSBY SHOW	34.0	29.1	30.2	23.5	22.0	32.8	32.7
Family Ties	30.5	27.5	28.2	18.8	20.3	29.7	27.6
Cheers	23.8	21.0	21.3	16.9	18.3	17.3	11.8
Golden Girls	21.9	16.0	17.9	9.2	10.6	14.8	14.6
Who's The Boss	21.4	17.7	18.5	11.3	12.5	18.5	15.4
Night Court	21.0	18.9	19.1	15.2	16.6	14.3	8.0
Kate & Allie	20.1	15.3	15.2	9.2	10.6	13.3	8.9
Growing Pains	19.8	17.1	17.6	11.0	11.9	19.7	13.8
Newhart	19.6	15.6	17.5	10.0	11.7	11.0	6.4
Webster	15.3	10.1	11.4	5.5	6.4	9.7	14.5

a specific show in delivering an audience that typically might stay loyal to a particular channel/network. The magic prime time hour of 8 P.M. EST has been found to be vital to a network's scheduling: "A strong eight o'clock show, such as *The Cosby Show*, can provide enough momentum for the network to dominate the entire evening's ratings" (Blum and Lindhelm, 1987, p. 135).

A senior vice president at the New York advertising firm of BBDO, Bob Riesenberg supplies this ratings information: "An average annual ratings point can be worth $50 million to $70 million in profits."[8] When translated into an estimated 92.1 million homes, the value of a single ratings point underscores how ratings rule the networks.

Demographics is where the real story of *The Cosby Show* lies. When the final year-end ratings were tallied in April 1986, "(n)o matter how you analyze them, *The Cosby Show* is a winner. Maybe the biggest overall winner in TV history," Dave Poltrack, vice president of research at CBS, is quoted as conceding. "It's unprecedented in terms of being No. 1 in all demographic areas."[9] Poltrack cites the following statistics:

• It was the top-rated show with kids, teens, adults under fifty-five, men, women, high- and low-income families.

• The number 2 show in virtually all categories was *Family Ties*, which followed *The Cosby Show*.

• *Cosby*'s 51 percent average share of the audience was the best for any series since *Dallas* in 1980–1981. It was the highest rated sitcom since *All in the Family* (1971–1972). On average, 28.9 million homes tuned in weekly.

These statistics were extremely helpful in selling *The Cosby Show* in syndication. Joseph Zaleski, former president of Viacom Domestic Syndication, stated: "There is no other property in the market that is achieving the kind of demographics that 'Cosby' is. It has definitely been the phenomenon of the '80s."[10]

Of particular interest to advertisers and media analysts were the figures on Black viewership of *The Cosby Show*. Although Blacks represent only 12 percent of the U.S. population, they are known to watch more television than any other target market (they make up 17 percent of viewership totals), and are emerging as a viable group of consumers. It is both interesting and encouraging to note that the advertisers of *The Cosby Show*, led by McDonald's, are using more and more Black actors in their commercials. Whereas the show has averaged ratings of 34 with audiences in general, it has drawn ratings of 47.6 among Black viewers.[11]

In an amusing chart entitled "Mouth–Eye Coordination," *Channels of Communication* reported on a Simmons Market Research Bureau report that divided the consumer population according to eating habits.[12] It states: "First there were demographics, then psychographics. Now lunchographics." Breaking down the Nutritional Segmentation System in the company's 1985 Study of Media and Markets, an annual survey of 6,000 households, it divided the (predominantly female) participants into five dietary groups:

Kids Around (soft drinks, spaghetti)	9.0%
Diet Conscientious (skim milk, salads)	18.8%
Meat and Potatoes (with gravy and coffee)	16.7%
Sophisticates (bagels, wine, and tobacco)	31.1%
Naturalists (wheat germ, yogurt, and vitamins)	23.5%

Where did *The Cosby Show* stack up? Sophisticates made up 30.8 percent of its viewing audience, according to this measure. Its popularity was next highest with the Naturalists (24.2%), then the Meat and Potatoes crowd (18.9%), the Diet Conscientious set (17.9%), and last, 7.5% for the mothers with Kids Around.

Where did *The Cosby Show* stand in the ratings? Figure 4 contains the Nielsen figures from 1988. The show was first, with an overall rating of 27.9, which made it the favorite of U.S. television households. *A Different World,* a *Cosby* spinoff, was second, with a 23.4 rating. Broken down further demographically, it significantly remained the top choice of all television programs among women ages eighteen and older, teens (ages twelve to seventeen), and children; it lost out, however, to *60 Minutes* and NFL football as the favorite of men aged eighteen and over.

In another unique television phenomenon, *Cheers* has continued to rise in popularity from its initial place in the cellar when it began ten years ago. Therefore, NBC is "hammocking" the 8:30 P.M. time slot between the two hits. It helps explain the popularity of *A Different World*, and it also becomes a good place to promote a new show.

Nielsen's 1988 report (p. 16) also shows that *The Cosby Show* garnered first place in ten out of seventeen cities in the top 100 television markets: New York (25.5), Los Angeles (24.8), Philadelphia (31.8), San Francisco–Oakland (25.6), Boston (26.1), Detroit (33.6), Washington, D.C. (26.7), Atlanta (31.5), Seattle–Tacoma (28.0), and Sacramento–Stockton (29.6). In Miami–Ft. Lauderdale, it came in second, with a rating of 22.6, and in Hartford–New Haven, it placed third, with a 20.6 rating.

At a time when the networks are concerned about losing prime time audiences to other broadcasting alternatives, these statistics are particularly impressive.[13] The phenomenon continues, but the question that arises is, for how long. An article in the *Los Angeles Times* (Donlon, 1990, p. 1D) reported that Carsey-Werner Productions had originally asked NBC for a $100 million bonus to renew *The Cosby Show* annually, later lowering the price to $25 million. *Broadcasting,* writing about the negotiations for what it called *The Cosby Show*'s "return of perennial powerhouse sitcom," stated that Carsey

Figure 4
Top 15 Regularly Scheduled Network Programs (Nielsen Average Audience Estimates, November 1988)

Total U.S. Television Households

	%
1.THE COSBY SHOW	27.9
2.A Different World	23.4
3.Cheers	22.8
4.Roseanne	22.3
4.Golden Girls	22.3
6.60 Minutes	22.2
7.Who's the Boss?	20.8
8.Growing Pains	20.2
9.Empty Nest	19.8
10.Murder, She Wrote	19.3
11.Dear John	18.3
12.Head of the Class	18.2
13.Hogan Family	17.9
14.L.A. Law	17.8
15.ALF	17.5

Women 18+
1.THE COSBY SHOW	21.7

Men 18+
1.60 Minutes	16.4
2.NFL Monday Night Football	15.7
3.CBS NFL Football Game 1	15.0
4.THE COSBY SHOW	14.3

Teens 12-17
1.THE COSBY SHOW	21.3

Children 2-11
1.THE COSBY SHOW	21.8

and Werner could radically change the whole financial structure of network programming purchases.[14] In the same issue of *Broadcasting*, Brandon Tartikoff stated: "When you're talking about renewing the No. 1-rated show in television, it's a question of how high you're willing to go. They have one level and we have another."[15] Supposedly, the producers would otherwise take their deal to CBS. Carsey-Werner, in addition to wanting a network to pay extra for the privilege of broadcasting and being affiliated with the prestige of *The Cosby Show*, were requesting the chosen network to pay the $1 million production costs per episode. It is but a small part of the ratings game.

ADVERTISING

Typically, a current thirty-second commercial during prime time costs about $100,000, ranging from $68,000 to over $150,000. History was made in February 1983 when the final two-hour episode of *M*A*S*H* commanded $450,000 per thirty-second spot, but that was a special occasion. So, too, are recent Super Bowl games; promising advertisers audiences of more than 100 million viewers, these games have been able to coerce spending of over a million dollars. World Series half-minute advertisements have escalated to $350,000, ABC's *Monday Night Football* can command $250,000 for thirty-second commercials, and the Academy Awards go for $450,000.

Currently, the networks worry and wonder about competition from cable television and other sources for the coveted advertising dollar. Coincidental with *The Cosby Show*'s beginning in 1984, television's advertising growth has slowed, its single-digit increases just barely keeping pace with the nation's economic growth. Still, the broadcast industry's advertising revenues increased from $5.1 billion in 1980 to nearly double that ($9.3 billion) by the end of the decade. During that same period, cable's advertising revenues grew from $53 million to $1.5 billion.

Popularity catapulted *The Cosby Show* into the highest-paid category for prime time advertising. In the beginning, NBC was charging $110,000 for a thirty-second commercial; the latest figures from *Advertising Age* place the cost at $380,000. During the first nine months of the 1985–1986 broadcast year, NBC collected $401.4 million from advertisers of the show alone. The selling point was the projection that one of every two people watching Thursday night television would be watching *The Cosby Show*. The following analogy gives these figures more meaning: If an advertiser were to send 15-cent postcards out to 28 million households (which is what the show typically draws), it would cost $4.2 million in postage alone. That is more than ten times the going price tag for a thirty-second commercial on *The Cosby Show*.

Over the last few years, advertisers on *The Cosby Show* in the Springfield, Massachusetts, area have included products and promotions such as McDonald's, Actifed, Toyota, Stouffers, Tylenol, the U.S. Postal Service, Campbell Soup, Ore Ida, Beef, Triaminic cough syrup, Levi's, Sears shirts, Domino's pizza, Advil, Sucrets throat lozenges, Burger King, Post Sugar Crisp cereal, York Peppermint Patties, Prego Spaghetti Sauce, Kellogg's Muesli, Kentucky Fried Chicken, Corning "visions," Revlon's Charlie, Special K, Primo perfume, Kinney shoes, and lots of NBC promos. Amazingly, this is only a partial listing.

One particular commercial that *The Cosby Show* aired on March 2, 1989, midway through the show was a two-minute MTV-type video featuring the rock star Madonna. In this highly stylized video, the only reference to its sponsor—Pepsi—came late in the tape when the singer picked up the soda can. There was a great deal of hype prior to the unveiling of the Madonna video, with special emphasis of *The Cosby Show*. Later in the week, distributors of Madonna's new single, "Like a Prayer," decided against its immediate release for Italian television because of protests from a Roman Catholic group that the video was blasphemous. Pepsi withdrew its sponsorship of *The Cosby Show* and therefore the show's identification with the rock star.

In its earlier seasons, production costs for *The Cosby Show* were reportedly around $450,000 per episode (Smith, 1986, p. 196). That figure escalated to about $575,000 per episode within a few seasons, and then, at the beginning of the seventh season, *Variety* (September 17, 1990) reported that the show was not only the most successful sitcom on the air, but also the most expensive. NBC was paying a whopping $900,000 per episode for the show. By way of comparison, ten years earlier *M*A*S*H*, as the highest rated sitcom of 1980, cost $240,000 per half-hour episode to produce. That same year *Dallas* cost $420,000 per hourly episode, whereas its production costs eventually grew to $1 million. Although costs include such items as licensing fees, production staff salaries, and pay for the actors, it is worth considering that NBC is currently paying $300,000 more for *The Cosby Show* than for *Cheers*, $350,000 more than CBS is paying for *Murphy Brown*, and $350,000 more than ABC is paying for *The Wonder Years*, and just $50,000 less per episode than ABC paid for its one-hour drama, *Twin Peaks*.

Advertising costs for *The Cosby Show* in syndication are yet another matter. Figures of $350,000 to $400,000 for thirty-second commercials make it the highest priced series in history. Yet Allan Banks, director of media for Dancer-Fitzgerald-Sample/Dorland Worldwide, has commented: "The fact of the matter is that 'The Cosby Show' is a phenomenon. The price for it is certainly not excessive relative to other shows, because of its huge audience."[16] Indeed, *The Cosby Show* reportedly will have grossed over $600 million for its first three and a half years of syndication. Peter J. Boyer adds that "(t)he show brought NBC from last to first, its enormous popularity cannily exploited to build an empire of hits and to ruin the strategies of the opposition" (1988, p. D8).

Even though he had some tough demands for the show, Bill Cosby has been a self-marketing genius, a quality that has been invaluable to the promotion of *The Cosby Show*. Cosby sold the network on a sitcom when people thought the genre was dead. He sold the network on a family show in prime time when by all accounts the nuclear family on television was not going to draw. He sold the network on an all-Black cast at a time when demographics on Blacks as viewers and consumers were just being seriously considered. And he sold the network on a Black family headed by professionals and supported by nonjiving and nonbacktalking children before television viewers realized they had to replace old stereotypes. Television critic Martha Bayles has commented: "Perhaps because Cosby has never gotten stuck on a dilemma about the social or artistic implications of his enormous popularity, he has been able to lift an entire network into first place" (1985, p. 25).

NBC, for its part, has remained dizzied by the success of *The Cosby Show*, but it clearly knows a hit when it sees the numbers, and Cosby continues to bring in the numbers. The network takes every opportunity to promote itself not only as number 1, but also as the "Cosby network." Whenever it can, as during the 1988 Seoul Olympics, it cites *The Cosby Show*, and sometimes it is even fortunate enough to talk Bill Cosby into doing guest spots.

SYNDICATION

The Cosby Show in syndication is yet another record-shattering story. Syndication, television programming that is sold by independent companies to local stations and cable networks typically in the form of reruns, is a business of distribution. *Cosby* is an example of "off-network syndication," the most successful "off-net" in television history, earning 32 1/2 percent of gross.

Producers typically hope to recoup their production costs through syndication, to profit from sales of their programs to independent stations, network affiliates, and countries around the world. With hours of programming for independent television stations currently projected to be about 40,000 per year, series producers hope to sell their programs to fill in the gap. In order for a program to qualify for syndication, it needs a requisite number of episodes—usually three years' worth—to make a package.

At the time *The Cosby Show* began, sitcoms for syndication were scarce, and industry executives were telling television programmers that sitcoms were generating higher syndication ratings than one-hour shows. In addition, sitcoms were known to have great flexibility in scheduling. The timing could not have been better. Opting not to negotiate but to sell *The Cosby Show* by a confidential bidding method, Viacom International made syndication history with its megahit, both financially and procedurally.

When Viacom International began its promotional campaign to get *The Cosby Show* syndicated, it ran an advertisement asking: "Can you name the fifteen top-rated network television shows of 1985–1986?" As shown earlier in this chapter, *The Cosby Show* had consistently been the highest rated program, with the exceptions of Super Bowl XX and its post-game show of January 26 (see Figure 4). At the bottom of the slogan, "The Cosby Factor:

Profit from it," on the ad page is a tiny designation saying, "Source: NTI, September through September." When one turns the advertisement's page over, there is a closeup of Bill Cosby's grinning face, broken up into fifteen parts, two of which contain footballs. In addition is the statement, "Now think what Cosby can do for *your* ratings beginning in 1988."

Bill Cosby himself also assisted in promotional efforts, helping to produce more than twenty separate filmed advertising spots and hundreds of personalized station tags. The idea was that local stations could see that Viacom stood behind its program and, reciprocally, that local stations would be willing to pay a premium to be a station associated with airing *The Cosby Show*. It was reasoned that some stations might even pay to have the syndicated series just to keep the competition from having it.

Always the first to capitalize on a good thing, the media joined the *Cosby* clamor from the moment the show's first high ratings point was announced. Newspapers, magazines, tabloids, and even broadcasting outlets all got on the bandwagon. Bill Cosby and/or the whole cast of the show appeared on the cover of every major publication (see Appendix 1).

Plans to market the show for syndication were put in place well over three years before the actual campaign began. Viacom Enterprises, which had won the honors, set a date of October 1988 for the beginning of syndication and put together a sales team to "successfully sell *The Cosby Show* in one of the most innovative marketing approaches ever used in television" (Vitale, 1987, p. 18).

At the time, the market for syndicated programs was ripe. Media watchers know that the syndication market, like so many others, is cyclical. In 1986, for example, *Facts of Life* was the only off-net sitcom offered into syndication with a full complement of episodes. Two years later, when *The Cosby Show* was ready to be launched into syndication in 1988, it was joined by three other programs: *Night Court, Newhart,* and *Kate & Allie.* The next year, three more were available (*Who's the Boss?, Growing Pains,* and *Mr. Belvedere*), and 1990 welcomed seven sitcoms: *Alf, Golden Girls, Amen, 227, Perfect Strangers, Head of the Class,* and *The Hogan Family.* Hot on their trails are *Full House, Married . . . with Children, Designing Women, A Different World, Roseanne, The Wonder Years, My Two Dads, Just the Ten of Us,* and *Murphy Brown.* Fortunately for Viacom, it was a seller's market when it was putting together its deal for *The Cosby Show.*

Joseph Zaleski had an optimistic prediction for the syndication: "Cosby is going to be the most important piece of syndication ever available for sale to television stations" (Behrens, 1986, p. 13). And his prediction was right on target: Syndication sales set an industry benchmark. What he might not have known was that the show's syndication example would become another integral part of the phenomenon.

On October 16, 1986, syndication was officially launched at a press con-

ference in the Starlight Room of New York's Waldorf Astoria. Viacom announced that it would be making available all barter inventory (unsold advertising time) in *The Cosby Show* on a competitive, closed-bid basis.

Although off-network shows most typically are sold per episode, *The Cosby
Show* was sold in syndication as a unique cash-barter deal for three and a
half years, 182 weekly episodes. Successful bidders were then allowed to use
the episodes once a day in any time slot of their choice. Because Viacom
sends *The Cosby Show* to television stations via satellite, its distribution
method enables the syndicator to demand that all stations involved in the
licensing agreement air the same episode on the same day. This arrangement
also facilitates national promotions of particular episodes for both syndicator
and station.

Six months into the campaign, fifty-six stations (48% of the country) had
signed up (see Figure 5). A feeding frenzy set in. By April 1987, nineteen
NBC affiliates, eighteen ABC affiliates, fifteen CBS affiliates, and four independents wanted the show in syndication. That same year Viacom underwent
a leveraged buyout, with Sumner M. Redstone becoming chairman of the
board, and Frank J. Biondi, Jr., president and CEO of Viacom International.

One year before the series' syndication debut, Viacom had sold *The Cosby
Show* to more than 137 stations for an estimated $520 million, with prices
surpassing even the syndicator's expectations.[17] The sales had an impact on
the schedulers' rekindled interest in sitcoms and caused independent television stations to worry about counterprogramming. For those who purchased
the potentially valuable program, the next decision was to decide on the best
way to use it; typically, *The Cosby Show* was utilized as a news lead-in.[18] Part
of what is called the halo effect, lead-ins and lead-outs affect a station's image
in terms of its programming. WWOR-TV in New York and KCOP-TV in Los
Angeles, for example, claim that they have had increased audiences as a result
of their syndicated scheduling of *The Cosby Show*.

By January 1988, a total of 165 markets had cleared the show for syndication—a figure representing 94 percent of all television households in the
United States. Although Viacom International has not released *Cosby*'s final
figure, industry sources generally agree that it is around $600 million aggre-
gate. To date, all but about twenty-five television markets in the country have
purchased the show, paying the highest prices for syndication ever recorded.

Viacom's key marketing ploy was to emphasize the strength of *The Cosby
Show* and its potential impact on local television programming. Viacom was
quick to point out that the show had remained first in its time period for
176 consecutive weeks, and that its barter was a unique media franchise
opportunity. Its "Cosby Barter Plan Checklist" stressed the following points:

• National "network" of 162 stations minimum; 10 independents, 53 CBS affiliates, 57
  NBC affiliates, and 42 ABC affiliates.

Figure 5
Syndication Markets for *The Cosby Show*

56 markets, 48% of the country,
sold by Viacom Enterprises as of 4/87

Market rank, station and affiliation	Closing date for bid submissions	Reserve price
1. WOR-TV New York	November 3	$125,000
2. KCOP (TV) Los Angeles	November 18	150,000
3. WFLD (TV) Chicago	November 14	100,000
4. KPIX (TV) San Francisco (CBS)	November 20	80,000
6. WCBV-TV Boston (ABC)	March 16	60,000
7. WDIV (TV) Detroit (NBC)	March 23	50,000
12. WPXI (TV) Pittsburgh (NBC)	April 7	26,000
13. KIRO-TV Seattle (CBS)	April 8	26,000
16. KARE (TV) Minneapolis (NBC)	April 13	24,000
17. Tampa, Florida (no bids)	January 21	32,000
19. KUSA-TV Denver (ABC)	March 23	26,000
22. KPHO-TV Phoenix	November 25	36,000
25. KGW-TV Portland, OH (NBC)	April 10	18,000
26. San Diego, CA (no bids)	March 4	16,500
27. WESH-TV Orlando, FL (NBC)	April 14	16,000
28. WISN-TV Milwaukee (ABC)	March 30	15,000
29. WLWT (TV) Cincinnati (NBC)	December 17	20,000
31. WKRN-TV Nashville (ABC)	February 25	12,500
32. WSOC-TV Charlotte, NC (ABC)	February 27	14,300
33. WCMH-TV Columbus, OH (NBC)	March 25	10,000
35. WIBV-TV Buffalo, NY (CBS)	March 27	11,000
37. WITN-TV Greenville-New Bern, NC (NBC)	March 23	2,200
38. WRAL-TV Raleigh-Durham NC (CBS)	March 30	15,000
40 WREG-TV Memphis (CBS)	March 18	10,000
42. WPRI-TV Providence, RI (ABC)	March 17	8,000
45. KENS-TV San Antonio, TX (CBS)	April 20	12,000
46. WTKR-TV Norfolk, VA (CBS)	March 10	10,000
54. WNEM-TV Flint, MI (NBC)	April 15	5,000
57. WALA-TV Mobile, AL (NBC)	February 13	3,800
58. WNEP-TV Wilkes Barre-Scranton, PA (ABC)	April 20	5,000
61. WTLV-TV Jacksonville, FL (ABC)	March 3	10,000
63. WXEX-TV Richmond, VA (ABC)	March 11	6,600
64. KSEE (TV) Fresco, CA (NBC)	February 13	6,600

Figure 5 (continued)

Market rank, station and affiliation	Closing date for bid submissions	Reserve price
66. WOI-TV Des Moines, IA (NBC)	February 18	$3,300
67. WTVH (TV) Syracuse, NY (CBS)	February 23	6,000
69. WAND-TV Springfield, IL (ABC)	March 11	4,000
70. KETV (TV) Omaha (ABC)	February 27	4,400
73. KCRG-TV Cedar Rapids, IA (ABC)	February 18	2,200
74. WQAD-TV Moine, IL (ABC)	April 7	4,000
78. KREM-TV Spokane, WA (CBS)	March 9	4,600
85. WJTV (TV) Jackson, MS (CBS)	March 23	2,200
87. WIS-TV Columbia, SC (NBC)	March 10	2,400
90. Lincoln, Nebraska (no bids)	March 3	2,000
91. WRBT (TV) Baton Rouge	April 13	2,500
96. KVBC (TV) Las Vegas (NBC)	February 18	6,600
99. KRDO-TV Colorado Springs (ANC)	March 25	2,200
101. WMBD-TV Peoria, IL (CBS)	March 16	2,200
105. WAGT (TV) Augusta, GA (NBC)	March 9	2,200
107. WINK-TV Fort Myers, FL (CBS)	February 18	2,500
108. WSAV-TV Savannah, GA (NBC)	April 17	2,200
109. Madison, Wisconsin (no bids)	March 18	3,000
112. KLFY-TV Lafayette, LA (CBS)	April 15	2,000
121. KIII(TV) Corpus Christi, TX (ABC)	March 25	1,800
125. KOLO-TV Reno, NV (ABC)	February 20	2,500
133. KVAL-TV Eugene, OR (CBS)	March 11	2,200
136. KIVI (TV) Boise, ID (ABC)	February 25	2,000
138. WJET-TV Erie, PA (ABC)	March 30	2,000
140. KHSL-TV Chico, CA (CBS)	April 14	1,600
148. KGET (TV) Bakersfield, CA (NBC)	April 15	2,200
151. WECT (TV) Wilmington, NC (NBC)	March 24	1,200

Note: there are nineteen NBC affiliates, eighteen ABC affiliates, fifteen CBS affiliates, and four independents.
Source: *Broadcasting* (April 27, 1987), p. 58.

- Limited exposure of *Cosby* episodes—no network daytime run; only five telecasts per week in syndication.

- $500 million as well as cash license fees—assuring heavy station promotion throughout the three and a half year term.

- True national coverage—90 percent guaranteed.

- In-program commercial pod (period); positions 2 A&B.

- Ideal commercial environment.

Viacom's strategy was unique in many ways. First, it decided on a gradual market rollout—one at a time, with no more than ten markets a week being opened. A great deal of time went into researching each market, and well-rehearsed presentations were developed that typically lasted one and a half to two hours. Second, the bidding process consisted of offering ten "blocks" of *Cosby* inventory, each block comprising one Monday-Sunday thirty-second unit; Viacom would establish minimum unit prices and accept all qualified offers at or above, with Price Waterhouse administering the bidding. The bidding terms included the following: offers were made for one to ten blocks for one year or three and a half year terms; Viacom would handle all commercial integration, distribution, and affidavits; and a 10 percent down payment and a payout period of forty-two months were mandated, with monthly payment beginning on October 1, 1988. Finally, stations could submit second free-form bids, and alternate bids improving payout were invited.

An important extra clause was added to the original *Cosby* barter agreement: Viacom was allowed to insert one minute of national advertising time—a contractual point that many affiliates feared and/or resented in terms of their sixty-second loss of local advertising revenues. Called a barter spot, it allows the distributor rights to withhold one minute of commercial time for its own use. This means that the station, for each half-hour of *The Cosby Show*, gets five and a half minutes of advertising time to sell, and the distributor gets another full minute to sell.

On January 27, 1988, press releases announced the syndicator's plans to bid that valuable minute.[19] It was another industry first for off-network syndication: bidding on cash-plus-barter terms to local stations. And so *The Cosby Show* was promoted via the *Cosby* sales team, sales kits, presentations, and press reports in what has become a model for future syndication sales.

Kathy Haley discusses Viacom's retention of "an outside firm, Los Angeles-based The Agency, to consult local promotion managers on campaign plans and to administer the *Cosby* co-op program" (1988, pp. 29–30).

The Cosby Barter Plan timetable, as prepared by Viacom International, was as follows:

January 27–February 5: Viacom available to discuss/meet

February 8: Offering letters with "reserve" prices delivered

February 8–18: Offers submitted to Price Waterhouse

March 9: Irrevocability period ends; winners will have been notified; all bids held confidential.

Dennis Gillespie, Viacom's senior vice president of marketing, labeled the company's selling approach the "fear and hope strategy": "We give the station *hope* by telling it all that *Cosby* can do for it, while also instilling *fear* in the station by telling it all *Cosby* can do for the competition."[20] That approach was not always appreciated, to say the least. Some stations felt bullied; some became angered; others thought the whole approach was arrogant; and many cheered at the NATPE (National Association of Television Program Executives) International Convention when Tampa–St. Petersburg didn't make a bid for the show.

The media jumped on the story. Articles with negative overtones appeared in *TV Guide* (Hill, 1988; Zacks, 1986); *The Wall Street Journal* (Kneale, 1988); *Broadcasting* ("Viacom Will Auction Sports in 'Cosby' Reruns," 1988); *Television/Radio Age* ("Programming/Production"); and *Variety* (Dempsey, 1988).

The first rights to air reruns of *The Cosby Show* went to station WWOR-TV of New York—a superstation that reaches 8.5 million households. The price for 182 weeks of the show was an unprecedented $365,000 per episode, "the highest ever for any television show going into syndication ... double the minimum price Viacom said it would accept in New York" (Barnes, 1986, p. 15). Prior to that, the highest current local price for a thirty-minute comedy was $80,000 per episode (for *Cheers*). WWOR-TV was not only banking on the show in its own time period, but was also allowing for audience flow for its next programs. WWOR-TV's purchase price for *The Cosby Show* became a public relations story in its own right.

Beginning in October 1988, a total of 175 local stations covering 96 percent of the United States had *The Cosby Show* reruns available to them five days a week. "Collectively, they paid close to $4 million for each of the show's half-hour episodes, almost *three times* more than any sitcom before had cost" (Hill, 1988, p. 3) Moreover, according to Betsy Vorce, vice president of public relations for Viacom's Entertainment Group, *The Cosby Show* is now available on every continent but Antarctica.[21]

The final step in Viacom's record-setting sales was completed with a deal announced in May 1988 to sell the program's barter minute for $60 million to Procter & Gamble, General Foods, and Group W. This meant that "the total take for sales of *The Cosby Show* in syndication [moved] to close to $600 million for the initial three-and-a-half years of its syndicated run, easily breaking previous off-network sales records for any show in syndication by a factor of almost three."[22] Profits will be distributed so that Viacom will get about one-third of the pie, with the other two-thirds going to executive producers Marcy Carsey and Tom Werner. Bill Cosby himself will be paid about $166 million (Hill, 1988, p. 3). From its domestic marketing plan, which yielded an unprecedented $600 million in gross sales, Viacom received its one-third of $200 million. In addition, Cosby's announcement that he would stick with the show through the 1991–1992 season obligated the syndicated affiliates to continue their commitments to the show for an additional six-month period, or a total of five years. In its off-network syndication, the series has helped catapult Viacom Enterprises to leadership in its field, the largest independent syndication company in the world.

Overall predictions are that the show will earn a billion dollars. Joseph

Zaleski has been quoted as calling the amount "A billion frigging dollars!" (Hill, 1988, p. 3). "Billion Dollar Bill" is considered a "quite conservative" estimate by Steve Behrens, who points out "the staggering effect of *Cosby's* success on the value of NBC's four Thursday-night sitcoms (*The Cosby Show*, *Family Ties, Cheers*, and *Night Court*) in their afterlife" (1986, p. 13). Already by the end of its first off-network season in syndication, *The Cosby Show* reportedly had grossed nearly half a billion dollars.

"Despite a high-powered publicity campaign, reruns of 'The Cosby Show'— the most expensive repeats ever telecast—fell short of expectations in their first week" (Gerard, 1988, p. 26). Viacom's predictions of 12 to 15 percent of television homes fell short, with only about 9 percent of nationwide audiences tuning into it; by later in the week, the numbers were up, and they have continued to climb. Some people blame the underperformance on the stations themselves, saying they took the show too much for granted and failed to do their own promotions. Before the seventh season even began, 124 episodes were already in syndication. By the spring of 1991, Paul Kagan Associates of Carmel, California, reported *Cosby* as number 1, having earned $4.4 million for its reruns.

The Cosby Show in syndication will no doubt become legend. According to an interview in *Television/Radio Age* with Joseph Zaleski, its lessons go beyond just the economic advances: "The show has brought to us a way of understanding the marketplace and broadcasting better because of the extensive research we did on every television station in the U.S. before undertaking the selling of *Cosby*."[23] That effort, Zaleski says later in Viacom's in-house publication, *Broadcast Daily*, was a combination of Viacom's marketing department and sales force: "Through marketing we developed a strategic plan blending all aspects of product, price, distribution and promotion. In addition, marketing had to evaluate the effects of political, regulatory, legal, technological, economic and societal forces and how these environmental factors might impact on our potential customers" (Zaleski, 1988, p. 1).

Defining "The Cosby Factor" as the unique combination of those elements that distinguished the series to make it the single most powerful marketing opportunity available in syndication, Zaleski (1988) reviews the innovative concepts Viacom created to sell *The Cosby Show*:

• We based our plan on a weekly licensing fee with Viacom Enterprises, retaining one minute of barter time.

• We encouraged competition among stations in each market to bid for "Cosby" at or above a minimum or "reserve" weekly license fee which Viacom set based on an in-depth analysis of competitive factors at work in each market.

• We also decided that we could further enhance the performance of the show by offering it on a week-and-date basis through a satellite feed so that the sample episodes would be broadcast nationwide in each market.

• The success of our marketing plan and its execution are proven not simply by the fact that "The Cosby Show" has earned nearly triple the cash generated by any previous show in syndication, but the techniques we developed to sell it are being studied and duplicated by other firms in the industry.

This case study undoubtedly will live up to Zaleski's belief that license fees for *The Cosby Show* will remain the benchmark for successful marketing of "premium-tiered" programming (programming that demands a top price from the syndicator, generating record revenues for the programmer).

During the summer of 1989, it was rumored that Viacom would tie second-cycle renewals of *The Cosby Show* to introductions of *A Different World* and *Roseanne*, *A Different World* being slated for syndication in 1991 and *Roseanne* in 1992. Under the management of the Redstone-Biondi team, the company's stocks more than doubled within these two years and revenues grew by 50 percent.

Yet, when second-cycle renewals were being negotiated later in that autumn of 1989, *Cosby* itself had such a lukewarm reception among the top twenty stations that a "package" seemed unlikely. According to *Broadcasting*, only one station, Viacom-owned KMOV-TV in St. Louis, had accepted the deal, whereas Los Angeles, Chicago, Philadelphia, Boston, Dallas–Ft. Worth, and Washington passed or submitted unacceptable counteroffers.[24] Although Viacom is reputed to get $700 million on its first-cycle revenues for *The Cosby Show,* with the second one—including *A Different World*—it is thought to garner less, about $120 million. With a thirty-second spot commanding $350,000, there were advertising revenues in excess of $130 million in 1990 alone.

But the story is not over. It will be curious to see whether NBC is willing to bend to Carsey-Werner's continuing demands to pay millions extra for continuing to broadcast *The Cosby Show*. Although the producers refuse to confirm it, the *Los Angeles Times* (Gerard, 1990, p. 81) reported in a front-page article that Carsey-Werner were demanding $100 million to renew the show in the 1991–1992 season.

Ironically, NBC, which took the original risk by giving Bill Cosby a slot for a sitcom about a Black family, has not received a dime of the hundreds of millions of dollars that Carsey-Werner and Viacom International made from *The Cosby Show* in syndication profits. Although the network has made a great deal from the show's high ratings, which translate directly into enormous advertising revenues, NBC is now finding that the show in syndication is cutting into audience shares of some of its other programming. Called the "fin-syn" issue (financial interest and syndication rule), concerned with whether or not financial interest and syndication rules are restraining free and open competition in program and syndication markets, the networks have long been seeking rule repeal by the Federal Communications Commission (FCC).

John Agoglia, a top executive at NBC, asks: "How is it that a show on which we risked millions can now turn around and sting us?"[25] The dilemma brings up the perennial issue of whether or not networks should be permitted to share in syndication profits, a regulation stemming from a 1970 FCC decision. The regulation was made stricter in 1980 by a ten-year consent decree from the U.S. Justice Department that further restricted network power by limiting the amounts of programming a network could own, produce, and/or syndicate. Concerned about the power of the Big Three (ABC, CBS, and NBC), most citizen groups applauded the decision in its day.

In 1980 most television stations in the United States were sole proprietorships; today only about 100 of the 630 network affiliates are single-station entities, and the market for program production and program syndication increasingly continues to belong to a privileged few companies. Yet the networks, which obviously want a part of the $5.7 billion global syndication business, only got a compromise from the FCC in its April 1991 fin-syn decision: they were restored the right to handle a portion of their program rerun sales domestically, and all of them abroad. Both they and the major movie studios remain unhappy, claiming that the entire set of 1970 restrictions should have been revoked. Although the networks had the support this time around of the White House, FCC chairman Alfred Sikes, and editorial approval from many pivotal American newspapers, they also launched a multimillion-dollar campaign, but to no avail. Not surprisingly, a plan to challenge this latest decision is already in the works.

Syndication of *The Cosby Show* continues to have repercussions. The backlash caused by its record prices and then its mediocre showing should greatly affect future syndication deals. In addition to reported Nielsen ratings of 6.9, anecdotes abound throughout the industry. For example, one West Coast station has moved *The Cosby Show* to 11 P.M. Yet, as Arthur Kananack, president of International Theatrical and Video Sales for Viacom Pictures, reminds us, they will own the show forever, in perpetuity.[26]

At least one thing is clear: Syndicators are more serious than ever, but statious are reciprocally more cautions. Inescapably, the marketing, advertising, ratings, promotions, and syndication stories about *The Cosby Show* underscore the fact that it is a phenomenon.

3

The Politics and Legalities of
The Cosby Show

The development of mass communications throughout the western
world and particularly in the United States in the twentieth century is a
product of both science and law.

Zuckman and Gaynes,
Mass Communication Law (West, 1977), p. 1.

As part of this study on *The Cosby Show*, it is appropriate to discuss the politics
and legalities surrounding it as part of a systematic approach to researching
a media phenomenon. This chapter will be brief, because obviously the real
political and legal issues pertaining to the program are undoubtedly considered—and usually cleared, canceled, and/or settled—behind closed doors.

Fellow communications researchers might be interested to know about
the legal roadblocks encountered in this project itself. From the start, Bill
Cosby and his various staff members were informed about this book. That
list of support staff included Cosby's personal secretary (Julie L. Phillips of
SAH Enterprises), his agent (Norman Brokaw of the William Morris Agency),
his publicist (David Brokaw of the Brokaw Company), the show's executive
producers (Carsey-Werner Company, c/o Laura Black, director of public relations), the show's syndicators (Viacom International—first, Gloria Rella as
director of public relations, and then Betsy Vorce, vice president of the
Entertainment Group), the show's script consultant (Dr. Alvin F. Poussaint)
and director of public affairs (Kim Tinsley), NBC's press representative to the
show (first Joann Alsano, then Mary Neagoy, and then Rosemary O'Brien),
and Carsey-Werner's counsel, Joella West, at the law offices of Stuart L. Glickman in Los Angeles (who later held the title of vice president of business
affairs for the Carsey-Werner Company at Studio City, California).

For some reason, the initial communications discussing plans for the book (examining *The Cosby Show* from an academic/communications perspective) were interpreted as a desire for cooperative involvement in it. Counsel issued a stern response, emphasizing that neither the Carsey-Werner Company nor Bill Cosby wanted to be involved in my project. It was made very clear that both the show's executive producers and its star are adamant about protecting all their material other than that which is considered in the public domain.[1]

The Cosby Show's Office of Public Affairs also maintained strict policies. In response to an initial query there, the office issued the following statement: "Unfortunately, Carsey Werner Company policy precludes the use of Cosby Show scripts, characters, locales, expressions or trademarks in conjunction with marketing proposals."[2]

Although it was not necessary, the major parties affiliated with the show have been consistently informed not only of this research, but also of reports relative to it.

David Brokaw, Bill Cosby's publicist, was most cooperative and helpful in this project. Recognizing the value of a publication that is so overwhelmingly pro-Cosby and pro–*The Cosby Show* in terms of its impact and implications, he has been an invaluable go-between. Upon request, he previewed a draft of this manuscript and shared it with both the star and its producers.

This chapter discusses a lawsuit that was filed over who originated the idea for *The Cosby Show*, the role of the show in the Writers Guild strike in 1985, the issue of closed captioning on the show, a particular problem of Bill Cosby's that was made public, and the legalities of the show in syndication.

WHOSE IDEA WAS *THE COSBY SHOW*?

In 1987 Hwesu S. Murray, a unit manager at NBC Sports, filed a lawsuit in Manhattan federal court claiming that he had submitted the idea for the show to the network's entertainment division. According to Murray, his idea suggested Bill Cosby as star, "head of a middle-class black family with five children, the eldest away at college. Both parents would be professionals, and the show would avoid stereotypes about blacks in favor of family situations."[3]

NBC rejected the idea. Once *The Cosby Show* premiered in the fall of 1984, however, Murray decided to sue for misappropriation and fraud. Lawyers for NBC argued that the idea was not novel enough; Federal Judge Miriam Goldman Cedarbaum sided with them, dismissing the suit and reasoning that there is no reason "a program based on the life of a middle-class family and resembling the 'Dick Van Dyke Show' or 'Father Knows Best' should be considered novel" (Landro and Power, 1987, p. 21).

With the recent success of Art Buchwald's lawsuit against Eddie Murphy's film *Coming to America* regarding idea authorship, no doubt many more people will want to seek legal redress. The *New York Times* (June 7, 1989,

p. B5) has cited a second suit filed over the idea for *The Cosby Show*, but to date the challenge has not been taken seriously.

THE COSBY SHOW AND THE WRITERS GUILD STRIKE

The Cosby Show became the first major casualty of the March 1985 Writers Guild of America strike (Sharbutt, 1985, p. 1 V–2). It was forced to shut down production minus three scripts before the walkout began.

As will be seen in chapter 4, final polishing of each episode tends to continue right up to the time the show is taped. Of particular concern about the loss of *Cosby*'s last scripts was the plan to consider one as a potential pilot for a spinoff series starring Tony Orlando as a social worker.

CLOSED CAPTIONING OF *THE COSBY SHOW*

An article in the *New York Times* (Boyer, 1986, p. C16) relative to *The Cosby Show* brought up an interesting concern in " 'Cosby' Captioning Sparks Dispute." At issue was whether or not the show would be close-captioned for the hearing impaired, and if so, who should pay for that service—NBC or the show's producers? The actual weekly tab was a minimal $1,250; the problem, it appeared, was more symbolic.

Thirty-six months later, I determined to find out who had won. The article had named a spokesperson for an agency called the Caption Center, a Boston-based organization that produced captions for television commercials. When contacted, a woman at the agency stated that captioning of *The Cosby Show* had been enthusiastically received. Aware that the Caption Center was "a non-profit center that is part of WGBH Educational Foundation," I telephoned Boston's public television station late on a Friday afternoon, with a request to be directed from there.

Annette Posell, the Caption Center's manager of marketing who was named in the article, came on line, introduced herself, and asked the reason and nature of the call. The initial response of this researcher was to begin with an apology for following up on a three-year-old newspaper article, but then went on to explain who the caller was, what project/book was being written, and why there was interest in wanting to get caught up on the captioning issue.

After a long pause, Posell explained that she herself was hearing impaired and that other people's comments had to be decoded electronically before she could decipher what was being said. As she explained it, the first season of *The Cosby Show* had not been captioned. But as it grew in popularity, a number of hearing-impaired persons (there are some 400,000 persons with decoders in the United States) wanted the show captioned during its second year. Closed captioning, which is announced on various programs, is made possible for hearing-impaired persons by means of particular decoding devices that they purchase for their television sets. Broadcasters have voluntarily provided closed captioning as a service since it began in 1980. Part of the cost is also picked up by the U.S. Department of Education and by commercial sponsors.

NBC, which was making an estimated $1.5 million in weekly advertising revenues from *The Cosby Show* at the time, refused to pay any of the tab for captioning. Thus, Bill Cosby and Carsey-Werner decided to split the costs with the Caption Center. Then Tom Werner, maintaining that the show made so much money for NBC, said that the network should pay for the captioning. NBC's vice president of corporate affairs, Robert Cornet, announced that it was against NBC's policy to pay for captioning of programs. And so the squabble stood.

Posell was able to fill in between the lines and beyond the report. It turns out that NBC was the only network in 1986 that did not support closed captioning. According to Annette Posell's version, Bill Cosby was upset and embarrassed by this fact, and he wanted to take the network to task. Cosby himself took this story to the *New York Times,* knowing that it would get quite a public response, which it did. And within a year, NBC had changed its policy.

As pointed out earlier, few people understand the power of media more than Bill Cosby.

BILL COSBY'S OWN LEGAL PROBLEMS

From his background in a Philadelphia ghetto, which he has since parlayed into comedy routines, Cosby has gone on to become a "one-man multimedia phenomenon: actor, comedian, pitchman nonpareil . . . he has made himself into the most ubiquitous presence in American pop culture" (Waters, 1985, p. 3). Yet, he has not forgotten his roots. *Jet,* a Black publication, reminds us that "Cosby knows what it is like to be poor and Black in affluent America" (Johnson, 1982, p. 13). Without great fanfare, he has long been a supporter of Black causes; his most recent donation has been that of $20 million to Atlanta's Spelman College, the largest gift in the history of the Black women's college. He and his wife, Camille, have also donated $325,000 each to four predominantly Black universities: Florida A&M University in Tallahassee, Howard University in Washington, D.C., Shaw University in Raleigh, North Carolina, and Central State University in Wilberforce, Ohio. Kathleen Teltsch discusses the challenges Cosby's gifts have posed to the traditional notion of Black philanthropy.[4] The list of his causes is too extensive to cite here, but they range from helping Winnie Mandela to serving as celebrity fundraiser and as sickle cell spokesperson. There is wide documentation of Bill Cosby's generosity including, in addition to monetary donations, his giving of himself and his talents to worthy causes. Most of Cosby's responses to solicitations have been in the name of education, particularly Black education, and most have also been politically relevant. It is important to note that he has remained loyal to family, old friends, Temple University, and many people who have helped him at various stages of his career.

Cosby may not have forgotten his roots, but he has also become quite aware of litigious lessons: He has an enormous legal staff on hand to protect him from both a prying public and a sensationalism-seeking media. Members of the press realize that there is another side to Cosby the funny guy, and that is Cosby the cautious guy. His dislike and distrust of reporters run deep. As in many other instances, Cosby wants control, and he is usually able to wield control, whether the issue involves consenting to an interview (if the questions are prescreened), letting his name or the show's title be associated with a particular sponsorship, or permitting his photo to be used (with approval and preferably on the cover). In addition to insisting on editorial control for personal interviews at the time of the series' debut, *The Cosby Show's* savvy star demanded front-page coverage; this is why he appeared on the cover of so many publications. Only *People* magazine, an interesting exception, held out; it refused to conform to Cosby's demands, claiming that they limited the magazine's editorial choice.[5]

A 1986 report in *Channels of Communication* included this item: "A corporation co-owned by television's squeaky-clean First Father, Bill Cosby, has been rejected for station ownership by a Federal Communications Commission official on grounds of questionable character" (O'Brien, 1986, p. 11). The "co-owned" designation is the key: It turns out that Cosby has co-owned a corporation called Cozzin Communications Corporation since 1980 with Cleveland broadcaster and sports promoter Joseph Zingale. Actually, Cosby owns 51 percent and Zingale 49 percent. The "questionable character" problem was relative to the minority owner. FCC law judge Walter Miller dismissed the application for a Boston radio frequency when he found out that Zingale had previously forged the signatures of his wife and three children on forty-six applications for low-power television licenses. John P. Schmidt, Cosby's New York lawyer, called his client a passive investor in Cozzin; in this case, he remains "squeaky-clean."

Cosby has had legal problems of his own of late, however. He and his wife, Camille, are pressing for an early start to the banckruptcy trial of their fired business manager, Mary Waller. After serving as chief financial officer to the Cosbys for more than eight years, earning $1 million annually, Waller was accused, according to court records, of cheating her clients out of more than $8.5 million.

As this book goes to press, lawyers are arguing whether the fraud and embezzlement allegations brought by the Cosbys merit an early trial. This trial will help decide whether Waller can manage her own assets while she reorganizes under Chapter 11 of the U.S. Bankruptcy Code, or whether her estate should be placed under the jurisdiction of a court-appointed trustee. Whatever the final outcome, it has been a difficult and disillusioning episode for the Cosbys.

It was a major news item in the summer of 1990 when Bill Cosby announced that he was leaving Doubleday book publishers for Putnam Berkley Group, a unit of MCA, even though Doubleday reportedly had offered him $4 million for a book on childhood. MCA owns television stations that run *The Cosby Show* reruns in syndication; it also owns Universal Pictures, with whom Cosby made the film *Ghost Dad*. Although figures were not disclosed on the book bonus, spokespersons for Cosby agreed that it was one of the biggest deals of its kind. As part of the arrangement, Cosby wrote *Childhood* (1991).

The ultimate political animal, Bill Cosby does his own homework, learns his turf, and seems to know both his strengths and weaknesses. Typically, his approach is through humor. As the star speaker at an October 1990 fundraising banquet for the University of Massachusetts, this was the scene:

After a few opening jokes about the timeless quality of institutional food, Cosby launched into a lively pep talk. Mixing laugh lines with serious advice, he exhorted employees and friends of the university to learn the political skills necessary to combat state budget cuts and stir up popular support for public higher education. "You've got to take it to the people," he urged. "If the people know about it, then they're going to care. And you've go to make them feel they can do something about it." (C. Smith, 1990, p. 11)

This statement of advice could be a credo for how Cosby the politician operates both personally and professionally.

THE LEGALITIES OF *THE COSBY SHOW* IN SYNDICATION

When promotion to get *The Cosby Show* into syndication was in place, the role of the legal department was key. Thomas P. Vitale, market strategy analyst at Viacom Enterprises, describes how the Counsel/Entertainment unit "was involved from the beginning, setting up the way the offering process and papers worked from a legal point-of-view . . . (and) the Legal Department was also involved in this process and in the first markets that were cleared" (1987, p. 21). Daily, throughout that period, these members of "The Cosby Team" prepared bid letters, including terms, conditions, and rules of the offering, and then formally accepted winning bids. They were also responsible for legal problems such as defining markets and exclusivity rights.

Viacom itself has had its own legal problems. In the spring of 1986, financier Carl C. Icahn posed a potential takeover threat of the corporation. Then, in mid-September 1986 the corporation received a $2.7 billion buyout offer from a management-led group. National Amusements, Inc., Viacom's largest stockholder, which held 6.91 million, or 19.6 percent of the company's 32.3

million common shares, made an offer to acquire the company in February 1987.

The next month, Carsey-Werner filed a suit in U.S. District Court in Manhattan against Viacom International, Inc., as it was "(c)oncerned that its cut of the syndication revenues might be jeopardized by the recently announced $3.4 billion acquisition of Viacom by National Amusements, Inc., a Dedham, Mass.-based theater chain operation."[6] The producers primarily wanted the court to order the syndicator to place Carsey-Werner's share of *The Cosby Show's* syndication proceeds in trust. That June, U.S. District Judge Charles S. Haight announced in an oral hearing that "he would decline to enter a preliminary injunction against the Viacom transaction."[7]

Although Viacom is still adjusting to ownership under Sumner Redstone, Hillary Condit of the syndicator's Corporate Relations office reports that the bottom line can be found in terms of higher profits.[8] The real story, however, is good morale since the acquisition.

4

Production of *The Cosby Show*

TV directing is always concerned with four basic issues:

- *The message*. The programme material. What we are trying to say to our audience. The emotions we hope to engender in them.
- *The mechanics*. The equipment we have available. What it can and can't do.
- *The methods*. The techniques we choose to enable us to build up an arresting, interesting presentation.
- *The organisation*. The behind-the-scenes activities that interrelate and coordinate the work of our production team.

This is our field of study.

Gerald Millerson,
Effective TV Production (Focal, 1976), p. 9.

To see how these four issues—message, mechanics, methods, and organization—come together each week in the actual process of producing *The Cosby Show*, this researcher traveled to the Kaufman-Astoria Studios in Astoria (Queens), New York. In this drab, gray, warehouse-like building, plunked incongruously in the middle of a high-crime area, I spent a day watching a group of professionals put together parts of what would become twenty-two and a half minutes of prime time viewing on a single episode of the nation's top-rated program.

This chapter, therefore, focuses on how *The Cosby Show* is developed—when, where, by whom, and how. Its cast and crew are introduced, Bill Cosby's role in the production process is discussed, and a behind-the-scenes description should help elucidate how episodes come together into a final product. A case study of the episode "Gone Fishing" highlights that process. Yet, this chapter goes beyond merely discussing the mechanics and methods of delivering messages; it helps explain a critical component of the show as a phenomenon in terms of its being a collective endeavor led by a single individual.

CAST AND CREW OF *THE COSBY SHOW*

First, let us review the Huxtable family and then take an opportunity to find out about the production crew behind their seemingly effortless performances.[1]

The key characters include the following:

Dr. Heathcliff Huxtable (obstetrician/gynecologist)—Bill Cosby

Clair Huxtable (lawyer)—Phylicia Rashad

Sondra Huxtable Tibideaux—Sabrina LeBeauf

> Sondra's husband, Elvin Tibideaux—Geoffrey Owens

> Sondra's twins, Nelson and Winnie

Denise Huxtable—Lisa Bonet

> Denise's husband, Martin—Joseph C. Phillips

> Denise's stepdaughter, Olivia—Raven-Symone

Theodore Huxtable—Malcolm-Jamal Warner

Vanessa Huxtable—Tempestt Bledsoe

Rudy Huxtable—Keshia Knight Pulliam

The wider, extended family includes Cliff's parents (Russell Huxtable: Earl Hyman; Anna Huxtable: Clarice Taylor), Clair's "distant relative" Pam (Erika Alexander), who has moved in with the family, and some of the kids' friends, such as Cockroach, Charmaine, Slide, and Kenny/"Bud." This is only a partial listing; for a fuller listing see Appendix 5.

A major reason for making the pilgrimage to Queens was to witness at first hand some of the operations that are not visible on the television screen. Some of the key players associated with behind-the-screen decisions and designs for the series include executive producers Marcy Carsey and Tom Werner, producer Caryn Sneider Mandalbach, director Jay Sandrich, and consultant Dr. Alvin F. Poussaint.

The functional job descriptions of television executive producers vary according to circumstances and contracts. Sometimes they want complete control of everything from storyline to personnel. Because of the title "executive," they are typically not under organizational restraints, and they are free to develop, package, and/or administer individual patterns and styles to best express their reasons for being involved in a show in the first place. Budgetary concerns take most of their time.

Correctly interpreting their role vis-à-vis the star of *The Cosby Show*, executive producers Marcy Carsey and Tom Werner have pretty much remained in the business end of the series. Not overly concerned with the tedium of weekly artistic creations, they prefer instead to surround themselves with competent persons to nurture and further develop the concept that they brought to the screen.

The Carsey-Werner Company, headquartered in Studio City, California, took the original gamble on producing *The Cosby Show* and has never looked back. Both Marcy Carsey and Tom Werner are considered unparalleled successes in producing not only a hit show, but also an enviable work environment. Yet, they give all the credit to the "team." In 1986, Warren Littlefield, then president of NBC Entertainment, declared that Carsey-Werner were "Hollywood's newest deities. . . . They know how to handle people. It's that simple. They've nurtured new writers and they've made people want to stay."[2] The team seems to blossom best in the collaborative atmosphere associated with developing and producing programs: "In addition to negotiating deals with the networks and financing whatever production and overhead costs the network fees do not cover, they work closely with writers, directors, actors and production executives in formulating ideas, writing scripts and attending to the myriad of details of putting a show on top."[3] The two spend much of their time in California, counting on that cooperative base that has been set.

Both executive producers Carsey-Werner and producer Caryn Mandalbach oversee the writing and production of *The Cosby Show*. Typically, a television producer is allotted a wide creative range, and Mandalbach is no exception. Writing about "the producer's medium," Newcomb and Alley (1983) discuss the role of the producer:

First, given the structures of the industry's economic organization the producer is often assigned legal and financial responsibility for the final television product. A commonplace within the entertainment industry is that television is a "producer's medium." Second, in series television, several episodes or even several series are under production at any given moment, and the producer is the one who must oversee entire projects. The producer must hire or fire other members of the production team, including line producers who often see to day-to-day activities. Directors, writers, editors, and guest stars may work only in a single episode of a series. The producer, involved with the project from beginning to end, sees to it that continuity is maintained, that peace is kept among other members of the team, and, most importantly, that the series concept remains secure. Even in productions that are not part of a series, the same formal and informal authority and responsibility belong to the producer. (p. xiii)

Mandalbach discusses her working relationship with Carsey-Werner: "They make decisions and back up the people they work with. The big thing they do is listen to what Mr. Cosby has to say and add their own thoughts. . . . You can't underestimate their skill. It's astonishing how easy they make it seem. It's a subtle and beautiful difference."[4]

Whereas the producer is in charge of finances, personnel, and overall supervision of a program, the director's job includes performing "three distinct operations: pre-production, shooting, and post-production."[5] Television directors have primary authority for taping a program, giving directions to crew members and assuming ultimate responsibility for the artistic compositions of sight and sound.

Jay Sandrich, director of *The Cosby Show*, has been called the "Ace of Pilots—He's a rare one: a thinking man's director with real clout. For Bill Cosby's producers, he was the only choice" (Meisler, 1986, p. 50). Sandrich was Tom Werner's first (and only) choice. He was called on to shoot the pilot for the show, direct the first two seasons, and even directed several of the twenty-five episodes in subsequent seasons, coordinating and overseeing "nearly every aspect of production—from script changes to the quality of light, the editing, the cameras, the action."[6] Asked in an interview with *Videography* magazine if there is a "Jay Sandrich signature," he replied: "No, my way of shooting a television show is to ask, if I were in the audience, what would I want to be seeing at that moment." Audience is key to Sandrich, especially, he thinks, with Cosby, who seems to thrive on the interaction. The director has found that with expert actors, such as those on *The Cosby Show*, the difficulties of taping before an audience are far outweighed by the performance results. Even though he prefers Los Angeles to New York, Sandrich has enjoyed working on the show and has been particularly gratified by its wide audience reach. He states: "That is very satisfying, not because we're reaching the number of people, but because we're reaching across the spectrum of audiences. It's really nice to be able to reach young audiences and old audiences and everybody in between. And I happen to philosophically like what we're doing. I think we're a positive show. I think we are trying to say there are other ways to deal with family relationships."[7]

Writing about *Television: The Director's Viewpoint*, John W. Ravage (1978) explains:

Both those who find fulfillment in television and those who do not seem to agree on its limitations. There is little room for the *auteur* style of direction. There are few visual or syntactical trademarks setting one television director off from another. A good show becomes its own reward, and the wise director lets it go at that. When a script and its production are truly superior, the director rejoices, but he must realize the transitory nature of his product. Then he can say, with Jay Sandrich, "I have been satisfied emotionally and intellectually by my work." (p. 8)

Every television show has its producers and directors, but not many have their own resident psychiatrists, as does *The Cosby Show* in Alvin F. Poussaint,

M.D. Bill Cosby called on Poussaint, a long-time friend, to be the show's consultant because he "wanted the show to be real, the psychological inter- actions of the family to be real. And he wanted the issues to be real issues, universal to families."[8] Dr. Poussaint has been variously called "the Cosby Show's Secret Ingredient,"[9] "the conscience of 'the Cosby Show,'"[10] and its "credibility watchdog." Each week, he reads the approximately fifty-page scripts, dissecting every detail of every scene, "to make sure that the family interactions are psychologically accurate, that the children act in age-appro- priate ways, and that the show creates the feeling of a loving and caring family."[11] Guarding against stereotyping, sexism, racism, inconsistencies, and/ or inappropriate behaviors, Dr. Poussaint makes changes and suggestions such as how to deal with marijuana- or cigarette-smoking friends, playing a game rather than telling monster stories at a slumber party, adding the names of predominantly Black colleges to a list of other potential ones, making a correction in an aspirin dosage, or deleting a negative reference to an ethnic group.

Poussaint, in a telephone conversation, said he wanted to help collaborate on a quality show to make the Black community proud and positive, reflecting caring and love through laughter and respect.[12] He has met those goals. Beyond the brief job description delineated here, Dr. Poussaint has been the subject of much literature relative to the show; see Appendix 6.

"For the series in particular," Cantor has argued, "the problems associated with high ratings take precedence over all other considerations. The creative people must satisfy the production companies (the program suppliers), the network that distributes the series, the advertisers, and finally a large segment of the audience to keep their show on the air" (Cantor, 1980, pp. 81–82). Meanwhile, Michael Real claims that the super media are more institutional than the individual; he states that "(t)he achievements of Spielberg, Coppola, Bochko, Cosby or Disney are collective endeavors in ways that those of Dostoevsky or Shakespeare were not" (1989, p. 257). Both Cantor's and Real's contentions get spun around, it will be found, in how *The Cosby Show* and its star are involved in the production process.

This is an enormous endeavor. Staff alone for the show numbers more than 150, and there are many additional people at NBC and at Viacom, in New York and in California. Each one is critical to the final product, but a single person is the ultimate decision maker.

BILL COSBY'S ROLE IN *THE COSBY SHOW* PRODUCTION

Not every star has, or wants, a role in production; Cosby, on the other hand, has, wants, and commands nearly complete control.

"Equally as important as his presence on camera is Mr. Cosby's deep involvement behind the scenes of his new series," wrote the *New York Times* in 1984: "From start to finish of each episode, Mr. Cosby dominates. And the challenge for the show's staff is to translate his ideas into stories crafted around his comedic style rather than the traditional comedy formula" (Smith, 1984, p. 27). Typically, Cosby introduces a thread for an idea or theme, and he lets his writers develop loose constructions into stories an audience can recognize from their own experiences. In this last step in the script process—the actual taping—one could easily see Bill Cosby's mark on touches like practical jokes and when and how he was to showcase his mugging talents.

Without question the show centers on Cosby. "Cosby is the focal point," states Michael Real. "The family emphasis and the centrality of Cosby are among the principal symbolic contributions of the show" (Real, p. 115).

In a distinct move away from formulaic sitcom jokes, *The Cosby Show* tests an idea on its studio audience for reaction and then decides whether to incorporate it into the final scene. That's why there are two different audiences for each "final" taping of the "live" show. It was very obvious to me, on seeing the finished product, which parts were from the first session, which I had observed, and which parts were dubbed either from the second session or from another entirely separate editing.

Paul Taylor has written about live sitcom audiences: "Until a program is actually performed in front of a large, expectant audience, no one can accurately predict where all the laughs are going to come. The presence of an audience raises performances to concert pitch and allows the creation of a relationship built on feedback" (1979, p. 24). No one understands that prescription better than Bill Cosby, concomitant performer and producer.

Editing for *The Cosby Show*, as one might well imagine, often continues right up until the last minute.

Director Jay Sandrich describes Cosby's manner as "purposeful but relaxed," so disagreements become useful and performers are allowed self-expression.[13] By way of example he cites Phylicia Rashad's contribution: "She can go along with whatever Bill's doing and at the right moment get him back on track. She's not a comedienne; she's something at least as rare: an actress who can do comedy." Reciprocally, Bill Cosby's television wife says of him, "(h)e's like a magnet. Nothing escapes his eye. He sees everything on the set, and he's always creating avenues for his supporting cast to shine."[14] The Huxtable parental team obviously works well together. What is apparent, however, is how completely professional Phylicia Rashad is—more so than any of the other performers on the set. Between takes, she typically stands back or sits down, but she is always ready to laugh, cry, or produce whatever line or emotion is called for. For her working on a *Cosby* set is serious fun/work.

"Cosby is uniquely suited to play the figure of flexible authority at the center of a new style of enlightened sitcom," writes Mark Edmundson, a teacher in the English Department at the University of Virginia.

He's the first TV dad with a body: He loves to move and shake. Gestures do half the work of communication for him. He also has a control of tone that puts any of the upstarts to shame. Then there's Cosby's magnificent face. His expressions are exquisitely subtle, and always just a shade out of joint with whatever lines he's speaking, providing a knowing but uninterpretable commentary on them. Cosby has a knack for ironizing everything he says without discrediting it or himself. (1986, pp. 71–72)

That centrality is apparent throughout *The Cosby Show*.

John J. O'Connor (1984) focuses on Cosby's comic routines, "ranging from electronic boogie to using Monopoly game money to teach his son a lesson in economics. He does slow takes and delivers fast joke lines. He is on a roll and making the most of it" (p. C30). The comedy can be verbal, or it can be nonverbal—or a combination of both.

THE COSBY SHOW PRODUCTION PROCESS

Television situation comedy, grounded in forms of theatrical comedy, is equally influenced by its structural and institutional characteristics. Hal Himmelstein discusses the apparatus of television comedy:

Lifelike characters are seen in enclosed spaces, are revealed in tight two- or three-shots and close-ups, acting out the mundane everyday world manifested in incongruous if not bizarre configurations. Situation and characterization are crucial to the success of this work. But beyond the aesthetics of television comedy lies its relationship to the real world of social relations. (1984, p.78)

No one seems to understand that concept of finding humor in our daily lives better than Cosby. Whether he is showing exasperation-with-love toward children or concern-with-cynicism toward patients, he touches a nerve. Furthermore, knowing that his series is being shot in a small space, he is savvy enough to capitalize on what could be a constraint. For example, occasionally he points to his face for a cameraperson, indicating a close-up might be in order.

"Effective control and manipulation of screen space" (Barker, 1985, p. 234) become critical elements in the notion of television aesthetics, and as such are of constant concern to both the star and the producers of *The Cosby Show*. David Thorburn (1990) has called television the *Story Machine*. He remarks on how television fits into an aesthetic anthropology—beginning with literary perspectives, then eventually taking the study of motion pictures seriously, and at last accepting the study of television as the principal medium of popular narrative. The various episodes of *The Cosby Show* have become part of our culture; the really intriguing thing is that so many of them only evolve during their taping.

According to John Ellis of the University of Kent at Canterbury, England, broadcast television "offers a radically different image from cinema, and a different relation between sound and image" (1982, p.127). Television is mainly differentiated by its capability of immediacy; seemingly live, it is right there in our living rooms. This effect may help explain why so many viewers of the show have remarked that they think various scripts have been stolen from their own lives and stories. It may also help explain how dextrously *The Cosby Show* producers make use of presence and immediacy in various situations and why.

The setting for the show is a New York City brownstone. The main focus is on the living room, which features a large couch and paintings by Black artists such as Oliver Johnson, Varnette Honeywood, and the late Ellis Wilson.[15] Off the living room is an equally spacious kitchen, with a garden visible through the back window. The sets also include a master bedroom, a child's bedroom that changes ownership depending on plot line, a hallway, bathroom, and a set of stairs off the living room that don't go anywhere but are the scene for a number of escapades. In many ways it's a very comfortable, very enviable home.

Before one reads too much into the fact that the family is homebound, and that most scripts are home-oriented, it is important to remember that financially, it is most beneficial to tape most of the shows in that existent living room. That revelation and others became clear at an invaluable session held on September 20, 1989, when the Museum of Broadcasting sponsored a seminar entitled *"The Cosby Show:* An Inside Look." Tom Werner, executive producer of the show, chaired a panel session that included the following creative staff: John Markus, co-executive producer and head writer; Gary Kott, co-supervising producer; and Carmen Finestra, supervising producer.

The participants uniformly agreed that the genius behind the show is Cosby himself. John Markus commented that their sitcom is different from others because of its star; production-wise, he pointed out, everything begins with a full-blown meeting with Bill Cosby. According to Carmen Finestra, Cosby maintains control throughout, until the final product has been delivered. Both the staff and the network give him free rein. Cosby knows what he wants, Finestra continued, and he has a unique vision: Cosby aims at positive means and solutions to the conflicts proposed during a half-hour sitcom. Gary Kott emphasized that scripts go right up to the last moment. With regard to audience responsiveness to the show beyond its formal ratings, Tom Werner stated that it is large, incredibly positive, and often very amusing.

Overall, a strict schedule for production is maintained. On Mondays, cast and crew get together to review the script, which typically takes about two weeks to write for a thirty-minute show. They meet with Cosby and discuss reactions to what has been written. The writers are responsible for revisions— sometimes minor, sometimes major. Rewrites can be done in twelve or more hours; sometimes as much as 30 to 50 percent of the original script is completely changed, according to Gary Kott. The head writer, for example, observed that Cosby would sometimes read an item in that day's newspaper, which he wanted to incorporate into the script. This gives the show added spontaneity; the material is brand new, and Cosby loves that immediacy. Likening their work atmosphere to that of the physician in an emergency room, John Markus nevertheless says: "It's fun. You have nine hours to fix it."

By 10 A.M. the next day the reworked script is incorporated into proper staging. This is team writing at its finest; often it is completed within a forty-eight hour period.

Wednesday is camera-blocking day. Shots and scripts are synchronized, scenes are plotted, and actors rehearse during the afternoon. According to Gary Kott, at this point, about 90 percent of the script is complete. Once the cameras have been choreographed, on a given day the crew can work on as many as three shows at a time. There are meetings with the director and talks with Tom Werner. There are talks, too, with the set designer, the wardrobe department, and the cast coordinator. For example, one episode called for a fireman, and at 6 o'clock the night before shooting the call went out for a Dalmatian dog and a mini fire engine.

Thursdays, as Michael Cieply has documented, "Spell Trouble for the Huxtables." "Thursday is tape day . . . when the crew goes hunting for funny bones" (1986, p. 28). Rehearsal runs from about 10:30 until 1 P.M., which is not a very long time, and deliberately so, for emphasis is on spontaneity. Cosby saves his routines for Thursday. The dress rehearsal is first taped around 4:30 P.M. before a live audience of several hundred people. The second taping occurs around 8:30 P.M., again before a live audience; that second run-through often lasts late into the night. Carmen Finestra comments that it is a "demanding and exhausting work week."

Depending on how it goes, Thursday often becomes Friday. That is the day when the job of the cast is finished, but Jay Sandrich's job is only beginning. He has the critical task of editing; as he told *Videography* in "Conversation with Jay Sandrich": "We work at Editel. We work with five monitors so I can see the same line five times in different takes. I literally will cut the show line by line by line. I'll look at the line in the afternoon performance, the line in the evening performance, and any retakes, and I can see absolute differences, some things just in inflection. It's a wonderful thing" (1986, p. 68).

Specifically, if Cosby has a funny line or makes a funny face and none of the ensemble laughs at it appropriately, the editor can insert one of their hearty responses from another time. The show yields image and illusion, as promised.

There is a "comedy rule of thumb" that says that parts that are funny are not cut, but that rule does not necessarily apply to *The Cosby Show*. John Markus points out that each episode is constructed to stand on its own and that you do not have to rush for the joke to get your message across.

To put all this into a clear example, it might be of particular interest to see detailed scheduling for a specific episode, "Theo's Holiday," which appears in Figures 6, 7, and 8.

Figure 6
The Cosby Show: "Theo's Holiday"—Short Rundown

NBC PEACOCK	:05
MAIN TITLES	:55
COMMERCIAL #1	1:03

ACT 1, Scene 1   (1)
INT. LIVING ROOM - EVENING (DAY 1)
  (Cliff, Theo, Vanessa)
ACT 1, Scene 2   (8)
EXT. HUXTABLE FRONT STOOP -THE NEXT MORNING (DAY 2)
  (Cliff, Theo, Vanessa)
ACT 1, Scene 3   (12)
INT. LIVING ROOM-CONTINUOUS ACTION (DAY 2)
  (Cliff, Clair, Theo, Rudy)
ACT 1, Scene 4   (14)
INT. THEO'S ROOM-CONTINUOUS ACTION (DAY 2)
  (Cliff, Theo)
ACT 1, Scene 5   (22)
INT. LIVING ROOM-A MOMENT LATER (DAY 2)
  (Cliff, Denise, Theo, Vanessa, Rudy)

TITLE BUMPER	:03
COMMERCIAL #2	1:03
NBC PROMO	:40

ACT 11, Scene 1   (28)
INT. THEO'S ROOM-LATER THAT AFTERNOON (DAY 2)
  (Cliff, Theo, Cockroach)
ACT 11, Scene 2   (34)
INT. DINING ROOM-MOMENTS LATER (DAY 2)
  (Cliff, Clair, Theo, Cockroach)
ACT 11, Scene 3   (39)
INT. KITCHEN--CONTINUOUS ACTION (DAY 2)
  (Cockroach, Theo, Denise)
ACT 11, Scene 4   (43)
INT. LIVING ROOM-CONTINUOUS ACTION (DAY 2)
  (Rudy, Vanessa, Clair, Cliff, Theo, Cockroach)
ACT 11, Scene 5   (50)
INT. THEOR'S ROOM-THAT EVENING (DAY 2)
  (Theo, Cliff, Clair)

COMMERCIAL #3	1:03
CLOSING CREDITS	:30

TOTAL PROGRAM LENGTH	28:34
PROGRAM LENGTH	23:12

Figure 7
The Cosby Show: "Theo's Holiday"—Tentative Rehearsal and Taping
Schedule

MONDAY, MARCH 10, 1986   NBC BROOKLYN
  9:00AM - 10:AM   SCHOOL FOR MINORS
  10:00AM - 1:00PM   READ THRU/DRY REHEARSALS
  1:00PM - 2:00PM   MEAL BREAK
  2:00 - 6PM   DRY REHEARSAL (RUN-THRU TBA)

TUESDAY, MARCH 11, 1986   NBC BROOKLYN
  9:00AM - 10:AM   SCHOOL FOR MINORS
  10:00AM - 1:00PM   READ THRU/DRY REHEARSALS
  1:00PM - 2:00PM   MEAL BREAK
  2:00 - 6PM   DRY REHEARSAL (RUN-THRU TBA)

WEDNESDAY, MARCH 12, 1986   NBC BROOKLYN
  8:30AM -9:30AM   CAMERA MEETING
  9:00AM - 9:30AM   ESU
  9:30AM - 12:30PM   CAMERA BLOCK W/STAND-INS &
                                SCHOOL FOR MINORS
  12:30PM - 1:30PM   MEAL BREAK
  1:30PM - 6:00PM   CAMERA BLOCK W/CAST

THURSDAY, MARCH 13, 1986   NBC BROKLYN
  9:30AM - 10:30AM   ESU/CAMERA MEETING
  10:30AM - 12:30PM   CAMERA BLOCK
  12:30PM - 1:30PM   MEAL BREAK
  1:30PM - 3:00PM   CAMERA BLOCK
  3:00PM - 3:30PM   WARDROBE, MAKE-UP
  3:30PM - 4:30PM   AUDIENCE IN, WARM-UP
                                CAMERA TOUCH-UP
  4:30PM - 6PM   VTR DRESS SHOW
  6:00PM - 7:00PM   MEAL BREAK & NOTES
  7:00PM - 7:30PM   AUDIENCE IN, WARM-UP
                                CAMERA TOUCH-UP
  7:30PM - 9:00PM   VTR AIR SHOW
  9:00PM-   PICK-UPS IF NECESSARY

Figure 6, "Theo's Holiday"—short rundown, begins with the NBC peacock prior to the main credit titles. There are two distinct acts in this show, both of which have five scenes. Most of the action takes place in the living room, although some occurs in Theo's room and elsewhere in the house. Most of the action, too, is continuous, merely moving from room to room. Most of the characters are Huxtables, the exception being Theo's friend Cockroach.

Figure 8
The Cosby Show: "Theo's Holiday"—Cast and Set

<u>CAST</u>

Cliff Huxtable...Bill Cosby

Clair Huxtable...Phylicia Rashad

Denise Huxtable...Lisa Bonet

Theo Huxtable..Malcolm-Jamal Warner

Vanessa Huxtable...Tempestt Bledsoe

Rudy Huxtable...Keshia Knight Pulliam

Cockroach..Carl Payne

<u>SET</u>

The audience appears comfortable with that house and that family, and even with the "outsider." We expect merely to be entertained; yet the entertainment lasts only twenty three minutes and twelve seconds out of the allotted half-hour.

Figure 7 represents an excellent guide for better understanding some of the concepts outlined above. With a clearer conceptualization of *The Cosby Show* scheduling process, this calendar might even make some sense. It is still incredible to think of going from "dry rehearsals" to full-blown taping before a live studio audience within such a short period of time.

Figure 8 presents yet another close-up of who and what is needed for production.

These examples from "Theo's Holiday" are from an episode that was written by John Markus, Carmen Finestra, and Matt Williams in March 1986. The information was obtained from Script City in Hollywood, California.

The team at the Museum of Broadcasting related some telling stories about production issues relative to *The Cosby Show*. For example, when Phylicia Rashad was pregnant in real life, it was decided not to have her character Clair also be pregnant, and to try and hide her growing waistline. Rather than have her appear walking around, she was often seen in bed—a bed that was properly "scooped out" so that her back was low down, and her front would seem normal. Another time, Bill Cosby was out of town for the actual shooting, but he was taped separately a month later and then edited in. Cosby has rarely missed a performance in his entire career, and he has been known to do shows even when he has a fever. The "fantasy show," featuring Rudy's dream, was scheduled on a day that she was sick—but it somehow worked out.

In response to questions from the New York audience, Markus admitted that the show does not tackle negative issues. In their minds (following Cosby's lead no doubt), the show is not about Blacks, but about family. Issues such as interracial dating and prejudice can be left up to *Newhart*, it was said. Gary Kott did point out, however, the episode that talked about the March on Washington in 1963 and reiterated the emphasis on Black culture in terms of including Black artists on the show.

The creative staff acknowledges the "fundamental thing Bill has done": that is, every Black family on television has been stereotyped, and this show merely seeks to introduce a new stereotype of a Black doctor and lawyer husband-wife team working together to raise a family. The message of the show is that all this is available through hard work. Beyond that, these producer-writers resent attacks about not being Black enough. It is Cosby's nature, they say, to look for "moments" in human nature, and to show not how different people are but the things they share. There is almost a tension in the creative process to avoid conflict.

Tom Werner claims he found the best people to do *The Cosby Show* and that its success can be attributed to them. "It's a team," he insists. Now that

Carsey-Werner have become involved with other shows, notably *Roseanne*, *Cosby*'s executive producer says he has to trust his staff. Werner also enjoys getting input in the creative process; for example, there were three different endings for the first episode of the 1989–1990 season, and his suggestion for the second one won out.

"Content is produced by people who work in organizations and who are limited or enhanced by government and industrial policies," writes Cantor (1980). "To study the impact of television it is necessary to know how the content gets on the air" (p. 99). She continues: "Writers and producers are creating for an audience, but that audience is not necessarily the ultimate audience. Rather, the shows are created for an audience composed of network officials, producers, other gatekeepers, as well as for the writers and producers themselves" (p. 112). These constraints, bound as they are to ratings and demographics, make Bill Cosby's power in his show's production process all the more important to examine.

The Cosby Show has made few bloopers over the years. As part of its February 1990 sweeps week, however, NBC decided to run a half-hour show called "The Cosby Outakes Show." Directed by Chuck Vinson, it ran Monday, February 12, which for many schoolchildren was the beginning of winter vacation. The main message intended for the viewer was that much fun goes on while the show is being taped. There were clips of Cosby teasing Clair, especially over her pregnancy, Cosby calling Theo "Malcolm" (his real-life name), Stevie Wonder mimicking Cosby, and then Cosby doing an imitation of Julia Child. The viewer also learned the value of editing, which was called "The Magic of TV," such as when Clair tried unsuccessfully at least four times to pin a flower on Theo's lapel; when Sammy Davis, Jr., took the white chess pieces off the chess board when he was supposed to remove the black ones; or when Cosby lapsed into a whole different script and ad-libbed about a date for Vanessa. We also learned that Bill Cosby likes to keep things loose on the set, and we were allowed to see the star's face as he picked up a bra off the floor in Theo's room. This look at the action behind the scenes reveals that rehearsals too are fun.

Because the literature on production processes for television is limited, the insights gleaned here should be particularly helpful to students of the media.[16] *The Cosby Show* is particularly interesting because of its expert collaborative team, the control wielded by the star of the show, and the key role the audience plays.

CASE STUDY: "GONE FISHING"

According to Newcomb and Hirsch, "It is in the economic interest of producers to build on audience familiarity with generic patterns and instill novelty into those generically based presentations" (1984, p. 65). The *Cosby* audience establishes a certain "contract" with the show, which is reminiscent of the ritualistic television-viewing theory. The viewer sets aside the night, Thursday, and knows what time it will be on, 8 P.M. EST; the show never disappoints, even when there are other "specials" on NBC that night. The length of each segment before the commercial break is also known, as is who will be on the show: the Huxtables, everyone's favorite family. The audience even knows what will take place, sort of—at least it knows it will be fun, and funny, and maybe even striking. The audience members know it will be something they can relate to. They know where the action will take place, mostly in the living room. Viewers also know that they may discuss what happens—maybe tonight with family or maybe tomorrow with friends. The viewers know something about how the plot lines will develop, how the characters will be dressed, how the scenes will move around, and how people not necessarily seen in one's own, regular lives will be seen. What is not included in the contract are the "why"s of the viewers' relationship to *The Cosby Show*. The case study that follows should begin to answer some of those questions.

On Thursday, March 17, 1988, came an opportunity for me to see the production process for *The Cosby Show* first-hand. Through the courtesy of the show's Public Relations office at NBC, two tickets were set aside for my attendance at the first taping of the show. My youngest son, then a senior in high school, joined me for what was to be a fascinating excursion.

The case study is of the episode titled "Gone Fishing," listed in this way in the daily newspaper's television section:

Theo (Malcolm-Jamal Warner) basks in the spotlight after reeling in the body of a mobster during a fishing trip. Meanwhile, Rudy (Keshia Knight Pulliam) and Kenny (Deon Richmond) become adopted parents to baby birds. Harriet Waters: Alanna Davis. Wayne Urich: Darrell Echols. Cliff: Bill Cosby.

These were the credits:

Produced by Terri Guarnieri
Producer Gary Kott
Carmen Finestra—Supervising Producer
John Markus—Coexecutive Producer
Created by Ed. Weinberger, Michael Leeson, and William Cosby, Jr., Ed.D.
Written by John Markus and Carmen Finestra and Gary Kott
Directed by Tony Singletary
Executive Producers Tom Werner and Marcy Carsey

Most of the audience for this show arrived in groups. There was a busload of predominantly Black choir members from a church outside of Philadelphia, who were having a wonderful time. Guests of Dr. Poussaint were sitting in front of us, and the mother of Tempestt Bledsoe (Vanessa), on my right, beamed proudly anytime her daughter appeared.

A host and hostess, Barry Barry and Angela Scott, warmed up the audience, asked where everyone was from, told jokes, and answered questions. The audience was also shown the prior week's program and a clip of some bloopers that had previously occurred on *The Cosby Show*. The atmosphere was electric. Everyone was watching *Cosby* on television, and there was the real Bill Cosby and his television family right in front of us.

On stage were four separate sets, with most action focusing on the living room. There were six monitors, four cameras shooting scenes from different angles, and a crew maneuvering everywhere. The director, Tony Singletary, came out to make some changes; the cosmetician would dab someone's sweaty face; the camerapeople would collaborate about positioning.

Takes were for real, but the reality was that this was the first of two "live audiences" that night. This group had assembled around 4:30 P.M.; the next one was due around 7 P.M. If it could be done right the first time, all the better; if not, there was always that other chance for change.

Cosby was about the only one who wasn't serious about the whole thing. He had great fun jiving with the choir members from the church group, focusing on their being from Philadelphia, and teasing them about where they had gotten their tickets. He also made a big point about introducing two old college buddies who were in the audience that afternoon. On two occasions he cracked up so much that filming had to be done all over again. It seemed like regular practice, and everyone in the audience reacted uproariously.

One scene proved to be particularly difficult. It involved Rudy and her friend Kenny finding some baby birds in a nest. The two read their lines perfectly, but the monitor showed the bird nest too high up, obliterating the children's faces. The scene was run twice more, but still it wasn't quite right. The decision was made to move on and to do that scene later. Whether it was done at the next taping, or whether it was edited even later than that, is not known but it was eventually included.

Back at home, we had someone videotape the show; when we got to preview it, it looked very different somehow. Although we had been able to see the action on monitors simultaneously while watching it taking place, at home on our own television set it seemed closer, more personal. We also noticed how many more full close-ups of Bill Cosby there were on the program.

Specifically, a content analysis of Cosby's facial antics shows that, although other people were talking, he dominated the screen during this episode by a ratio of 8 to 1 for any other cast member. Most of all, the ending was surprising. It was a complete turnaround from what the first viewing audience had seen. Truly, a first-hand viewing of the production process is an invaluable experience.

Reading a sentence in David Marc's study comparing stand-up with sitcom humor sheds some light on the experience of watching the taping. "To attend such a taping is to witness the preparation of a drama, not its performance," Marc writes about being part of the audience for a taped sitcom.

Crew and equipment, heedless of a nonpaying audience's prerogatives, move in and out of the line of vision at will. Second takes are by no means unusual. Most important, the members of the audience are more conscious of being a part of a television program than of seeing one performed, and this creates an almost irresistible incentive for enthusiasm. The audience knows that its negative reactions are irrelevant and that its only possibility for participation is tied to its approval. (1989, p. 28)

And so now it is time to explore the *real* audience for *The Cosby Show*—the one that counts, beyond the ratings.

5

Audiences for *The Cosby Show*

> The study of media organizations is essential for understanding how the media operate as links to the larger social system. Probably the most visible linkage the media provide is to the audience. Just as the media share certain organizational realities in which they produce content, so do media audiences share certain social and personal realities in private and social play.
>
> Sandra Ball-Rokeach and Muriel Cantor,
> *Media, Audience, and Social Structure*
> (Newbury Park, Calif.: Sage Publications, 1986), p. 17.

As a global broadcasting phenomenon, *The Cosby Show* has continually attracted high ratings and large audiences both in the United States and, in syndication, to more than seventy countries around the world.

Who are these viewers, demographically and psychographically? How often do they tune in to the show, and how do they rate it? With which members of the cast do they identify? Which members of the cast are their favorites? Which episodes are their favorites? And what are their perceptions of *The Cosby Show*: do they see the Huxtables as a typical family? A typical American family? A typical Black family? A typical wealthy family? Would they like to be in the Huxtable family? Do they see the show as one about being Black?

The search for some concrete data on the audience (audiences?) for *The Cosby Show* produced a host of other questions. Do audience responses to the series differ depending on gender, age, ethnicity, occupation, and/or typicality of television viewing? Do Europeans interpret the show differently from Americans? Is that enormous American audience in unison? Do Black audiences from the Caribbean react differently from Black audiences in South

Africa? Would there be similarities or differences between various target markets in the United States, and then between American and global responses? A survey of viewers from around the world could touch on some of the broader issues in audience response and audience impact that media specialists have begun to explore.

TELEVISION AUDIENCE RESEARCH

Increasingly, mass communication scholars are beginning to recognize the need to research media audiences. Grounded in the functionalist approach of uses and gratifications theory, which recognizes a goal-directed media experience, most recent work tends to extend effects research by seeing the audience member as active, selective, and responsive to both media and nonmedia choices. As a competitor with many other sources to satisfy our needs, our individual television consumption patterns tell a great deal about the viewer.

In terms of television utilization, this study on the audience for *The Cosby Show* most appropriately fits under the heading of "reception analysis," integrating both quantitative and qualitative variables, and social-scientific and humanistic perspectives. Its underlying concern follows that of Muriel G. Cantor; that is, what is the problematic relationship of audience influence on program content? Recognizing the tremendous role that ratings and demographics play in what she calls audience control, Cantor contends that "the one major reason for the conflicts that arise between creators and decision makers is because of the class and educational differences between popular culture creators and their audiences" (1980, p. 112). The key, she notes elsewhere (1990, p. 282), is the target audience, who should not be offended by writers, producers, and advertisers. In the case of domestic comedies, typically the target audience is made up of women and children, and the message focuses on social and sexual relationships as central and all-important.

Extending the argument on the importance of understanding audiences, Victoria Billings, a student of Cantor's, writes:

The audience, regardless of the medium, has not historically been passive or inconsequential in shaping its participation in, or the content of, popular culture. Rather, audiences emerge as significant spurs to innovation once they are considered in various media, in a variety of historical settings, and as collectivities rather than an amorphous mass. (1986, p. 200)

Her perspective of the "audience as innovator" is evidenced in various audience members' reactions to *The Cosby Show*.

As early as 1972, sociologist Herbert J. Gans stated: "If one looks at the mass media as institutions which deliver symbolic content to an audience, there are three major and interrelated areas of study: the institutions themselves, the content, and the audience" (p. 697). The present study aims to address those three subjects by discussing *The Cosby Show*'s network and syndicator; its topicality regarding race, sex, class, and family relationships; and specific target audiences globally.

What follows here, then, is an attempt to find out about audiences for *The Cosby Show* both at home and around the world.

THE COSBY SHOW SURVEY

A survey instrument designed to answer the various research questions posited here is included in Figure 9.[1] Note that the questionnaire was simplified so that a wide range of age and literacy populations could be included. It was constructed to encourage participation and look like "fun." The complete survey is limited to a single page. It has simple directions, it flows easily from one section to another, and, most importantly, it is meant to appear nonthreatening. Certainly, too, the topic helps—many people undertook the survey with enthusiasm, and some even sought out this researcher so that they could participate. A series of "checks," circles, and fill-ins was deliberately chosen as part of the questionnaire format. Aesthetically, the instrument looks pleasing; it contains only a few questions but it also allows for expanded responses. Emphasis is on the positive, such as using "not very good" at the low end of the "excellent" scale, rather than a more negative term, or asking for one's "favorite" and not necessarily one's least favorite characters or episodes. It was of extreme importance to keep the instrument nonsexist and nonracist; for example, the cast was listed according to age, with Cliff (Cosby) first, as he typically appears in the show's listing. A decision on whether or not to capitalize "Black" was difficult to make, but the lowercase "b" designation appeared to draw less attention to the racial connotation. Rather than using the academic term "demographics," that section was deliberately labeled "Some information about you"—helping it yield nearly unanimous responses. Finally, a note of thanks and encouragement for further commentary, along with listing the author's name and address, elicited numerous extra replies, as will be documented later.

The questionnaire was also constructed with cross-cultural research in mind, so its simplicity had yet another purpose. It has since been translated into eight languages: Dutch, French, German, Greek, Indonesian, Italian, Spanish, and Swedish. In some instances changes were made in the demographics section, such as excluding the term "race" from South Africa and instead determining it according to area of residence. Race in Australia brought particularly interesting responses; although there were no Blacks per se, many of the respondents indicated nationalities after the designation asking for race in their own terms, such as Greek or Greek Cypriot (7), Vietnamese (4), Italian, Filipino, and Macedonian (3). Rarely did the others just say "white,"

Figure 9
Questionnaire: *The Cosby Show*—A Survey

1.Have you seen THE COSBY SHOW?
___No (skip to #8)   ___Yes

2.If yes, how often have you seen the show?
___Only once   ___Several times   ___Regularly

3.On a scale from 1-10, 1 being the lowest, circle your rating of it.
Not very good   Excellent
    1   2   3   4   5   6   7   8   9   10

4.Which member(s) of the cast do you identify with/relate to:
___Dr. Heathcliff ("Cliff") Huxtable--Bill Cosby
___Clair Huxtable (wife/mother/lawyer)--Phylicia Ayers-Allen
___Sondra Huxtable (college student)--Sabrina LeBeauf
___Denise Huxtable (17-year old daughter)--Lisa Bonet
___Theodore Huxtable (only son, aged 14)--Malcolm-Jamal Warner
___Vanessa Huxtable (11-year old daughter)--Tempestt Bledsoe
___Rudy Huxtable (youngest daughter, age 5)--Keshia Knight Pulliam
___None

5.Which character on THE COSBY SHOW is your favorite?_____

6.Which episode on THE COSBY SHOW was your favorite?_____

7.Circle your opinions on the following issues:

	Agree	No opinion	Disagree
a.The Huxtables are a typical family.	1	2	3
b.They are a typical American family.	1	2	3
c.They are a typical black family.	1	2	3
d.They are a typical wealthy family.	1	2	3
e.I'd like to be in their family.	1	2	3
f.The show is about being black.	1	2	3

Some information about you:
8.Sex: ___Male   ___Female
9.Race:
10.Age:
11.Occupation:
12.How much television do you watch:
        ___Less than 1 hour/day   ___1-3 hours/day   ___3+ hours/day

Thank you very much. Please feel free to add any comments about
THE COSBY SHOW.

Linda K. Fuller, Ph.D.
Media Dept/Worcester State College
Worcester, MA 01602 USA

but instead chose descriptors such as anglo, white/caucasian, English/anglo, Celtic, white Anglo-Saxon, and so forth.

From a global network of media scholars (mostly through membership in organizations such as the International Communications Associations, the World Communication Association, and the International Association for Mass Communication Research) and media representatives, this project has involved impressive cooperation worldwide.

This chapter examines audience responses to the questionnaire on *The Cosby Show* from thirteen countries (see Figure 10). In addition, the show's programming ratings and results are reported for an additional fourteen countries: Austria, Canada, Denmark, Greece, Indonesia, Ireland, Italy, Japan, Malaysia, Malta, Mexico, Norway, Poland, and Singapore.

Attempts were made to get audience survey data from a number of other countries, such as from Canada and Mexico, or Eastern Europe, parts of the Middle East, and Asia, but to date no usable replies have been received. (The complete list of participating countries and their number of respondents to the questionnaire is presented in Appendix 3.) Note that the figures include 192 respondents from the United States and 617 worldwide—809 survey responses in all, as well as much other audience input in addition to and/or separate from the survey instrument.

Audiences participating in this questionnaire included men and women, young and old, Black and white television viewers from these countries: Australia (35 survey participants), the Bahamas (17), Finland (18), France (10), Germany (32), the Netherlands (36), South Africa (49), Spain (231), Sweden (37), Turkey (118), the United Kingdom (13), the United States (92), and the West Indies (Barbados, Jamaica, St. Vincent, and Trinidad—21).

Methodology

Because participation conditions differed according to the settings in which the survey was administered in the thirteen countries listed here, results cannot be interpreted by a strict standard. Some of the questionnaires, for example, were administered to closed, captive audiences, such as those in elementary school classrooms in the United States, or university classes in Finland, Germany, Turkey, Australia, and Sweden. Some were undertaken voluntarily, such as at a California health club, by Black residents of the United Kingdom, or at Unesco's headquarters in Paris. Others were informally solicited in neighborhoods, such as in Spain, the Netherlands, and the Caribbean. Still others were sent on request, such as via the articles in the Johannesburg and Durban newspapers on this project.

With regard to time, the surveys also cover a range. The earliest were administered in 1986 to affluent New England sixth graders; from there, it was determined to get comparisons. The most recent are results from the

Figure 10
Countries Participating in *The Cosby Show* **Survey**

Country	# of survey participants
Australia	35
Bahamas	17
Finland	18
France	10
Germany	32
Netherlands	36
South Africa	49
Spain	231
Sweden	37
Turkey	1 18
United Kingdom	13
United States	192
West Indies	21
Total	809 survey participants

thirty-two German college students, who took the survey in the spring of 1990.

Because participation means, rates, and responses vary greatly, each country included in the survey is discussed individually following some overall comments.

Demographically, there were both similarities and differences among the various participating survey respondents. Target markets within the United

States, for example, were composed of population profiles from a wide cross section, even though the show had great appeal for most of them. The 116 affluent New England sixth graders were predominantly white (97%), but they also included two Blacks and one Indian. There were four Blacks·in the sample of twenty-eight Florida retirees, the same number as Asians among the forty-eight members of a California health club. One interesting aspect of the American samples is a similarity in television-viewing time: The majority of persons in all three groups reported watching one to three hours per day.

A number of the survey participants were students: 35 were in Australia (60% of them age 21), 18 in Finland, 32 in Germany, and 183 in Spain. The Spanish sample also included four nurses, two economists, two engineers, three administrators, as well as an architect, a secretary, teacher, journalist, psychologist, doctor, and hair stylist. With the exception of Germany, where 56 percent reported watching less than one hour of television per day, the students typically watched one to three hours: 43 percent of the Australians, 61 percent Finns, and 63 percent Spanish, respectively.

Overall, only 8 percent of the entire sample was Black: In addition to some Blacks from South Africa and the United States, 94 percent of the seventeen Bahamian respondents, all thirteen persons who participated in the survey from the United Kingdom, and 95 percent of the twenty-one West Indians. Although most were "regular" viewers and gave similar responses rating the show, their overall answers did not differ appreciably from those of other survey respondents. *The Cosby Show* clearly crosses color boundaries. As some critics maintain, the show offers positive Black role models, but white audiences also respond favorably.

The Bahamian sample, composed of slightly more women (53%) than men, comprised the following occupations: social worker, youth officer, clerk/secretary, administrator, civil servant, housekeeper, conciliator, psychotherapist, technician, and sales. Most (88%) of the seventeen respondents were between the ages of twenty-one and thirty-five, and only about one-fifth watched television three or more hours daily.

Women also edged men out in the Dutch sample (58%) of thirty-six, and included an occupational range from student to professional to retired to housewife; 50 percent reported watching one to three hours of television per day.

So did the forty-nine South Africans; 86 percent were white (there were also four Indians and three Blacks), they had an even gender split, and they reported the occupations of librarian, receptionist, social worker, secretary, teacher, and union organizer. One was unemployed and seven were retirees.

Just over half the Swedish sample of thirty-seven respondents were women, 73 percent were between the ages of twenty-one and thirty-five, with these occupations: teacher, student, nurse, editorial assistant, boss, secretary, computer operator, receptionist, sociologist, researcher, and economist. None of them reported watching much television, with 57 percent checking less than one hour per day.

Turkish respondents included fifty-six women and sixty-two men, most of whom were middle class; their professions included housewife, laborer, retiree, student, employee, businessman, and academic. All the laborers, most of the retirees (83%), and nearly three-quarters of the housewives reported watching more than three hours of television daily, whereas 48 percent of the businessmen and 56 percent of the students watched one to three hours per day.

The nine males and four females who made up the all-Black sample from the United Kingdom included some students, an accountant, a dress maker, lecturer, researcher, teacher, and trainee accountant; 54 percent reported watching one to three hours of television daily.

The predominantly Black West Indian survey respondents included seven males and fourteen females, nearly half of whom were between the ages of twenty-one and thirty-five. Their numbers included civil servants, teachers, administrators, students, researchers, clerk/typists, a nurse, a social worker, and a salesperson, with the wide majority (71%) reportedly watching one to three hours of television a day.

Audience Ratings

"On a scale from 1 to 10, one being the lowest," survey participants were asked to circle their ratings. Not surprisingly, the show got nearly unanimous high marks.

The show drew the top spot in all three target markets in the United States. Sixty-two percent of the sixth graders, 50 percent of the Florida retirees, and 32 percent of the California health clubbers gave a number 10 rating. Looking at figures from number 7 upward, we find that the show was rated very highly by 85, 97, and 95 percent of these populations, respectively. Consistent with formal ratings services, Americans who took this survey really liked the show.

Supporting their high praise for *The Cosby Show*, many of the New England schoolchildren added extra comments to their surveys, such as: "I like the Cosby Show alot. It seems like there family gets along"; "It's so funny, my grandmother watches it"; "Its pretty nifty dude"; "I think 'The Cosby Show' is a great, funny show!!!!!"; "If they took the Cosby Show off the air I would just die!"; "The Cosby Show is the best show! It's my favorite"; and "It's a great show!" One of the teachers added, "A great family show." The 54 percent of this sample who watch one to three hours of television per day is particularly interesting when correlated with the high ratings these children gave the show (see Figure 11).

A former teacher, now a retiree in Florida, commented: "A lot of family questions [are] answered." Other comments from the retiree group included:

Figure 11
Correlation Between TV Viewing and Rating *The Cosby Show*: New England Affluent Sixth Graders

RATING OF THE COSBY SHOW (1 - 10)

Count	5, 6	7, 8, 9	10	Row total
FREQUENCY				
Only once	1 33.3 33.3 .9	1 33.3 2.6 .9	1 33.3 1.4 .9	3 2.7
Several times	1 5.3 33.3 .9	13 68.4 34.2 11.6	5 26.3 7.0 4.5	19 17.0
Regularly	1 1.1 33.3 .9	24 26.7 63.2 21.4	65 72.2 91.5 58.0	90 80.4
Column total	3 2.7	38 33.9	71 63.4	112 100.0

Raw chi square: 25.54949 with 4 degrees of freedom

Significance: .0000

"It is an excellent show"; "The chemistry of the actors is magnificent, but I don't derive any social statement. I simply like to watch this show—I find it 'non-threatening' "; "I wish that more parents would realize that discipline means love"; "They make me laugh my brains off"; "Cleverly written, witty fun."

The members of the California health club said: "My favorite show. I got my husband to watch it"; "Over all it's a pretty entertaining show as far as *value* goes"; "It is a nice show"; "I love the show but it is a bit far-fetched at rare moments when parental understanding is so easy-going, etc. Otherwise it is a very REAL show." A survey participant who had never seen *The Cosby Show* observed: "I understand the show is wonderful...and therefore am gratified that it's constantly No. 1 in the national Nielsens."

Many of the survey respondents who knew about the present book wanted to talk at length about it.

One fourth grader exclaimed, "I like it [the show] because it's funny. I usually watch it with my mother and sister, and if I don't understand something they tell me about it. I also like it because Bill Cosby reminds me of my father. They are both real funny." Or his friend: "It reminds me of my family, all the things that happen in the show reminds me of stuff that happens in my house. I like the way their family is always doing things together, just like mine does." A secretary wrote: "I never really watched any t.v. except the Cosby Show. It's the best show that ever went on the air!"

In addition to the specific target markets from the United States, a number of other people wanted to take this survey. A doctor added the following comment on her questionnaire: "Perhaps their universal appeal comes from the fact that while they really aren't typical of anything they embody *ideals* that we all seek. They have created a MYTH of the ideal family, in the original and powerful sense of the word." A businessman/entrepreneur acquaintance said that he never missed the show and that he particularly liked the kitchen scenes where everyone has a hidden agenda. People talk, but all anyone is really thinking about is food. Another man, a Black CEO, added this comment to the survey instrument: "The show crosses racial lines, uses humor and creatively addresses issues that confront people in their daily lives. The show provides an effective model for families to emulate." Recently, an octogenarian at a women's club luncheon talked about how cute she thinks the bedroom scenes are—"Just enough for the imagination!"

Abroad, the show got highest marks from the predominantly Black viewers in the Bahamas. One-third rated it number 10 and 94 percent at 7 or more—much as did the Black fans in the United Kingdom, where 85 percent rated it at 7 or higher. The single non-Black Bahamian was also the only one who added a further comment: "*Good, clean* humour that the family can watch. Also it is *one* show at least that does *not* harp on about the coloured bit."

What may be surprising is that approximately the same percentage of viewers from South Africa, though predominantly white, rated the show at 10; 57 percent in the 9 to 10 category; and 80 percent at 7 or higher. Some of the comments were: "I like it because it is so amiable, agreeable, and amusing"; "My diplomas come from lifes experience. . . . The Cosby Show is great simply because it has a well balanced viewing appeal, humour, stable family relationships, as well as a typical teenage approach to situations"; "What I love most about The Cosby Show is that it is very amusing with no sordid sex and bad language and I can relate to my own married life raising children. A very fascinating programme which I *never* miss"; "I am interested in your studies re the Cosby Show which I & everyone I know consider the highlight on our low standard TV viewing. 1. The show is realistic—deals with real-life issues. 2. Warmth, love something we all can relate to. 3. A lesson learned in amusing scenes. 4. Finally I guess by watching it we all yearn to be part of it"; "I very much like the love and affection shown by all members of the family, the kindly and understanding manner in which problems are dealt with and the total lack of aggression. Also the clean sense of humour. I very much like the family commitment"; "A superb family series—can touch us so very, very much. Wouldn't the world be a wonderful place with their philosophies?"; "Every show was equally enjoyable!"; and "I consider the Cosby Show to be one of the best shows for general viewing for the following reasons: a. It deals with family problems, concerning a wide range of ages, of a type faced by most families. b. It is clean and wholesome without relying on sexual inuendos."

Nearly half the predominantly Black viewers of the West Indies rated the show at number 9; 85 percent gave it a 7 or higher. They commented: "Great evening entertainment!"; "The family life and style is true to life and the programme really projects this highly"; The love and admiration which my daughters and I have for the cast, as well as for the lessons learnt/taught from the family setting provided/portrayed, have driven us to record/capture many of the shows which appear on our television screen."

From France a teenager rated the show at 9 and commented: "C'est une très bonne emission, très comique, qui me fait rire. Bill Cosby est très 'cool.' Chaque fois que cette serie passe à la télé, et que j'ai le temps, je la regarde." This respondent has only seen the show a few times (he does not have the time to watch much television), but it makes him laugh; Cosby is cool. Another respondent in France, a sixteen-year-old girl, added that the show is funny, the family "cool," and their problems are those of young people all around the world.

While 22 percent of the German respondents rated *The Cosby Show* at a modal rating of 8, 65 percent circled 7 or higher. Nearly half (43%) of the Dutch viewers rated the show at 8, and 74 percent at 7 or higher. These comments were made by fans from the Netherlands: "I think that the Cosby Show is a funny and relaxing program. It handles family problems which happen every day in normal life"; "Always funny and original ideas!"; and "I liked the show a lot, but unfortunately I can't see it a lot because I always have to work when they broadcast the show."

More than one-third of the Spanish survey respondents gave the show an 8, and more than three-quarters a 7 or more. Some Spaniards added: "I like very much this show, it is very nice, and lovely and of course smiley"; "It is an American series, very human"; "It is a good show that coincides with the other series of its type in this season, with 'The Golden Girls.' " Nationally in Spain, Ente Publico RTVE's *Audiencia Media de "La Hora de Bill Cosby"*, based on 40,000 interviews per year, found these results:

OLEADA EGM (research date)	AUDIENCIA (% Population)
May-June 1987	16.2
October-November 1987	22.0
February-March 1988	18.0
Media	18.7 (5,404,000 individuals)

Figures were given for "La Hora de Bill Cosby" on TV–1 for 1987 and 1988, and it typically received numbers ranging from 8.1 to 8.8.

One-quarter of the thirty-seven Swedish survey participants also rated the show at 8, and 64 percent at 7 or higher. Although a number of them added comments, a particularly insightful one is included here in its entirety:

The family is an idealistic type of family, within a frame of our wishful dreams. The producers have succeeded in presenting a believable picture of a happy family and of how it is working. The series admits family conflicts, but 'the happy family' doesn't really have any trouble solving them. As a Swede, perhaps I think that the show could be classified as something that confesses [*sic*] to the well-known American cliché about how you would like reality to be (in this case the family kind of reality). The Cosby show, however, includes some more fresh aspects and differs from other American soap operas. The family is a black one; the dialogue has a swift sense of humor which, within the frame of decency, has a scent of freedom; the relations of the family members are colored by a free outspokenness, and of mutual confidence.

Contrary to most other similar series, there is in the Cosby show a pedagogical ambition. You can see "a good example of family life," "it's possible to solve conflicts," "keeping together is important," and so on and so forth. Probably this is the reason of the series' popularity; there is a sort of open-minded realism which never worries you since the family is an ideal family, performing a complete harmony beyond accidental conflicts, sorrows, disappointments. People embrace, subconsciously for sure, the positive pedagogics in watching a family life that really works ("then it can work for us too.") The fact that the family is black is, in my opinion, likely to be a new grip of catching a TV audience—even though it may also work as fighting against prejudices; it's encouraging democracy and equality.

However, the family actions are adapted to a "white" behavior; the family appears to be white and Anglo-Saxon—despite a certain amount of black culture characteristics like the special sense of humor, the language, the clothing (the enchanting, positive colors).

Among the 118 Turkish participants in the survey, housewives and laborers rated the show the highest, and academic people and businessmen the lowest.

Only among the Australian survey participants did the greatest number (37%) rate the show at 7, but cumulatively 83 percent rated it at 7 or higher. Some of the students, most of whom were regular viewers, added comments: "I think it's great because the humour is down to earth. I enjoy it very much!"; "The Cosby Show is a very entertaining show. It is something for everyone"; and "Favorite? Almost all."

Although, as noted, the comments were overwhelmingly favorable, some negative opinions were also expressed. One twenty-three-year-old Macedonian-Australian male who saw it once declared: "This show stinks." A fellow classmate commented that "(e)arlier episodes had some originality. I used to enjoy the program but now it lacks substance." Two of the German students said they were turned off by the laugh track (although, in fact, there is no laugh track); a Belgian said he didn't like programs with the Cosby grandparents. These comments were made by various South Africans:

- I find it inane and geared to the level of intelligence of a five year old. I'm not racist, but I think it's time the SABC was a little more fussy over the decadent rubbish they buy.
- The setup is pretentious. The show is not as funny as it is supposed to be. There is never much of a storyline. Cosby's grimacing is embarrassing. The Huxtable family is unconvincing, ranging as it does from white to Negro.
- The Cosby family is unconvincing. Colours range from white to Negro.
- Cliff is inane, Clair too bossy, Sondra uninteresting, Denise and Vanessa too full of themselves, Theo mindless and stupid, and I'd love to put my hand to Rudy's backside. I have no objection to it being black. I love "Benson" and "Charlie" and both [are] full of wit.

One student from Bilbao wrote, "I like it enough, but I like the British series better." Two Swedish students commented about the programming: "I liked the earlier episodes better," and "Nice series but most often a bit *too* nice—that is, too comfy-cozy. Everybody is *so* happy." Another one, referring to the survey, asked, "What do you mean by asking RACE!? That's offensive! But maybe you are members of the Ku Klux Clan."

American survey participants also had a few critical comments. One of the sixth graders said, "I think it is a fun show—but sometimes, occasionally, farfetched—still a good show." Another noted, "Some shows are o.k. Some are bad." A Floridian considered: "The show was much better in early episodes. It regressed as this season progressed. I don't watch it any more."

From the West Indies came these comments: "This show I believe is uncritical of 'bourgeois' values and presents a false vision of the black reality. It also is built so much around 'The American Dream' which is being spread to Third World countries where it is shown. Does not seek to realize other forms of 'family'"; "Good that it shows a black family that has respected, professional parents, well educated and well brought up children. However, it's unrealistic because everything is *too positive* and they never seem to have *real* problems."

Identification and Favorite Characters

The questions of identification and favorite characters were kept distinctly apart on the survey instrument, but the two did overlap in the various responses. One South African survey participant underscored the identification question and added: "Being White and English, I cannot truly 'relate' to any. One appreciates the blend of humour and discipline in the Cosby household. My husband, like me, never misses an episode if he can help it."

For the most part, Bill Cosby as Dr. Huxtable/"Cliff" garnered the most votes for these two categories. From South Africa came this note: "I identify with Bill Cosby because he is Black like me. His T.V. programmes are fantastic and most enjoyable. His T.V. household sets the guidelines for homes and children worldwide. Bill Cosby's programme is also extremely humourous and entertaining." An elderly white South African widow added: "Dr. Huxtable is the epitome of what every father should be. He creates a stable and happy family life, is supportive and loving in his relationships and above all has a wonderful sense of humor. He loves life and is so human that we all identify with him and his problems. Wish we could all do the same!"

Clair claimed her fair share of approval too, especially with Bahamians, South Africans, and West Indians. One white South African wrote: "Being a retiree I can appreciate and identify with Clair, but each member of the family displays moods and fancies that each of my children affected in their teens and I now see the same thing repeated in my grandchildren. So I think that is why it is so difficult to relate superficially to any one person in the show. Cliff as the central character is the sheet-anchor usually. I cannot see the family as other than an ideal family—one we would all like to have had and should aspire to. I do not think it is about being black or white but about how to live in a family." A member of a health club in California was moved to add, "I like Clair's independence!!!" It's particularly interesting that many Caribbean women—some 60 percent—chose Clair as the person with whom they most identify/relate, perhaps because they recognize that she is on an equal footing with Cosby as head-of-house (if not more important).[2]

Among some Finnish students, Dutch residents, Bilbaoan Spaniards, Swedish students, and American sixth graders, Cliff also had competition with Rudy as favorite character. One of the American sixth graders wrote, "Rudy is my favorite, but I most relate to Dr. Huxtable and Theo." An equal number of Turkish respondents voted Cliff (67% of the 56 men) or Clair (67% of the 56 women) as the person with whom they identify.

There were a few surprises: Australians voted Cliff their favorite character, but more than a quarter of the sample named Denise as the cast member with whom they most related—as did nearly the same percentage of Bilbaoan students. One Melbourne student added, "Theo is unreal!!!" Barcelonians claimed to identify most with Theo, but liked Cliff the most.

One South African, a twenty-three-year-old white male, wrote, "I never miss the Cosby Show if I can help it. My father (73), mother (51) and brother (19) enjoy it as much, and we all identify with various aspects of the family life and all get tremendous laughs from it!"

Favorite Episodes

Methodologically, this was an important question to ask. On the one hand, it is just the kind of non-threatening question that a survey participant likes to answer; reciprocally, it makes for an easy check on the researcher's part that the respondent is indeed familiar with the topic.

The grandparents' anniversary was the walkaway winner in the category of favorite episodes. It was mentioned by two Australians, three Bahamians, three Finns, one Dutch respondent, several South Africans, a Black from the United Kingdom, seven U.S. sixth graders, two Florida retirees, three California health clubbers, and four West Indians.

Other favorite episodes cited include: Rudy in the shopping center; the camping/wilderness store; Sondra and her new husband; Father's Day; Stevie Wonder; Rudy playing football; a snowball fight; "when they want to fool their Dad"; Theo and the "real world"; Cliff when he does a "do it yourself"; when Cliff and Clair sold Theo his room and its belongings; "the one where Rudy plays a little old lady with a posh accent"; when Cliff explains to Rudy (all in bed) about germs that "party party" inside the body; Theo's earring; Monopoly money; the fire drill; Denise buying her first car; Theo's shirt made by his sister; the prize awarded to the best doctor; Halloween; the dentist (with Danny Kaye); having a teacher over for dinner; the first day of school; Denise deciding on colleges; Thanksgiving; the card game; Theo growing a mustache; Clair breaking her foot; Sondra's friend doing a research project; Rudy with the juicer; the art gallery; Rudy's story; and "reviews of past experience with the family." One Swedish respondent added, "I liked it when Dr. Huxtable imitates his son playing (in a horrible way) the clarinet, and when the son slices the Christmas turkey." A Californian liked it "when Rudy teases Cliff." And a middle-aged South African school secretary commented, "We have most of our shows on tape and have watched them over and over. Looking through my note book with the names of the shows, I really can't pick *one* that is my favorite."

This audience quite obviously reacted most positively to very simple stories. For example, they responded most favorably to intergenerational plots, holiday celebrations, school concerns, food incidents, and some celebrities.

Audience Social Commentary

Researchers Brown, Austin, and Roberts (1987) chose *The Cosby Show* to examine how children process both familiar and unfamiliar images. They state that it

provides a unique context in which to evaluate the realism perception process. The Huxtable family represents at least two domains of experience. The first—the family—

is familiar even to very young viewers. The second—a sophisticated, advantaged, minority family—may be less familiar, even to many older viewers. (pp. 3–4)

Following are reports on responses to the opinion questions on the questionnaire.

1. *"The Huxtables are a typical family."* While the Swedish and Finnish students both registered a resounding 83 percent "no," and the German students were close behind, one of the Swedes commented: "In my opinion *The Cosby Show* is an entertaining series. By watching it you get some nice relaxation. It's more close to reality than for example *Dallas* and *Falcon Crest*. The persons appear to be pretty real, and the series itself gives an impression of reality, although I don't believe that it illustrates a typical family." Another wanted to add, "This is my favorite program. It's the only program on TV that I wouldn't miss for anything in the world. Concerning question 7, I want to say that there are no 'typical' families. The Cosby family is an ideal one."

Many other survey target markets said "no," the Huxtables are not a typical family: Australians (57%), Bahamians (50%), Dutch (60%), English (46%), Florida retirees (57%, one specifically citing "much higher parental ed. and financial status than typical"), and California health clubbers (52%, although nearly one-quarter agreed on their typicality).

Whereas the French population was mixed in its response, 59 percent of the South Africans considered the Huxtables typical as a family, although a thirty-five-year-old white female teacher wrote: "They communicate with each other too much to be typical." A retired white male teacher speculated that "(i)t's a pity they are not a typical family—the divorce rate might not be so high. May it last forever!!!" Another, a white middle-aged landlady, wrote: "I think that the family is not so much typical of any of the suggested categories— rather it is the *idealised* version of the 'typical' upper-middle-class family of any race, in America. I don't think I'd fit into their family, but I do admire their gregariousness, humour, warmth and high morals."

More than half the Barcelonese considered the Huxtables to be a typical family, whereas the Bilbaoan students' estimates were just under that figure. From Turkey, 62 percent of the women in the sample of 118 voted yes, as did 38 percent of the men. Most (62%) of the American schoolchildren see the family as typical, although one young man noted: "The Huxtable family is not a typical family that is made up to make you laugh." And one of the West Indians put it this way: "The Huxtables are a typical loving family."

For the most part, then, this audience as a whole interpreted this opinion question on the Huxtables as a typical family positively, by whatever definition of typicality they might have been using. While often that vision might be an idealized one, it is interesting that race does not seem to contaminate the responses.

2. *"They are a typical American family."* Again, the Finnish and Swedish students were in agreement; 72 percent of both samples said "no," whereas

half of the Australians, the Florida retirees, and just a bit more than that of the German students and California health clubbers would agree with them.

Not surprisingly, more than 69 percent of the predominantly white American schoolchildren considered the Huxtables typically American. So did 80 percent of the Barcelonians and 44 percent of the Bilbaoans, 57 percent of the Dutch respondents, and 40 percent of the South Africans. One middle-aged white receptionist in South Africa added:

I see the Cosbys as a typical American family (of any colour). The clean, wholesome family communication/bond they portray is a good influence to all viewers. Their attributes as good civilised human beings shine through and the parents have and do instill their principles and sets of values into the children. The time that Dr. Cosby and his wife devote to their children, although limited, is definitely quality time!!!

French, British, and West Indian respondents were mixed in their opinions on this issue. Their waffling may be explained by varying perceptions they might hold about American families in general.

What is a "typical American family"? Whereas nearly everyone can answer the earlier question on typicality as a family, images of American families worldwide often depend on media portrayals rather than on first-hand exposure.

3. *"They are a typical black family."* This question was nearly uniformly answered in the negative. It received a resounding "no" from 73 percent of the Australian survey participants, 89 percent of the Finns, 74 percent Germans, 66 percent Dutch, 47 percent South Africans (although 35 percent voted "yes"), 81 percent Swedes, 68 percent Florida retirees, 56 percent California health clubbers, and 55 percent West Indians. A Black female government officer from Christ Church, Barbados, commented: "Good that it shows a black family that has respected, professional parents, well educated and well brought up children. However, it's unrealistic because everything is *too positive* and they never seem to have *real* problems."

Although 56 percent of the predominantly Black Bahamians and 62 percent of the same racial group in the United Kingdom registered "no opinion" on this question, and the French, Spanish, and New England schoolchildren had mixed opinions, one of the New Englanders added: "I think that the question about being a typical black wealthy family is absurd." And finally, consider this comment from a Black woman from Barbados: "I find the Cosby Show is an excellent show especially because it portrays blacks generally and women in particular in a positive and realistic setting. Basically, I find it very educational, especially as it relates to parent-child relationship and ways of dealing with teenage problems."

R. G. Sherard's (1987) telephone survey of realism in *The Cosby Show* found that most adults do not consider the Huxtables an accurate reflection of Black family life in America, whereas Brown, Austin, and Roberts' 1987 survey of 627 third, sixth, and ninth graders revealed that "more frequent viewers, younger children and minorities judged the family as more real." The Black children in their study who were exposed to an episode from the series differed significantly from other ethnic groups. Forming 8 percent of the sample, more Blacks than other groups thought that the Huxtable family was distinctly different from other television families, yet they could identify with them. The authors offer several possible explanations: an effect of racial group identification, an unbalanced design that included minority children from more affluent than average subgroups, and/or other salient criteria, such as the family's problem-solving style.

Yet another Black perspective on realism in *The Cosby Show* emerges from Venise T. Berry's (1990) study of perceptions of fathers and sons between this series and that of *Good Times*. Using a sample of fifty-four Black youths participating in an Upward Bound summer program at Huston-Tillotson College in Austin, Texas, Berry found that the majority of these Black teens considered the father image of James Evans as stronger and more manly than that of Heathcliff Huxtable. This sample was nearly evenly split gender-wise (28 females, 26 males), and 89 percent came from single-parent families, most typically living with a mother only. In terms of dominance and control, as well as his harsh disciplinary approach, James Evans' image won out over Cliff/Cosby's "sensitive, soft-hearted nature." Among this population, the strong father figure appears to be one who uses physical punishment, takes control of a situation, and dominates.

4. *"They are a typical wealthy family."* The replies to this statement produced no consensus. Australians, for example, were divided in thirds between agreeing, disagreeing, and having no opinion; 63 percent of Bahamians had no opinion; Finns were evenly divided between yes and no; the French were mixed; 40 percent of the Dutch had no opinion, whereas a nearly equal percent agreed that the Huxtables are a typical wealthy family, and South African, Swedish, and American responses were nearly similar; 46 percent of the British respondents had no opinion.

Some 65 percent of the German students declared that the Huxtable family was not a typical wealthy one, as did half the West Indians, but only 27 percent of the Spaniards agreed.

This is an amazing finding, since an undeniably blatant consumerism is associated with *The Cosby Show*. With its fancy "designer" sweaters, allowances for new cars, all the latest kitchen gadgets, and expensive paintings, one of the underlying motifs of this popular program has been its emphasis on the "good life" that can be had from spending—albeit purposeful, worthwhile spending. Although interpretations might be tainted by race, hardly anyone, American or otherwise, would consider the Huxtable wealth typical. With Blacks so closely associated with poverty in the United States, the most likely answer is that more viewers see the family as a typically wealthy one rather than a typically wealthy Black one.

5. *"I'd like to be in their family."* Joining nearly half the Australian sample,

one student commented, "I probably would like to be in their family because it apparently never has any problems." The French (63%) agreed, as did 40 percent of the Dutch sample, 47 percent of the South Africans, 62 percent of the Turkish women and 32 percent of the Turkish men, and more than half the American schoolchildren and most of the Californians.

Yet, there were divisions. Whereas 35 percent of the Bahamian sample said they would like to be in the Huxtable family, half had no opinion; this was a nearly comparable figure with the figures for the Finnish, Spanish, and British students. Just over half the German students declared "no," they wouldn't like to be part of the family, as did the Swedish ones—but nearly one-third contradicted that decision. Florida retirees were caught in a three-way (yes/no/no opinion) tie, and West Indians were also torn between 35 percent of those surveyed saying yes and 40 percent no.

Overall, these findings support those of researchers Brown, Austin, and Roberts (1987), who found frequency of viewing *The Cosby Show* to be most strongly correlated with how much a child viewer "would like to be a Huxtable child."

This question about one's idealized relationship with the Huxtable family turns out to have been a good one to ask, as it elicited interesting responses that crossed the line between real and ideal. Although most people said "yes," they seemed to sense the importance of tempering that statement with reality. An initial response might be, "Of course"; a more considered one might be, "Of course, but..."

6. *"The show is about being black."* Of all the opinion questions, this one had the strongest answer—and it was almost universally "no." "No," said 97 percent of the Swedes, 91 percent of the American schoolchildren ("I really like the show, but don't think that being black makes any difference," wrote one), 86 percent of the sampled Dutch, 83 percent of the Australians and Finns, 82 percent of the Germans, 79 percent of the Californians ("The one thing I like about the show is that it doesn't seem like 'white' writers for a 'black' show. It seems pretty realistic."), 75 percent of the West Indians, 72 percent of the Barcelonians, 64 percent of the Floridians, 63 percent of the Bahamians, and half the South Africans. (One man wrote me directly to say, "I don't see why every question relating to colour should be tied to race and racism. The Cosby Show is a *cultural* and *not* a *colour* thing. Black South Africans, with whom I grew up, do *not* relate with white humour and do *not* relate with American Negroes or 'people of colour.' The Cosby Show portrays life as you would (or *could*) find in a white South African household, *not* in a Black one.") Only the French, Spanish, and British were mixed in their answers to this question; yet none tended to think that the show was about being Black.

Programming Reportage

Although survey results could not be obtained for all the countries, programming reportage for *The Cosby Show* will now be discussed from the following countries: Austria, Canada, Denmark, Greece, Indonesia, Ireland, Italy, Japan, Malaysia, Malta, Mexico, New Zealand, Norway, the Philippines, Poland, Singapore, Sweden, Turkey, the United Kingdom, and the former USSR.[3]

Austria: Josef Andorfer of Osterreichischer Rundfunk in Vienna reports that the show is called "Bill Cosby's Familienbande" and that it ran there from May 27 to September 1987 at 6 P.M. It averaged about 7 percent of the viewing audience and received sparse but varied critical response.

Canada: CTV Television Network, Ltd., in Toronto continues to broadcast *The Cosby Show* in Canada.

Denmark: Niels-Aage Nielsen of the Media Research of Danmarks Radio, wrote me the following letter:

I am glad to inform you that the first showing of Cosby on Danish television (DR) took place July 11, 1985. The third episode (July 25, 1985) was seen by 28% of the population aged 13+, i.e. 1.2 million. On a scale of 1 to 5 [1 being the highest] it had an average evaluation of 1.64, which is rather good for fiction.

The following year the show was measured twice with these results:

February 4, 1986: 62%, 2.6 million, evaluation 1.34
October 28, 1986: 66%, 2.8 million, evaluation 1.35

Thus the rating and evaluation went significantly up during the first six months of the showing in Denmark.

The high level of rating and evaluation has been stable since then. (The show has not been broadcast permanently during these years though.)

October 27, 1987: 61%, 2.6 million, evaluation 1.48
February 9, 1988: 63%, 2.7 million, evaluation 1.55

This shows that Cosby has been very successful and has enjoyed great popularity in the Danish television audience. Two-thirds of the adult population has been watching it.

From October 1, 1988 a second channel (TV 2) has started in Denmark. Continuous audience ratings have been introduced. DR still broadcasts "Cosby"—now in the "best hour" of the week on Saturdays at 8 pm. And during the first two weeks of Danish multi-channel television it has been 1, respectively 2, among the ratings of fiction programmes from both channels.

Greece: As in Denmark, *The Cosby Show* is shown in Greece during the popular 8 P.M. time slot.

Indonesia: Reports from visitors there indicate that *The Cosby Show* is very popular, a family favorite—even though it is broadcast in English, without subtitles.

Ireland: Robert K. Gahan, assistant director general of the RTE in Dublin, reported on August 9, 1990: "The Cosby Show has been carried by Radio Telefis Eireann for a number of years and in the past season was transmitted on Sunday evenings between 6:30 and 7 P.M. In this slot it tended to attract an audience of around 15%, which places it about 16th in our TOP 20 and at a similar level in adult and housekeeper TOP 20." He added that a book about Bill Cosby has been a big seller in Ireland.

Italy: The Cosby Show is also popular in Italy, where it is dubbed into Italian. A friend studying in Rome reported that they changed the name Huxtable to Robinson, but that information has not been corroborated.

Japan: Sports writer William May of the Kyoto News Service in Tokyo reported on September 2, 1988, that *The Cosby Show* was aired at 10 o'clock Saturday mornings on Tokyo Hoso (TBS) for about six months during 1987. On February 13, 1989, Kazuto Kojima of the Institute of Journalism and Communication Studies at the University of Tokyo asked his undergraduates whether they had watched the show, but no one had. Professor Youichi Ito of the Institute for Communications Research at Keio University in Tokyo was unaware that *The Cosby Show* had ever been telecast there, but in correspondence on January 18, 1989, commented: "Comedies are extremely difficult to enjoy internationally or interculturally. For example, a sense of humor is very difficult between different cultures."

Malaysia: On March 1, 1989, Brajesh Bhatia of the Asia-Pacific Institute for Broadcasting Development in Kuala Lumpur provided this information about the show:

After a break, the show was resumed on the Radio Television Malaysia Channel 2 in November 1988 in the 2030 hours to 2100 hours slot and the audience figures were: 289,000 for November and 360,000 for December. On the other two channels, i.e., Radio Television Malaysia Channel 1 and Television 3, *The Cosby Show* had to compete with Bahasa Malaysia (the national language) programmes. Radio Television Malaysia is part of the Government, while Television 3 is a privately owned station. The estimated total audience in Malaysia is 9.02 million out of a total population of 15.8 million.

Malta: Calling *The Cosby Show* one of his "favorite family comedies," on March 8, 1989, A.J. Ellul, chief executive of the Malta Broadcasting Authority sent me a copy of his program magazine that prominently features the Cosby family, and added:

Malta Television has, so far, shown four series of *The Cosby Show*. The last one consisting of 25 episodes finished its run last January. The programme is very popular with Maltese viewers and over the years it has built up quite a substantial following. The show is normally scheduled for screening either during early afternoon on Saturday or on Sundays during the family viewing slot at around 6.30 p.m. Programme sponsorship as such is not allowed in Malta but I believe that *The Cosby Show* attracted satisfactory advertising support.

Mexico: Unfortunately, we have little information on the Mexican audience for *The Cosby Show*. Pablo Casares, general secretary of CONEICC, the organization that represents the major faculties of mass communication in Mexico, stated that it had been taken off the air by 1989.

New Zealand: Although his source isn't cited, Whetmore states: *"The Cosby Show* was #1 in New Zealand, watched by an estimated 42 percent of the audience in 1987" (1992, p. 232).

Norway: Norsk Rikskringkasting, Norwegian Broadcasting Corporation in Oslo, reported that *The Cosby Show* ran at regular season intervals from November 1985 to the time of this writing. Ellen M. Almaas, of the Light Entertainment Department, Television division, responded:

The series in Norway got the title: "COSBY MED FAMILIE" (translated: "Cosby with family"). The first episode of 14 was sent here on Nov. 16, 1985, and the last of these on May 16, 1986.

This was a great success!!—so we continued: on August 30, −86 we sent the first of a series of 18, and the last of these ones was transmitted on Dec. 27, −86. And then en suite 7 more; from Jan 3rd −87 till Feb. 14th −87. Further we sent a series of 10 more, from Sept. 26 −87 till Nov. 27 −87. And then a series of 12, from April 16 till July 8, 1988. And the last series here—till now!—started Jan. 14 −89 and was running till Mar. 18 −89 (6 programmes), and 7 more of these all together 13 episodes will be sent this early summer, today stipulated from May 20th till July 1st −89.

The Philippines: Whetmore (1992, p. 232) places *The Cosby Show* in ninth place in the Philippines as of February 1987, joined by a number of other American shows: *The Equalizer* (no. 2), *Miami Vice* (no. 3), *The A-Team* (no. 4), *Family Feud* (no. 7), and *The Love Boat* (no. 10).

Poland: Professor Dr. Walery Pisarek, director of Osrodek Badan Prasoznawczych, the press research center in Krakow, wrote on February 10, 1989, to say, "I would like to have your welfare at heart but unfortunately so far the Cosby Show was not broadcast in Poland." His response was echoed by a later correspondence from Sergiusz Mikulicz, director of Polskie Radio I Telewizja in Warsaw.

Singapore: Lim Heng Tow, head of public relations for the Singapore Broadcasting Authority, described his country's experience with *The Cosby Show*:

(a) The show was telecast in Singapore since March 1985. Subsequent series were telecast soon after they have been aired in USA.
(b) The show was shown without a change in its title or sound track.
(c) It was shown once a week during prime time. Ratings have been consistently high.
(d) The show was not open to sponsorship but the commercial break within the show was fully loaded with spot commercials.

Sweden: Charly Hulten of the Audience and Programme Research Division of Swedish Television has provided a demographic breakdown of *The Cosby Show* audience in Sweden (See Figure 12). Hulten explains that all figures

Figure 12
The Cosby Show **Frequencies by Demographics—Swedish Television, 1985–1988**

Date	Order in series	Total	Sex M F	Age 9-14	15-24	25-44	45-64	65-79	Ed L M H	Appreciation Index
Season 1: Spring, 1985 Fridays 7:35pm, following news										
5/10	5:9	22	19 26	34	21	22	18	26	24 21 15	3.8
5/17	6:9	26	23 30	53	29	19	23	31	31 20 11	3.9
5/24	7:9	22	17 27	53	26	13	24	13	18 20 18	4.1
Season 11: Fall, 1985 Sundays 7:50pm, following news										
9/8	1:13	35	31 38	59	37	29	29	36	32 36 29	4.0
9/15	2:13	31	29 33	58	29	27	25	36	28 32 25	3.9
10/27	4:11	42	41 44	67	30	34	45	51	46 38 23	4.3
11/3	5:11	40	38 43	51	42	34	43	42	45 38 30	4.3
11/10	6:11	48	42 53	62	47	36	46	66	53 45 31	4.5
Season 111: Fall/Winter; 1986 Sundays 7:00pm, preceding news										
9/28	6:25	44	42 45	54	65	38	32	43	42 49 37	4.5
10/5	7:25	45	45 44	66	57	43	44	25	42 46 37	4.5
10/12	8:25	44	38 51	59	65	37	38	36	44 45 35	4.5
10/19	9:25	47	45 49	77	63	40	40	40	43 43 46	4.4
12/28	19:25	47	43 51	67	64	42	36	41	45 53 28	4.5
1/4	20:35	51	52 49	76	59	40	57	38	48 56 37	4.4
Season IV: Fall, 1987 Saturdays 8:00pm, following news										
9/5	1:10	35	30 39	45	28	25	42	46	39 34 23	4.4
10/3	5:10	38	33 42	73	26	26	40	49	39 32 27	4.3
10/10	6:10	31	30 33	49	22	23	34	43	36 25 23	4.1
Season V: Spring, 1988 Saturdays 8:00pm, following news										
5/7	14:25	22	18 27	35	21	19	18	31	27 20 10	4.0

indicate shares of the population, or demographic group. That is, they include people who did not watch television at all. Sweden has two channels, and just over 10 percent of Swedish households have access to satellite/cable services, none of which are in Swedish. Her letter of September 16, 1988, amplifies Figure 12:

Here you see steadily rising figures in all categories until Season IV. A second indication of increasing popularity is the decrease in differences between frequencies for men & women, for the different education groups and, to a lesser extent, age groups.

Success story it is, but there are two factors at work here. First, the familiar pattern of establishment: the audience becomes aware of the program and there is a snowball effect, as people start talking about it. The second factor, though, has to do with Sweden's very northerly position on the globe. The equinoxes (mid-March and mid-September) mean a great deal up here.... Swedes watch a lot more television in the dark months of Autumn and Winter.

All the above-mentioned indicators suggest that COSBY's popularity peaked in the 86/87 season. It was very popular then. Indeed, it was the only foreign series to make it onto the top-ten list that season.

Another complicating factor is the day of the week. Fridays and Sundays are about equivalent, but Saturdays are typical "nights out" here in Sweden.

Pensioners and children remain loyal, and all viewers continue to give the show high ratings on the appreciation index, but all in all, it appears that Swedish enthusiasm is beginning to flag.

A Swedish free-lance writer named Anna Wahlgren has written an article entitled "Njut av Cosby—Och Lar!," which loosely translated means "Enjoy Cosby—and Learn." Wahlgren states that she came to write the article in a roundabout way. An editor wanted her to do the piece, and she was simultaneously fascinated by how her son was drawn to the show, although she had never seen it herself. So she set out to analyze the show's popularity, writing on November 11, 1988, when she hit upon its secret: "Cosby. In this era of great confusion, when a father doesn't know how to be a father and a man doesn't know how to be a man, Bill Cosby provides an ideal model. He does it lovingly, without losing authority."

Kay Pollak (1987), a Swedish film director noted for sensitive and gripping films about today's young people, has written that "the 'Cosby' series has something wonderful and rare. In program after program we see two grown people who love each other. A Mom and Dad who LOVE EACH OTHER! It seems entirely true, and it shows, and they show it."

Before the start of the 1988 season of *Cosby, Roster 1 Radio*, Sweden's answer to *TV Guide*, asked two writers, a child psychiatrist, a pediatrician, and an "ordinary" family why they thought the show was so popular. In its March 18 edition, Lars H. Gustafsson, child psychiatrist, offered these thoughts:

Three things strike me when I see the Cosby series.

First, there's the father-figure. Sure, he can be stubborn and childish, but he is 100% *there* when he relates to his kids. He cares, is genuinely interested in them.

Second is the fact that the Cosby parents can make fools of themselves without losing face. Their relationships with their children are strong enough to take it. I think that is a relief for many parents.

Third, the Cosby series is very imaginative and resourceful when it comes to solving conflicts.

Kristina Lugn, poet and author, said: "I think the Cosby family is a dream-come-true, and that's why it's so popular. . . . I think the fact that they are black also plays in. It makes it a little special. They are so much more attractive than white people." The Pavlica family say they like the program because it puts them all in such a good mood. Daniel Atterbom, critic for *Dagens Nyheter*, adds, in the March 15, 1987, issue: "Without Cosby's personality the show would seem a lot cornier."

Turkey: The Cosby Show ran for several years with great popularity on Turkish Television (TRT) but is no longer on the screen.

United Kingdom: Writing about family television viewing in Great Britain, David Morley (1986, pp. 22–23) of Brunel University reminds us that only about 13.8 percent of households there can be described as traditional, nuclear families, that there is an overall decline in average household size, and that the country is increasingly becoming a home-centered culture.

Barrie Gunter, head of research for Britain's Independent Broadcasting Authority (IBA), offered to gather audience data on *The Cosby Show*, but it was not actually being televised at the time. The reader is directed to Gunter's collaborative work with J. Mallory Wober (1986, pp. 26–27) on audience research at the IBA during 1974–1984, particularly the sections on viewing fiction and comedy.

"*The Cosby Show*: Some Black and White Audience Perceptions and Possibilities" is an exceptionally relevant publication. Compiled by Fazal and Wober in November 1989 under the auspices of the IBA, it is introduced by the statement:

At one level it is simply a situation comedy. At another level it is a well designed exercise at role playing in situations which gently display the kinds of problems that Blacks meet in a largely white society, and which dramatise ways of dealing with those problems so as to enhance their self-esteem and success in the wider world. (p. 1)

Recognized as one of Channel 4/IBA's most widely watched programs, *The Cosby Show* has consistently achieved very high Appreciation Scores.

Stating that the program's success "has been attributed to its use of the conventional situation comedy genre within which new definitions of the Black family are offered," IBA's Television Opinion Panel decided to poll its weekly sample of 3,000 viewers as part of the Broadcasters' Audience Research

Board. In a move inconsistent with its usual procedures, it was determined that just this once the IBA could ask if respondents were Black, or knew a Black family, so that they could then explore possible viewer identification with the Huxtable family and reasons for liking/not liking the show. As it turned out, exactly half the sample (50%), or 679 members of the panel, did not know any members of Black families, and only another 32 percent were "slightly familiar" with any. Eighteen members of the sample (1%) were members of Black families. From this small number, the authors concluded that Blacks are slightly more likely than others to follow *The Cosby Show*, marking its characteristics more intensely than others do, and to find the characters more believable, the show funnier, and the characters more interesting than non-Black viewers. Yet, as can be imagined, the sample is too small for statistical significance.

Next, based on the questionnaire prepared for the present book, Shehina Fazal and her colleagues at IBA constructed the following table:

| | **Personal Status** | | | | |
	I am Black	Knows Blacks Well	Knows Blacks Slightly	Don't Know Blacks	No Answer
I'd like to belong to such a family	3.7	3.1	2.9	2.9	2.6
They are a typical wealthy American family	3.8	3.3	3.3	3.4	3.4
They are a typical American family	3.0	2.4	2.9	2.9	3.1
They are a typical black American family	2.7	2.6	2.6	2.7	2.7
The series is about being black in America	1.9	2.4	2.2	2.3	2.4
Base	18	156	431	679	68

Fazal and Wober interpret their table as follows:

Black viewers do not see the Huxtable family as being a typical black one, nor even particularly as being a typical American family; rather, they see it as a typical wealthy family—and they would like to be like them. (White) viewers who either know a black family only slightly, or who don't know any blacks, see the Huxtables as a typical wealthy American family; but by a slight margin they would rather not belong to such a family. No group thought that the series is about being black in America. (p. 8)

The British viewers who know no blacks personally are not "taken in" by any supposed idea that the Huxtables are a typical black American family, or that the series is about being black in America; rather, they realise it is about a "typical wealthy American family." (p. 9)

This is a most intriguing conclusion on the authors' part.

Overall, *The Cosby Show* was found to be "well liked by all viewers, with the characters found interesting and believable and the programme as a whole, good for all the family and funny." Fazal and Wober continue:

Herein lies Bill Cosby's opportunity to do good by stealth. Viewers and indeed the critics may be wrong in one of their crucial perceptions—that the show has little to do with being black in America. In fact, although we've dealt in the stereotypes promoted by use of average scores, these hide the fact that there is still a range of opinion across viewing. Thus, 5% of all its viewers agree strongly that *The Cosby Show* was about being black in America, and another 11% agreed, though not strongly. There may be some validity in these opinions. Content analysis of some of the episodes will show that these have indeed tackled issues of black advancement, achievement, esteem and the negative temptations and forces that harm the real black community. It is possible that Cosby considers that too obvious didactic treatment would "give the game away" and may alienate white viewers without telling the blacks any more than they already know. (p. 9)

The authors also posit some questions for further research relative to the show:

- Do the Huxtables win *respect* from white as well as black viewers?
- Do the Huxtables win *affection* from white as well as black viewers?
- Do viewers think that many black people would like to become like Huxtable characters, or to have some of their characteristics?
- Which Huxtable characteristics do viewers think are desirable, and which others not?
- Would viewers want to see any or more white characters enter the programme—and if so in what kinds of role?
- Is there interest in a friendly white neighbour?
- Is there interest in a hostile white neighbour? (p. 10)

Simon Hogart's article, "Black Gold" (1988), deals with the question of why *The Cosby Show* has not taken off in Britain as it did in the United States. Hogart offers his own speculation on the topic:

Race may have something to do with it; British people aren't used to the notion of middle-class blacks.... More likely, it's because American situation comedies have a different role from ours. The joke in most sitcoms derives from unsuitable, mismatched people living together ... (but) American sitcoms are mainly designed to offer comfort, warmth, and reassurance, which *The Cosby Show* delivers in full measure. (p. 8)

As the former Soviet Union's demand for American films and television programs continues to escalate, Moscow has reportedly expressed interest in *The Cosby Show* as one of several sitcom offerings.

A SPECIAL CASE STUDY: SOUTH AFRICA

This section could be an entire book on its own. It began back in 1986, when this researcher contacted the South African Broadcasting Corporation (SABC), headquartered in Johannesburg, to verify the statistic/rumor about *The Cosby Show*'s being number 1 in South Africa.

Dr. D. P. Van Vuuren and Dr. Aliza Duby of SABC reported the following findings in response to a nationwide postal panel they performed. Although figures and methodology are not explained, these were responses to the question, Do you think this program (*The Cosby Show*) is:

	April 15, 1985	January 18, 1986
Very funny	59%	69%
Funny	31	25
Somewhat funny	7	3
Not really funny	2	1
Not funny at all	1	2

Joy Morrison (1986), a white South African studying at the University of Iowa, reminds us that television has only been operative in South Africa since 1976, and that it was initially introduced with the explicit intention of further dividing the races. She documents the introduction of *The Cosby Show* as a complete reversal of previous broadcast policy, and notes how, with its meteoric rise to top place in popularity, it is a contributing factor in breaking down racial barriers in the country.

South Africa, with a population of around 30 million people, has distinct ethnic groups: whites comprise 5 million people, Blacks 22 million, and Indian/Asians 1 million, and "mixed races" 2.7 million. The government's ideological policy of apartheid operates on a separate but equal doctrine, but that execution is far from workable. Nowhere is that discrepancy more evident than in the current broadcasting situation. The reader is particularly encouraged to read Tomaselli and Tomaselli's (1986) chapter, "Between Policy and Practice in the SABC, 1976–1981," for an explicit explanation of the struggles within the state broadcasting system between pro- and anti-apartheid staffers.

The Cosby Show came to South Africa in 1985 and was greeted with the same enthusiastic response it had been receiving in the United States. First broadcast on TV4 at 10:30 P.M. Mondays, a typically late-night entertainment channel geared toward whites and broadcast in English, the program has caused ripples throughout the society. For whites with little or no social interaction with Blacks, it is quite amazing to consider how many have invited the Huxtables into their living rooms. For some Black viewers, the show has reportedly been an inspiration.

The Wall Street Journal's Steve Mufson writes that *The Cosby Show* in South Africa "reaches 17.2% of whites over the age of 16, 21.6% of people of racially mixed origin, 31.8% of Asians and Indians, and 18% of blacks." By way of perspective, he adds: "Today, television sets can be found in the homes of 93.7% of whites, 22.1% of blacks, 92.6% of Indians, and 61% of people of racially mixed origin. There are four stations, all owned by the government" (1986, p. 17).

In trying to find the Blacks' reaction to *The Cosby Show*, Joy Morrison got responses from eight Blacks who thought the show was a good example of the socioeconomic levels all people could attain, given equal opportunity. She received comments like these:

- I regard the Cosby family as role models that act as a spur for me to work hard to attain that level of success.

- It depicts a Black family in a very positive light, which should happen as much as possible in South Africa.

- The show makes me proud of being black.

- The show makes black people not ashamed of being black.

- All ethnic barriers have been broken down in this show. There is no such thing as "because you are white you are entitled to certain privileges."

- To us these programmes are our champions. They are helping us fight against inequality by changing the white attitudes. It gives us pride to see a black man on top.

- So the Cosby Show in other words is saying, "Come on you white guys [in South Africa], the blacks are not so bad as you make them out to be. Look at us, we are having a good life and normal family problems here in America. Give those guys down there a chance. Let's change for the better and live together, not apart." (1986, pp. 28–30)

These Black respondents report that watching *The Cosby Show* encourages them to work hard to attain a higher standard of living. Meanwhile, whites are being educated to another perspective of Blacks than they perhaps would have considered. Bill Cosby himself has commented: "It does not surprise me that people of all colors enjoy the fun, the humor, the love that the Huxtable family puts across."[4] The real impact might be on children, who hopefully are being socialized to reconsider and reconceptualize some racial stereotypes.

SABC tried to assess the impact of *The Cosby Show* on children. In a draft paper he faxed on December 28, 1988, Dr. Van Vuuren and his colleagues report on a study of "Children's Perception of and Identification with the Social Reality of 'The Cosby Show.' " The study begins with a discussion of the fact that television is thought to be mostly viewed in the family context in South Africa. *The Cosby Show* has consistently been among the top ten programs, reaching first position during the week of March 23–29, 1987. Deciding that "the family portrayed in *The Cosby Show* portrays economic and personal roles countering racial and economic stereotypes," the SABC's research unit decided to compare its viewership reaction to the show and compare it to a study by Brown, Austin, and Roberts done in 1987.[5] A sample of 467 children in the Transvaal (117 English-speaking whites, 116 Afrikaans, and 234 "black pupils speaking a variety of languages in the Nguni and Sotho language groups") were randomly assigned one of three episodes from the show, and pre- and post-viewing English questionnaires were administered, "regardless of the respondent's home language." Results differed from the study by Brown, Austin, and Roberts (1987), which indicated a significant relationship between frequency of viewing *The Cosby Show* and perceived realism. For South African children, the show's popularity can better be explained as "mere entertainment" rather than as a model for cultural transition.

The popularity of the show in South Africa should not be underestimated, however. In fact, an editorial in *The New Republic* suggested that *The Cosby Show*'s very popularity should be used as a bargaining chip: "If the intent of sanctions against South Africa is to communicate outrage at apartheid, and to do so in a way that puts more pressure on whites than on blacks, then why not impose a ban on the export of American TV shows to South Africa?"[6] Later letters to the editor of *The New Republic* were intriguing, particularly one by Ronald Lightstone, senior vice president, Corporate and Legal Affairs for Viacom International, who proclaimed the company's commitment to *The Cosby Show*'s access for all South African viewers and defended it as revolutionary in its inherent message.

Just how powerful is *The Cosby Show* in South Africa? In an effort to help find out, in November 1988 Keyan Tomaselli, director of the Contemporary Cultural Studies Unit (CCSU) of the University of Natal, ran announcements in two South African newspapers. Forty-nine responses were received from people living in Natal (see Appendix 16). All the respondents had seen the show, and most (73%) were regular viewers. They rated it very high: 76 percent at 8 or higher.

While gender was fairly even, race was predominantly white (86%). (CCSU removed the label "race" from the original questionnaire and substituted "suburb," which they were then able to decode for color.) Age range varied, as did occupation. Overall, this was a heavier television-viewing audience than was found in other countries, a statistic corroborated by other South African television surveys. Following are some of their comments on *The Cosby Show*.

- It is unique in that although it is made up of incidents in the family life of the Huxtables, the "incidents" are far from striking or exciting, in fact [they] are quite homely—and yet they have captured the imagination of a vast audience. The parents are good, sensible, and understanding, and are always available if any of the children should need them.

- I feel that the Cosby Show is a very good show but it is a bit hard to believe because

I don't think that families can be as happy like that ALL THE TIME. I enjoy watching this family show as it has comedy, variety, drama and emotive values. It does not rely on "SOPPY" shows to boost its rating!!

• I look forward to another series of the Cosby show—one can learn so much from their situations. I am not colour conscientious [*sic*] and believe all people basically have the same problems in family life.

• Having brought up three children, the programme constantly reminds me of situations we experienced, especially regarding boy/girl friends, using make-up, borrowing each other's clothes and entering each other's bedroom uninvited.

• If the show was too typical, it would be too normal and then become a bore. I became anti Bill Cosby after reading derogatory remarks he made about Rep. of S.A.

• I must say that when we first watched the show it did seem rather strange to see how "normal" everyone was. It didn't take long before we stopped thinking of the Huxtables as a Black family and began to relate to them as one would to any show about a middle-class family. It really helped us to better understand the fact that they were in fact no different from us, despite the colour of their skins.

   Hope that we will have the pleasure of many more hours of the "Bill Cosby Show" (*sic*).

• White friends are included in a most natural way. The whole series shows that people of other colours are very much alike.

• A little concerned as I am a true S. African—and I have been told Bill Cosby is anti S.A.,—so therefore I refuse to watch his show any longer! even though he/family are great.

• I don't see why every question relating to colour should be tied to race and racism. The Cosby Show is a *cultural* and *not* a *colour* thing. Black South Africans, with whom I grew up, do *not* relate with white humour and do *not* relate with American Negroes or "people of colour."

• The black population are mostly un-educated . . . consequently, these people do not find much to be amused about. Furthermore, they do not see any humour in seeing other black people finding it "so easy" and most probably even feel a little resentful.

In summary, South African survey participants in the main viewed the show favorably. Some of the positive comments use terms such as agreeable, typical, unique, having homey incidents, understanding parents, being reminiscent/ something to relate to, not "soppy," realistic, loving family, touching, humorous and entertaining, clean and wholesome, Cosby as the ideal father, and blending humor and discipline. Those who reacted differently considered it inane, pretentious, not funny, unconvincing, critical of various characters, and not a typical family but an idealized version; moreover, some survey respondents added pointedly anti-Cosby sentiments.

Some specific comments about race from these South African survey participants merit closer scrutiny. One ninety-four-year-old white woman commented that "(t)he amicable mixing of skin colouring from white to very

black should be a lesson to those South Africans who wish to segregate."
Another viewer noticed how quickly her family stopped thinking of the Huxtable family as Black and began to relate to them as any (middle-class) family.
One of the few Black respondents liked the fact that Bill Cosby includes white
actors on the show, stating "otherwise these programmes will be labelled
discriminatory." An Indian added that "(t)he ideas of colour and inferiority
fall away when people are uplifted and educated as seen in the Huxtables."
For a retired teacher, *The Cosby Show* has this benefit: "The whole series
shows that people of other colours are very much alike mentally, and it
should help break down South Africans' unfortunate way of condescending
to 'lesser intelligences.' " In contrast, another retiree finds the show "unconvincing—colours range from white to Negro." One man was angry that the
questionnaire brought up the race question at all. "The Cosby Show portrays
life as you would (or *could*) find it in a white South African household, *not*
in a Black one." And yet another respondent added, "I do not think it is about
being black or white but about how to live in a family."

Fifteen months after the South African newspaper appeal, an unidentified
Afrikaner wrote: "When you Americans think about blacks in this country you
automatically equate them with your Negros (*sic*) which is impossible for the
following reasons." The writer then went on to enumerate differences between growing up in urban/Westernized areas as opposed to rural/tribal areas,
the different ethnic groups or nations to which Blacks in South Africa belong,
and the groups' cultural differences in terms of humor. "A very interesting
fact that was found out by our own TV ratings is that the Cosby Show was
tops when shown on our TV 1 (whites) and scored miserably when moved
to the TV 3/4 (Blacks) channel," the letter continued. "The greatest divide
between black and white in this country is not the colour of one's skin but
the first- and third world values and attitudes displayed by the different race
groups.... Therefore, we do not see the Cosby show as being about black
people but we see it as a very entertaining sit-com displaying beliefs and
values we can associate with."

DISCUSSION

McQuail, Blumler, and Brown (1972), in a study of the television audience,
believe that media use is most suitably characterized as an interactive process.
Their model is of an open system, and their methodology is based on a
concern for moving from a qualitative and descriptive approach to a quantitative one, developing instruments to operationalize media-related gratifications that could be treated statistically. The authors have constructed a
typology of media-person interactions:

I. Diversion

    A. Escape from the constraints of routine

B. Escape from the burdens of problems

C. Emotional release

II. Personal Relationships

A. Companionship

B. Social utility

III. Personal Identity

A. Personal reference

B. Reality exploration

C. Value reinforcement

IV. Surveillance

The audience for *The Cosby Show* apparently fits under various parts of the model depending on the audience's various orientations toward the program. Although for most viewers the half-hour sitcom offers a fun-filled respite from daily activities, others have a deeper personal involvement with it, seeking meaning through family relationships. In its transmission of values, showing a positive portrayal of parenthood and family life, *The Cosby Show* has been held up as a classic example of socialization, maintaining a cultural heritage.

Audience research typically includes the following characteristics: (1) Demographic variables (sex, age, race, educational background, occupation, income, etc.); (2) knowledge variables (what do audiences learn from their exposure to media?); and (3) belief/action variables (how do audiences believe and act differently because of their exposure to the media?)

Researchers are increasingly discovering that television audiences are different from other media audiences. The television spectator, John Ellis reminds us, has many competing claims for his or her attention: "So TV cannot assume that its viewers have given it their attention in advance. The position given to the TV viewer is that of someone whose interest has to be courted over a short attention span: a viewer who is seeking diversion moment by moment, and accords little importance to this diversion" (1982, p. 163). This disclaimer attains greater importance when we count how many "regular" viewers of *The Cosby Show* put aside the time each week to watch it, even though many of them would not be otherwise considered heavy viewers of television. David Morley notes of television: "It is being used to provide the reference points, the ground, the material, the stuff of conversation" (1986, p. 22).

James Lull discusses television viewing as a family activity: "(It) involves an intermeshing of the constantly changing personal agendas, moods, and emotional priorities of each family member with the fluctuating agenda of programs that emanates from TV sets.... Further, television viewing is constructed by family members; it doesn't just happen" (1988, p. 17). That family-viewing context was found to be a frequent one for survey participants here. Thursday evenings become special times. *The Cosby Show* becomes part of a weekly, cultural ritual, a phenomenon Lull elsewhere terms "manifestations of microsocial (family) and macrosocial (cultural) *rules*.... These rituals embody extensions of the normative values, mental orientations, and day-to-day behavior of individuals and families that are at least tacitly understood by everyone as rules of social interaction and communication" (p. 238).

When we review all these statistics and statements, we are perhaps reminded most of Van Vuuren's study of reality perception. Nationally and internationally, cross culturally and interculturally, these audiences for *The Cosby Show* seem to be in firm agreement: They like the show, they rate it highly, and they have favorite characters and episodes, even if sometimes they have differing opinions about what it all means. By allowing for both quantitative and qualitative responses, this survey sought to obtain not only individual opinions about what this popular program means, but also data on viewing patterns, such as learning "This is the only time our family gets together."

It is one thing to know that *The Cosby Show* has been a ratings success story in the United States and quite another to get behind some of the statistics to understand actual personal feelings. Overall, this survey shows that its popularity crosses gender, age, and racial boundaries. Obviously, its humor appeals across a wide cross-section. It may even have helped make some inroads into promoting tolerance.

On the one hand, advertisers and syndicators don't really care about ideological perceptions as much as sheer numbers. On the other hand, the demographics of the audience—cutting across cultural boundaries as it does—puts a whole new face on the study of television audiences. Or perhaps it all just boils down to one American schoolboy's comment about *The Cosby Show*: "One of the best shows I've ever seen."

6

Kudos and Criticism for
The Cosby Show

> Until the audience understands what it sees in larger contexts, until it
> develops its own critical facilities, we will live in a world dominated by
> one-eyed monsters. When all of us participate in the critical climate we
> will live in a world more thoroughly humane than any other.
>
> Horace Newcomb, Introduction to
> *Television: The Critical View*
> (New York: Oxford University Press, 1987), p. 11.

This book has dealt mainly with the positive aspects of *The Cosby Show*,
describing its success in terms of ratings, its record-breaking advertising and
syndication revenues, its ability to save not only a network but also the sitcom
genre, the precedent it set for syndication, its production style which gives
freedom to the actors and the show's star, its content which has become a
model for family relationships, its introduction of a potentially new positive
image for Blacks, and its ability to cut across demographic and cultural boundaries both in the United States and around the world. *The Cosby Show* has
won more than its share of Emmys and accolades from both the public and
the television industry.

This book has also included kudos from individual audience members who
marvel about how amusing and how fulfilling the show is to them personally.
Without question *The Cosby Show* does make most people laugh. Yet, views
are not unanimous on interpreting typicality, believability, uniqueness, realism, and even the show's idealism. Clearly, the survey participants' frame
of reference must be taken into consideration in any final evaluation of the
show.

The Cosby Show has received praise for portraying blacks generally and women in particular in a positive and realistic setting and for relating well to parent-child relationships and ways of dealing with adolescent problems.

Yet, for all the raves, *The Cosby Show* is not without its critics and skeptics. Next we discuss some of the issues that are a necessary part of a critical system-theoretical perspective, including the escapist/unrealistic complaint, the show's deliberate decision not to deal directly with Blackness, Cosby himself, the storyline and style, and what it all means.

ESCAPIST/UNREALISTIC COMPLAINTS

In 1987, *TV Guide*'s Richard Turner asked the "experts" to rate television's best and worst sitcoms (p. 2). The panelists included:

- Garth Ancier—senior vice president of programming for Fox Broadcasting Company
- Martha Bayles—TV critic, *Wall Street Journal*
- Stuart Bloomberg—ABC vice president of comedy and variety series development
- Allan Burns—co-creator/co-executive producer, *Mary Tyler Moore Show* and *Lou Grant*
- Ellen Chasset Falcon—director whose credits include *My Sister Sam, Designing Women, A Different World*
- Jerry Katzman—senior vice president, Worldwide TV, William Morris Agency
- Scott Kaufer—vice president of comedy development at Warner Bros. TV
- Dennis Klein—director and comedy writer whose credits include *The Odd Couple* and *All in the Family*
- Thad Mumford—supervising producer of *A Different World*; also produced *M*A*S*H* and *Alf*
- Joel Segal—executive vice president, Backer Spielvogel Bates advertising agency
- Fred Silverman—programming chief successively at CBS and ABC; then president of NBC; now a producer (*Matlock, Jake and the Fatman*).
- Brandon Tartikoff—then president of NBC Entertainment

Turner began his discussion of *The Cosby Show* by saying, "We wouldn't even be doing this article if there hadn't been a COSBY show. In the early part of the year 1984, the sitcom was 'dead.' Three years later, of course, we're looking at wall-to-wall comedy." The panelists didn't credit the show's success simply to its star, "since he's failed in previous shows." They didn't give all the credit for its timing—the "Reagan-era" when audiences are supposed to want comfort and reassurance. Credit instead went to "something special about the rhythm of these shows; instead of rat-a-tat jokes, the episodes meandered around trivial incidents, where action was incidental rather than story-driven." The panel of "experts" gave particular credit to the youngest cast members, to the overall chemistry of the Huxtable family, and to director

Jay Sandrich's mechanics. Overall, however, they thought the show was slipping. Was it running out of material? Or were audiences getting tired of the too-perfect family?

David Lerner (1986, p. 88), Vice President and broadcast supervisor of Foote, Cone & Belding, praises the show but finds two weaknesses:

1. The first relates to the excessive time the Huxtable parents spend around the home, considering the demands of their professions. Clair seemingly logs more kitchen duty than Betty Crocker; Cliff occasionally reminds us of Ozzie Nelson, with a designer pullover in lieu of Ozzie's dowdy cardigan. There is a degree of validity in this grievance. However, television programs are not so much a reflection of society as they are a reflection of other television programs.

2. The second complaint questions the degree to which "The Cosby Show" exaggerates intrafamily harmony...it may simply be offering just another form of escapism.

One of the panelists, Martha Bayles, wrote an article for *The Wall Street Journal* (1988) in which she discussed Clair's role as going from "preachy" (sermons about women's rights) to preening. Picking up on early critics' gripe that the Huxtables were too affluent to be Black, Bayles turns it around:

I have to say that, in a different sense, their lives are too easy to be real. The problem isn't money. It never was. A husband and wife can earn two upscale incomes and still be human, especially if they fret and bicker about money as much as the Huxtables. No, what makes these folks unreal is the fact that they never fret or bicker about other scarce resources, such as time and energy. (p. 22)

She goes on with the familiar complaint that no one is ever seen housecleaning, but she is especially upset that the characters seem to be too self-indulgent.

Bill Cosby has responded to these "unreal" criticisms: "There are people who misread this show and feel that nobody's family is that perfect. We're not aiming for the perfect family. We're saying that there are certain situations that come about and this is the way it was handled. And we're saying, 'Does anything look like you?' "[1]

When associate professor of English Mary Helen Washington asked her students for their reactions to *The Cosby Show*, she was concerned about some of their specific responses: (1) On the question of the show's treatment of women, the class was divided between those who would give it an A+ for showing women as equals and those who saw a residual, between-the-lines kind of sexism that undermines the attempt at fairness and equality. (2) Race was simply avoided as a fact that influences their lives. (3) On the question of affluence, most of the students defended the family's upper class status.

Washington caused quite a stir with her *TV Guide* article, which ended with hoping the show would take more risks: "So far the Cosby show has been wonderful entertainment, charming and funny and as comfortable as ham and grits on a cold morning; but it could go much further in delivering us from the pretenses we live by—that racial problems have been solved, that sexism can be undone by having the husband help out in the kitchen, that being rich is the measure of success" (1986, p. 4).

The wider question is: Does Clair's profession serve to assuage special interest groups, or is it simply an easy plot device? Perhaps the answer is merely one of economics, as Phyllis M. Japp proposes:

Claire epitomizes one strategy for resolving the conflicts of woman and work—keep work invisible and peripheral to both plot and character. Just as television fathers— Ward Cleavers and Jim Andrews of the past—returned to the home from a mysterious, unseen workplace, so now do its wives and mothers. Women's work is essentially window-dressing, designed to enhance viewer appeal. (1991, p. 60)

Feminist media watchers argue that it hardly matters for "reality" that Clair is a professional, as she hardly could count as a role model for young women considering work as a lawyer. Japp, for example, writes,

Claire Huxtable glides smoothly in and out of her living room, ostensibly going out to engage in professional duties. She might as well be going shopping, in terms of the impact of her professional identity upon her character's attitudes, values, behaviors. Of course, Claire's path is well lubricated by money. She obviously doesn't need to work. With Cliff as a husband, she really need not mother either; he is apparently the family's chief provider and major nurturing figure. (pp. 59–60)

Discussing the show's idealization of Black families, Darrell Y. Hamamoto (1989, p. 137) stated:

While *The Cosby Show* might possibly have been an accurate portrayal of those black professionals who had broken through ethnic and class barriers, it was pure fantasy for the many more members of the black underclass who could only dream of the material comfort and security enjoyed by the Huxtables and their brood.

THE BLACKNESS ISSUE

"The real problem with *The Cosby Show*," writes *National Review* critic Terry Teachout (1986), "is that it fails to dramatize its vision of black assimilation in the context of the world outside of the four walls of the Huxtable household. Not only are the answers too easy, the questions never even get asked" (p. 59).

From the start, the press registered a negative reaction to the show's color-blindness. Frequently quoted are comments by *New York Magazine* that the show was *Leave It To Beaver* in blackface, by the *Village Voice* that the

Huxtables were "quite determinedly" not Black in anything but their skin color, by *Ebony* that it was not "Black enough . . . [or] not dealing with more controversial issues, such as poverty and racism and interracial dating, for focusing on a Black middle-class family when the vast majority of Black people survive on incomes far below that of the Huxtables."[2]

Cosby has responded to the criticism that the show "white-washes" its Black family: "What would be unique is if you had some Africans who came over here and set up a house like that. To say that we're acting white means that only white people can do this. It denies us being Americans. We go to college, we go to medical school. Now how then is this doctor [Cliff Huxtable] supposed to act?"[3] Columnist William Raspberry, in answer to the question "Cosby Show: Black or White?", adds: "Besides, there is value in letting white America understand that blackness isn't necessarily a pathological condition" (1984, p. A27).

One of the most frequent charges lodged against Black television shows is that they have predominantly been handled as Black images in white hands. As discussed in this book, however, that has not been the case with *The Cosby Show*. "Not until the advent of Cosby's show had there been a program in which the governing sensibility—the absolute first and last word on just about every detail—lay in black hands," writes Bogle (1988, pp. 247–48).

Moreover, Cosby had not taken the easy route out. He had refused to fall back on the standard raucous ghetto family that cracks jokes or sounds off on one another. Instead, his was a richly humorous depiction of black upper-middle-class life, a study of people, in so many respects, no different from white America, yet in other very specific and subtle ways, quite different. His series had shown the connective tissue between two separate cultural experiences in America.

Michael Dyson (1989) has criticized Cosby for not accepting responsibility on his shows for addressing racism. Labeling him "the reigning national icon," recognizing him as an innovator in shattering African-American stereotypes, and locating *The Cosby Show* in the folklore of family relations, Dyson still questions the images of the Huxtables as an authentically Black family. Dyson cites the show's ability to combat the system, and urges both the star and his writers to acknowledge the racism in our society. One of Dyson's suggestions, about a less-fortunate visiting relative, was actually incorporated into the storyline with the introduction, in the seventh season, of Erica Alexander as "Pam," a cousin of Clair's.

Labeling Bill Cosby "the most visible black bargainer on the American scene today" and *The Cosby Show* "a blackface version of the American dream," Shelby Steele (1990) argues that the series is devoid of racial guilt, and that the Huxtable family, "with its doctor/lawyer parent combination, its drug-free, college-bound children, and its wise yet youthful grandparents . . . never discusses affirmative action":

The bargain Cosby offers his white viewers—*I will confirm your racial innocence if you accept me*—is a good deal for all concerned. Not only does it allow whites to enjoy Cosby's humor with no loss of innocence, but it actually enhances their innocence by implying that race is not the serious problem for blacks that it once was. If anything, the success of this handsome, affluent black family points to the fair-mindedness of whites who, out of their essential goodness, changed society so that black families like the Huxtables could succeed. Whites can watch "The Cosby Show" and feel complimented on a job well done.

The power that black bargainers wield is the power of absolution. On Thursday nights, Cosby, like a priest, absolves his white viewers, forgives and forgets the sins of the past. And for this he is rewarded with an almost sacrosanct status. Cosby benefits from what might be called the gratitude factor. His continued number-one rating may have something to do with the (white) public's gratitude at being offered a commodity so rare in our time; he tells his white viewers each week that they are okay, and that this black man is not going to challenge them.

Dr. Venise T. Berry, head of the Mass Communication Department at Huston-Tillotson, a Black college in Austin, Texas, has studied the relationship between Black youth and television. She has found that most of them, particularly low-income Blacks, are deeply influenced by the box. They watch more often than whites, they identify with it to a greater extent, and they perceive it as reality more readily than their white counterparts. Comparing sons' attitudes toward fathers on *Good Times* (J. J. toward James Evans) and *The Cosby Show* (Theo toward Cliff), she found that most (87% of her sample, 28 Black male and 26 Black female teens) found James to be stronger and more manly than the Heathcliff character, who was described as sensitive and soft-hearted and, therefore, was seen as weak and unmanly. Berry concludes that "while it may be true that 'The Cosby Show' is presenting new definitions of black manhood and black family, the failure of the show to address class status differences may be affecting the show's ability to actually deliver those images to the lower-class audience as anymore than entertainment" (1990, p. 10).

Responding to the criticism that *The Cosby Show* is too soft, too idealized, "not focused enough on the type of realities most black families had to contend with," Bogle retorts (1988, p. 248): "Regardless, an important new step had been taken in television.... 'The Cosby Show' had revealed what some new blood—and new color—could do for the tube, infusing it with a new perspective and taking it in a new direction that grasped the attention and respect of almost everyone." A colleague of mine, categorizing himself as "representative of the black professional and middle-class population," wanted to go on record as saying that, in his opinion, *The Cosby Show* is about "positive values and family. This crosses and transcends race, black or white."

COSBY HIMSELF

Some criticisms have been leveled at Bill Cosby himself. *Time* (Zoglin, 1985) calls the star a problem:

He is, quite simply, everywhere. His name is listed five times in the credits: as star, co-producer, executive consultant, co-author of the theme music and, as William H. Cosby Jr., Ed.D., one of the show's creators. On a typical episode, he appears in virtually every scene. Children run in and out of the frame at a sprightly clip, but the center of attention is always Dad; no bit of action goes by without a quip, double take or comic harangue. It upsets the show's balance and throws off its rhythm. (p. 85)

A content analysis of several dozen actual televised episodes and scripts designed to determine Cosby's centrality verified *Time*'s criticism.[4] Similarly, when both Cliff and Clair were together, Dr. Huxtable was singled out by a ratio of 9 to 1. Typically, when one of the children entered a room when both parents were there, their opening salutation would be "Dad... "—rarely "Mom and Dad," and absolutely never just "Mom."

Cosby has been parodied for his many commercial ventures,[5] and has been called "a product" like his own programs and books.[6] *Rolling Stone* (Mc-Williams, 1987) labeled him a "segregationist when it comes to sex: women are cute when they get mad, and they're tasty only when they're second bananas" (p. 125). *Entertainment Weekly* (Appelo, 1990) ran an article entitled "Father Time Has Caught up with Father Cosby."

Bogle (1988, p. 374) again comes to Cosby's defense: "Most importantly though for the first time in television history, a black performer had complete control of his own series. And he had come up with an astounding winner, proving that black creative talents, if given a chance, could invigorate old television forms and formulas."

STORYLINE AND STYLE

"By most objective standards, 'The Cosby Show' is an unlikely candidate for through-the-roof success," wrote *Time* critic Richard Zoglin (1987). "In contrast, say, to the Norman Lear comedies of the early '70s, it breaks little new ground in style or subject matter. It has none of the gag-writing brio of *The Mary Tyler Moore Show* or a half a dozen comedies that followed it. Indeed, 'The Cosby Show' might be a classic illustration of ex-Network Programmer Paul Klein's theory of Least Objectionable Programming" (p. 87).

This argument, Cosby would say, is exactly the point. While some critics call the show too cosmetized, too simple in plot line, too moralistic, even too goody-goody, *The Cosby Show* has self-styled itself deliberately in that mold.

Fazal and Wober (1989) have encouraged the show's creative staff to take some of these criticisms to heart:

It could be possible for the Cosby production to make one or more episodes with more poignant or distressing contents, say to show an adolescent friend who is overcome by drug addiction or a patient of the doctor who has an anxiety neurosis brought on by racial victimisation. It is possible, then, for research to examine whether the series with a light emotional tone could "carry" such "heavier" episodes without alienating viewers but also gaining in esteem especially amongst black viewers. (p. 10)

In terms of its insularity, plot conventions on *The Cosby Show* have been criticized both literally and symbolically. "Because it never gets out of the house it causes cabin fever," declares *New York* critic John Leonard (1984, p. 154). "The world outside 'The Cosby Show' appears both diffuse and down-right perilous, to the degree that it exists at all," writes Ella Taylor (1990, pp. 162–163). "The Huxtables have friends who drift in and out of their lives but no discernible community, indeed no public life to speak of aside from their jobs, which seem to run on automatic pilot."

With regard to plot, Mark Crispin Miller (1986) claims that the show "is devoid of any dramatic tension whatsoever. Nothing happens, nothing changes, there is no suspense or ambiguity or disappointment" (p. 209). Taylor (1990) agrees: "Nothing, in the classical dramatic sense, ever really happens . . . (it) is a virtually plotless chronicle of the small, quotidian details of family life, at whose heart lies a moral etiquette of parenting and a developmental psychology of growing up" (p. 161). Blum and Lindhelm (1987), authors of a book on network television programming, point out that "(c)omedy series now touch the lives of ordinary people in recognizable situations," adding that *The Cosby Show* "epitomizes the appeal of recognizable settings and characters played by identifiable stars" (p. 4). Recently, *Entertainment Weekly*, noting the continuing success of *Cheers* to remain fresh, commented on how *The Cosby Show* could/should have ended after four seasons—which, it stated, were "more than enough for that old bonbon" (Appelo, 1990, 35).

Yet, as has been documented here, storyline and style in *The Cosby Show* are very carefully considered and executed. If it is criticized for lack of innovation in these areas, that too has been deliberated and deliberately pushed aside in terms of wider goals.

CRITICAL PERSPECTIVE

As stated in the Preface, this book could have been written from any number of theoretical perspectives, and/or combinations of them—say, from a Marxist, neo-Marxist, even feminist-Marxist point of view, or from a semiological, psychosocial, narrative, or many other frameworks. Although several of these approaches have been considered here within our overall systems-theoretical perspective, particular attention has been given to ritualistic television-viewing notions. Sandra Ann Dickerson, a Ph.D. candidate in educational media, has written a lengthy reaction, both positive and negative, about *The Cosby Show*. It is reprinted here, with her permission, in its entirety.[7]

Favorable

1. The nation gets to see a Black *FAMILY*—a rare occurrence in the American media for television or the movies. Although in reality *most* (more than 50%) of Black people live in a nuclear family. This is the norm. It always has been. I grew up as an only child with a mother and a father who were each other's first marriage and who were married to each other for 36 years. This was the case with most of my friends. It was the case with the majority of people I knew.

2. We see a strong yet gentle father figure in Cliff—another rare image.

3. Cliff and Clair are seen weekly in a loving relationship in which an open display of sex is not tangent to this love. An extremely necessary image in light of the role which is often mistakenly attributed to sex in a love relationship; and in light of the stereotypical notion of "the sexual buck" that has shrouded the Black male since slavery.

4. The nation has become used to looking at Black people on a weekly basis. The range of skin tones has made white America aware that skin colors can vary greatly within a Black family. It has forced America to look at other skin colors besides the lighter ones as being beautiful.

5. These Black people do not worry about money. They are well off. This has caused white America to grapple with and try to accept the Black middle class. However, there has always been a Black middle class since there was a Black presence in America. Most of the Black colleges were established during reconstruction. They have been graduating Black doctors, lawyers, teachers, etc. for generations. Even before the Black colleges there were always Blacks who struggled under the pain of death to learn and to educate others. History is replete with these examples. I know scores of Blacks who live like the Huxtables; but it is truly a new image for White America.

6. Most of the plots and central themes on the show examine conflicts over the rights and feelings of individual family members. None of the family members seem to have priority over another. For example, Rudy's friends, anxieties, problems are no less significant than Theo's or Denise's or any of the other children or adults. This is an excellent lesson in parenting. It teaches that children are people too. Sometimes the older generation of Black Americans have operated on the principle that "children should be seen and not heard."

7. The presence of Cliff's father and mother demonstrates the stability of Black family life. It glorifies older Black people and teaches that there is something rich about interactions with grandparents. It teaches that Black love exists generationally over time, too.

8. The show has had a remarkable effect on the grooming of both White and Black America. I do believe that Bill Cosby has brought the sweater back for us all. In 1984 when the show started, many Black males were wearing either bald haircuts or "gerry curls" [chemically processed hair]. As Theo's hair got longer, so did the

majority of Black teenagers. Longer natural hair has returned for both men and women. It is more sculptured than in the sixties, but natural hair is here to stay, I hope. I saw an interview on TV with Tempestt Bledsoe who plays the next to youngest. She indicated that Mr. Cosby strongly advised her to wear her hair natural. She did. Additionally, Tempestt has been seen frequently wearing the Braided African styles. Within the next ten years Black women have been fired or not hired for wearing this hairstyle—to wit, the Washington, DC Hyatt. Rudy's hair is never straightened. She has a "common" grade of kinky hair and it is styled in very "basic" styles which most of us Black women can identify with.

9. Those plots which emphasize education are exceptional. This is very realistic for the Black family. We all have had it pounded into us that education is the way out; not only for boys but also for girls. College is the end goal for all of the children.

10. Clair seems to be in an egalitarian relationship with Cliff. In respects of making decisions concerning the children, she does not give the classic "wait until your father gets home." Instead, she takes initiative and acts. The reverse is also true with Cliff. Clair is not demure and passive as many middle-class White women are found to be on sitcoms. The fact that Cliff is a doctor and Clair a lawyer sets an excellent role model for both Black and White youngsters. White children need Black role models, too.

11. All of the characters on the Cosby show speak clear clean crisp standard English. There is a burden of language among some Black youth that speaking standard English is "talking white." The show removes that burden. The characters are natural with language and occasionally lapse into inflections that are clearly "Black," but the emphasis is on language—standard English for the best communication. I have noticed this more in Rudy lately.

12. *The Cosby Show* is a watershed for departing with the common stereotypes of Black males and females which webb through most other Black programs and images. Such programs as *Gimme a Break, 222, Amen*, the former *Good Times*, and *What's Happenin,* and many others.

Unfavorable

1. For the most part, the show's plots are trivial. On one particular episode a whole half hour was taken up with Cliff's trying to find a quiet place to sleep.

2. The writers of the show ignore the fact that the Huxtable family is a Black family who lives in a predominantly White world. This does mean that combating racism is a fact of life for Black Americans at every and all economic strata. Because the show blatantly skirts the issue of racism, it does not confront White America with its own problems. Likewise, it does not teach Black America how to deal effectively with issues of race and class.

3. The Huxtables seem to exist in a vacuum of social issues and social pain. They have no opinions on social issues. With the exception of one anti-apartheid poster on the back of Theo's door, the show could take place on Mars.

4. There are only middle class Blacks on the show. There is a clear absence of interactions with other classes of Black and White people. This creates a fantasy illusion that "all" Blacks are as well off as the Huxtables.

5. Cliff does not have enough activities outside the home. In reality middle class Blacks are heavily involved in the Black church, and in performing many civic duties and volunteer services. The family has never gone to church nor discussed church to my knowledge. This is a major fallacy in any portrayal of Black life.

6. Although the color range is wide within Black families, I feel that Denise and Sondra are much too light for the median skin tone in the Huxtable family. I wonder what message is sent to Black America that Denise was the character for whom the spin-off *A Different World* was created. I may be stretching the point, since Denise was the only character of college age at the time. I would have felt more comfortable if Sondra's husband were darker. I think that this union again reinforces the false notion of the superiority of light skin tones.

7. Clair's character needs to be developed more. We need to see her with a circle of friends, in her courtroom and in general engaged in other activities outside the home. Clair seems not to have a background. Where did she grow up? Who are her parents, brothers and sisters? She seems to have no interests outside the home. This contrasts with Cliff who has college buddies, fraternity interests, reunions, parents, etc.

8. Theo needs a girlfriend. His character at this point seems to be moving toward asexuality. Perhaps this is an over-compensation to overcome the sexual image of the Black male. If you compare this with the role of Vanessa who has had a platonic relationship since pre-adolescence, there is an awkward mismatch. Theo talks about girls and in the last episode that I watched he was jealous over his so-called girlfriend's attention from another young man. We do not see him in a sustained relationship with a young woman. I believe that this is an imperative role for young Black teenagers because of the teen pregnancy epidemic.

9. Too often the success of an episode on the Cosby show depends on making Theo the brunt of many jokes. This is an old theme: "making fun of the Black male that needs to be squashed." As I think about it, Theo's character is not growing in proportion to Vanessa's, Rudy's, or the other Cosby children.

10. *The Cosby Show* has lasted this long because it is funny, light-hearted and offends only the most overt racists. Can we afford this luxury?

11. Because of the Bill Cosby Show, many people nationally and internationally labor under the false assumption that Blacks have "made it" in America. Nothing could be further from the truth. We have lost ground in the last 20 years in every economic sphere. The intrusion of one type of Black family does not equalize the plight of millions of Blacks and other peoples of color.

12. There could be some de-emphasis on clothes and looking good. It is a reality that middle-class Blacks dress well. But, it is also a reality that poorer Blacks dress well also. Part of the crisis in Black America is the struggle over material goods, particularly clothes, leather goods, gold chains, etc. I have actually seen a life lost because of a gold chain in a high school setting. Some of the root of the drug culture is encouched in "looking good" and having clothes like the Huxtable children wear. I would like to see them dress down a bit or wear a variety of types of clothes. For the most part it seems that each Huxtable child wears a $200-$300 outfit during each episode. Our youth in the schools try to do this also on $6.00 per hour McDonalds jobs.

Another teacher, Ella Taylor at the University of Washington's School of Communications, is concerned about shows like *The Cosby Show* in terms of fostering notions of a "Yuppie Paradise," with emphasis on the pleasures of commodities and "no public life outside the family ... (with) easy parental authority."[8] In her book *Prime-Time Families* (1990), Taylor writes:

Surrounded by the material evidence of their success, the Huxtables radiate wealth, health, energy, and up-to-the-minute style. Indeed, "The Cosby Show" offers the same pleasures as a television commercial—a parade of gleaming commodities and expensive designer clothing unabashedly enjoyed by successful professional families. (p. 160)

Mark Crispin Miller takes up this theme of conspicuous consumption (1986):

Everything within this spacious brownstone is luminously clean and new, as if it had all been set up by the state to make a good impression on a group of visiting foreign dignitaries. Here are all the right commodities—lots of bright sportswear, plants and paintings, gorgeous bedding, plenty of copperware, portable tape players, thick carpeting, innumerable knickknacks, and, throughout the house, big, burnished dressers, tables, couches, chairs, and cabinets (Early American yet looking factory-new). Each week, the Huxtables nearly vanish amid the porcelain, stainless steel, mahogany, and fabric of their lives. In every scene, each character appears in some fresh designer outfit that positively glows with newness, never to be seen a second time. And, like all this pricey clutter, the plots and subplots, the dialogue and even many of the individual shots reflect in some way on consumption as a way of life: Cliff's new juicer is the subject of an entire episode; Cliff does a monologue on his son Theo's costly sweatshirt; Cliff kids daughter Rudy for wearing a dozen wooden necklaces. Each Huxtable, in fact, is hardly more than a mobile display case for his/her momentary possessions. (p. 208)

In chronicling the history of prime time, Donna McCroban (1990) makes a positive assessment of the series: "Indeed, of everything *The Cosby Show* set out to accomplish, its achievements on behalf of human beings—including fathers, mothers, children, blacks, and people in general—top the list ... (it) presented a father who asserted parental authority, guidelines, and the difference between permission and permissiveness. He demanded, and commanded, respect. In turn, he respected his youngsters." (pp. 330–331).

The Cosby Show should be credited, then, for its humorous but also humane presentation of a loving, intact Black family that emphasizes caring for one another, the value of education, and strong middle-class American values. It merits criticism for its insularity and concomitant refusal to confront "real" issues, buying into the advertising/consumption ethic, and not allowing for more individual character development.

John D.H. Downing (1988) concludes his study in this way:

On one level "The Cosby Show" may function as a kind of televisual Doctor Benjamin Spock manual on family interaction: detailed, humane, rational, helpful, enjoyable, insightful. For families suffering from tortured, tense teenage relationships, that can be a contribution. On another level, "The Cosby Show" may operate as a reinstatement of black dignity and culture in a racist society where television culture has generally failed to communicate these realities, and has often flatly negated them. On another level, it may celebrate the virtues of upper-middle-class existence as the most desirable way of life to which the vast mass of citizens can reasonably aspire. (p. 67)

What, then, are the social and cultural ramifications of *The Cosby Show*? The last chapter attempts to address this point.

7

The Sociocultural Implications of *The Cosby Show*

> The message systems of a culture not only inform but form common images. They not only entertain but create publics. They not only satisfy but shape a range of attitudes, tastes, and preferences. They provide the boundary conditions and overall patterns within which the processes of personal and group-mediated selection, interpretation, and image-formation go on.
>
> George Gerbner, "Cultural Indicators."
> (New York: John Wiley, 1973), p. 567.

Typically, students who are new to the study of mass communication are introduced to the field in terms of its nature and functions, particularly its symbiotic relationship to other interdisciplinary systems. From a macroanalytic perspective, mass communication's sociocultural functions are considered to include information, surveillance, interpretation, linkage, persuasion, entertainment, and transmission of cultural values. This chapter concerns itself with the last function: in what way(s) does *The Cosby Show*, with its enormous, if diverse audience, transmit messages about its social and cultural heritage? What is it saying, and being interpreted as saying, about families, about Americans, about Blacks, about the (upper) middle class, about sitcoms specifically and about the media in general?

In other words, what does all this in-depth study mean? This final chapter looks at the sociocultural implications of *The Cosby Show* phenomenon. It discusses the universality of its star and the show's overall appeal, with a special eye to its ramifications by and for Blacks. Consideration is given to the show's uniqueness, particularly in terms of its enculturating values. Its effect on the sitcom genre is also explored. Finally, an evaluation of this case study of a media phenomenon is attempted.

THE UNIVERSALITY OF BILL COSBY AND *THE COSBY SHOW*'S APPEAL

Grant Tinker, former chairman of NBC, has said that NBC's research has shown that all ethnic elements accept Cosby as the current father figure of his country—"an Everyman, who happens to be black."[1] The audience data collected from the 809 survey respondents worldwide support that notion. Most of all, according to John J. O'Connor (1988), "(t)elevision's racial attitudes will be profoundly altered (by *The Cosby Show*).... That's bottom-line reality, and that's Mr. Cosby's lasting achievement" (p. C26).

As has been evidenced from more than one source, Bill Cosby himself has been singled out and credited with his show's runaway success—not by chance, certainly. Ever since his 1965 breakthrough on *I Spy*, when he made the record books as the first Black performer in a starring role on a television drama, Cosby has set high sights and standards for himself. He has also been smart enough to develop his own image—from "funny man" to "father"— and smart enough to figure out how to use the media to further those images. "Part of the appeal of Cosby's character is that he's so fallible: a knowledgeable man who's also sometimes goofy (he seems to relish strutting about showing off his pot belly)," writes Donald Bogle (1988, p. 264), "and frequently obstinate. Everyone knows he'll always end up by understanding his children, but what makes him special is that he always has to go through a ritual of being 'Dad' first: saying no to whatever they request, then testing them, then halfway giving in."

For these antics, Bill Cosby has become universally recognized as a father figure for the times. In some circles, he is called a genius, comic and/or otherwise; in others, he is called an icon. Bill Cosby has calculated "an immediate sense of what the largest portions of the public will respond to," according to Michael Real (1989, pp. 119–120). He has developed "an ability to operate in the middle register between the heights of elite culture and the depths of brutal culture. For Cosby this means a sense of 'popular taste' perceptively and humorously presented in books, records, television, and live appearances. He is obviously a maestro of modern super media."

Adding to his public persona, Bill Cosby's recent announcements of $20 million donations to Black institutions of higher learning have been duly noted, reported, and discussed in the media.[2]

RAMIFICATIONS OF *THE COSBY SHOW* BY AND FOR BLACKS

According to the Black publication *about...time* (Dupree, 1985): "Bill Cosby may be credited with rediscovering the black family. The key to that discovery is self pride" (p. 11). The show's psychological consultant Alvin F. Poussaint thinks that the singular universality of the Huxtable family may have a potent subliminal impact on society: "This show is changing the white community's perspective of black Americans. It's doing far more to instill positive racial attitudes than if Bill came at the viewer with a sledgehammer or a sermon."[3] In a later article published in *Ebony*, Poussaint suggests that the Huxtables are dispelling negative stereotypes of Blacks:

It should be apparent by now that "The Cosby Show" presents a high level of positive images that are far ahead of other Black sitcoms, and it is racist to suggest that the series is merely "Father Knows Best" in blackface. The Black style of the characters is evident in their speech, intonations and nuances; Black art, music and dance are frequently displayed. Black authors and books are often mentioned; Black colleges and other institutions have been introduced on the show, perhaps for the first time on network television.

There is ample evidence to suggest that as the show has raised Black self-esteem, it has simultaneously lessened stereotypical views of Blacks among Whites. It is even possible that "The Cosby Show" will produce changes in American attitudes that are not yet apparent. (1988, p. 74)

There are numerous examples of Black culture on *The Cosby Show*, including the well-known "Abolish Apartheid" sign in Theo's bedroom, the March-on-Washington show, regular mention of Black people and places, the suggestion of Ralph Ellison's *Invisible Man* for a book report, Denise's choice of an all-Black college, music by Ray Charles and the Raettes, the picture of Martin Luther King, Jr., in Denise's room, the paintings by Black artists in the living room, Afro hairstyles and clothing, Black History Week, a special dinner at a West Indian restaurant, and reminiscences of the old Negro baseball league. In addition, a number of Black performers and personalities have been incorporated into various episodes; as can be seen in Appendix 4 on celebrities, particular attention has been devoted to Black musicians, especially jazz artists like Dizzy Gillespie, B. B. King, and Max Roach.

"Black language," however, is deliberately not heard on *The Cosby Show*. Although Theo and Cockroach deliver a riotous rap version of "Julius Caesar" during one episode, and although there are various Black friends who "high five" one another, a conscious decision has been made to refrain from using jive language or nonstandard Black dialect.

Black fashion, especially in terms of hair styles for the Huxtable children, has been an integral part of the planning on *The Cosby Show*. Sweaters, African-American clothing and jewelry worn by both family members and friends, nonstraightened/natural Black hair, and many other features have all been reportedly noticed by the viewing public. Emphasis, whether regarding educational values or clothing styles, has been on Black dignity. Cantor notes that, although *The Cosby Show* represents a traditional family, modern roles are assigned:

For example, the mother is a working lawyer. Yet, in spite of her considerable independence, the father is clearly in charge. Most episodes revolve around him and his escapades, and the mother and children, although talented and entertaining, are secondary. However, in one very important aspect, *The Cosby Show* is different from other family shows. It portrays TV's version of *black* middle-class family life. (1990, p. 280)

That middle-class Blackness is continually underscored in various episodes, as various family members happily review and reminisce about their origins and ancestors.

It is clear, however, that the Huxtables don't live in a Black neighborhood. At some point their classy New York brownstone would undoubtedly have been part of a gentrification project; yet, we never see participation in neighborhood activities or at neighbors' houses. On a visit by Cliff's ninety-eight-year-old Aunt Gramtee (Minnie Gentry), the family is seen going to church together, but it is not made clear how far away the predominantly Black church was located. A decision was made on *The Cosby Show* to show an upper-middle-class Black family, and to make them look perfectly natural in that role. Downing (1988) has observed:

The treatment of social class in "The Cosby Show" is not simply a matter of blanking out the ugly realities of continuing oppression, but also of offering some sense of resolution to the grinding everyday realities of racial tension and mistrust in the United States, as well as some vision of what a financially secure family life might be like. The hopes and fantasies nurtured a little in this communication are *also* the stuff of continuing resistance to a harsh reality, not simply its denial. (pp. 69–70)

Several other Black-related issues arise of necessity. Black male sexuality—a carryover stereotype dating at least from D. W. Griffith's 1915 film *Birth of a Nation*, which portrayed the mythic Big Black Buck—has remained embedded in the American psyche. Depending on one's frame of reference, the sexuality associated with Black men has frightened some people or titillated others, and caused reactions ranging from abject terror to jealousy. *The Cosby Show* decided to have the Huxtable parents be sexy—cute sexy, that is: they cuddle, they coo, they communicate. Besides, he is a doctor, and he is good old Bill Cosby. There is nothing to worry about; he is no "threat."

Ever since Spike Lee's 1988 *School Daze,* the formerly taboo topic of the Black skin shade has been brought into the open. *The Cosby Show* has also been remarkable for introducing characters of differing shades, especially within the immediate family, and treating them all equally. But again, that decision also has been contingent on performer ability, with skin tone a much lesser consideration.

The success of *The Cosby Show*, several critics have argued, can be traced to its use of conventional situation comedy within new frameworks of Black consciousness. Michael Real (1988) asserts that the show has wrought limited but real change, "particularly in inserting a positive icon to replace negative stereotypes of Black males in family life" (p. 129). In contrast, R.G. Carter (1988) has labeled this phenomenon a "black comfort zone" for white viewers. Neale and Krutnik (1990) contend that "racial difference is made acceptable within the parameters of traditional family unity—the Huxtables are an idealized family who 'just happen' to be black. *The Cosby Show* can flaunt its 'modernity' in its positive representation of blacks but can at the same time hold this in place through a 'commonplace' sense of family unity" (pp. 243–44).

Nielsen Media Research data ("Television Viewing Among Blacks") report that Blacks watch more television than others—typically, twenty-three hours more per week. Viewership of sitcoms is 33 percent higher in Black households. These data are extremely interesting to advertisers, because Blacks are the largest demographic subgroup they have targeted. Professor Paula W. Matabane of Howard University, aware that Black viewers consume heavy diets of all-white prime time, has been particularly concerned that television's influence seems "most evident in isolating pockets of black dissidence among young and better-educated Afro-Americans" (1988, p. 21), and may conceal existing inequalities and injustices in the relations between Blacks and whites. Her unease about this acculturation process points up yet another concern that many of us have: the widening information gap in our society.

Because of the show's success, a number of other Black-related shows have appeared. Cosby himself has long been concerned about stereotyping, a practice dating to his *Fat Albert* days.[4] But, as *Newsweek* points out, "As their bottom line shrinks, the networks are stretching their color line."[5] Sensing a "new racial hue," the television industry has set out to woo Black audiences. "It's Bill Cosby, of course, who proved that such revisionism could be eminently commercial," Waters states. "But the always-in-control Cosby also sent a message to blacks who are following him into the TV factory: to take pride in the product, one must try to influence its design" (1988, p. 52). Still, some researchers are concerned that Blacks other than those on *The Cosby Show* (or *Frank's Place,* or *Snoops,* or the Black soap *Generations,* all of which received critical acclaim but limited runs) continue on the positive path set by Cosby. Joanmarie Kalter, for example, remarks that, although there are more Blacks on television, most of them still appear in comedic roles (1988, p. 26).

Many supporters of the Black movement point out wide discrepancies and discriminations that still exist today.[6] Donald Bogle chronicles the 1980s:

And so in marched the 1980s: a mixed bag of a decade if ever there was one. It was the age of Reagan and the yuppie, of the New Right and the Moral Majority, of scandals on Wall Street and of bands of the homeless wandering in cities around the country, of punk and funk in the world of music, of New Wave and neon, of campus protests against apartheid in South Africa, of the emergence of Third World powers, and of the rise of a new brand of political conservatism. For black Americans, it was a time to move fully into the system, rather than to remain outside it. Never was that social philosophy more apparent than in the candidacy of Jesse Jackson for president of the United States. The 1980s also was the era when the black superstar reigned supreme in the entertainment industry. Michael Jackson and Whitney Houston shot to the top of the music charts. "The Cosby Show" became the country's number one prime-time television program. Perhaps it was not surprising then that many Americans frequently lulled themselves into the assumption that the races were at peace with one another, that inner city blight and decay as well as social tension and racial inequities had ceased to exist, that indeed America's past history of racism had vanished. Consequently, when racial incidents sprang up in an area like Howard Beach in New York, many were jolted. Perhaps the nation had not changed so much after all. (1989, pp. 267–68).

Times are as tough as ever for Blacks, and in some instances more so because of that "lulling" influence to which many whites have succumbed. We read alarming reports such as the one from the Federal Sentencing Project that states that more young Black men in the United States are under the control of the criminal justice system than are enrolled in colleges, or that 60 percent of all Black children here are born out of wedlock. We read that minorities in the United States still hold less than 1 percent of management jobs in the media field. Dr. Alvin Poussaint for one has emphasized that underrepresentation of minorities in the media power structure remains a critical obstacle to accurate, diverse representations.[7] We read about the pervasive influence of race in the American political process, especially "resentment over the extent of the government's attentiveness to the demands of blacks," in the words of Citrin, Green, and Sears (1990, p. 1) on covert racism.

For many people *The Cosby Show* brings out in the open problems relating to Black families. Several prominent Blacks cited in a *Boston Globe* article warn against seeing the show as a model for all Black families (McCain, 1986, p. 69). Harvard sociologist Charles Willie applauds the show for its display of respect for the human condition but worries about the "image-consuming mainstream that is destructive of human values." Clyde Taylor, English professor at Tufts, does not see it as "helpful for anybody, including blacks. It recruits blacks into the image dream world that nobody profits from, except the networks and its advertisers." Herman Gray, a sociologist who teaches at Northeastern University, describes *The Cosby Show* as a breath of relief but adds that the Huxtables' achievement of the American Dream is "a real easy way out. It deflects attention from unemployment, the drop-out rate." Tommy Lott, a philosophy teacher from the University of Massachusetts at Boston adds, "It's bearing a burden heavier than any TV show ought to bear. It has taken on a meaning we ought not to attribute to it. It is not a focus for Afro-American identity." On the other hand, however, Jessica Daniels, a psychologist affiliated with Boston's Children's Hospital, finds *The Cosby Show* "uplifting and positive. Black youngsters who don't have ready access to black role models can see a slice of life that's attainable to some degree." Barbara Simmons, former president of the Greater Boston Association of Black Social Workers, finds the show "a good model for all families to aspire to. I think it's very realistic."

In 1986 Herman Gray analyzed Black male roles in *Benson*, *Webster*, *Different Strokes*, and *The Jeffersons*. All four sitcoms emphasize images of Blacks who have "achieved middle-class success, confirming in the process the belief that in the context of the current political, economic and cultural arrangements, individuals, regardless of color, can achieve the American dream" (p. 224). Labeling these programs predominantly assimilationist in tone and texture, Gray worries that their televisual impact will detract attention from issues of racism, inequality, and differential power:

Television's idealization of racial harmony, affluence and individual mobility is simply not within the reach of millions of black Americans. To the extent that different realities and experiences are not mentioned or addressed in television programmes featuring blacks, the effect is to isolate and render invisible social and cultural experiences of poor and working-class black Americans. (p. 239)

Gray actually wrote his article before *Cosby* went on the air, but many of his concerns persist. In November 1989 a feature article appeared in the Sunday "Arts & Leisure" section of the *New York Times* that has had loud reverberations throughout both the scholarly and popular worlds. Henry Louis Gates, Jr., a former Andrew W. Mellon fellow at the National Humanities Center in North Carolina, states:

Even black Americans sometimes need to be reminded about the deceptiveness of television. Blacks retain their fascination with black characters on TV: Many of us buy *Jet* magazine primarily to read its weekly television feature, which lists *every* black character (major or minor) to be seen on the screen that week. Yet our fixation with the presence of black characters on TV has blinded us to an important fact that "Cosby," which began in 1984, and its offshoots over the years demonstrate convincingly: There is very little connection between the social status of black Americans and the fabricated images of black people that Americans consume every day. Moreover, the representations of blacks on TV is a very poor index to our social advancement or political progress. (1989, p. 1).

Singling out *The Cosby Show*, Gates says that it makes some people uncomfortable: "As the dominant representation of blacks on TV, it suggests that blacks are solely responsible for their social conditions, with no acknowledgment of the severely constricted life opportunities that most black people face" (p. H40). Comparing its popularity to that of *Amos 'n' Andy*, Gates claims that the phenomenal success of *The Cosby Show* is equally troubling not in its actual representation, but in its representative role in the culture:

As long as *all* blacks were represented in demeaning or peripheral roles, it was possible to believe that American racism was, as it were, indiscriminate. The social vision of "Cosby," however, reflecting the minuscule integration of blacks into the upper middle class . . . reassuringly throws the blame for black poverty back onto the impoverished.

"As the eighties draw to a close, a new awareness of the unfinished struggle with racism seems to be emerging," writes David Ehrenstein (1988, p. 11). Citing Bill Cosby's domination of the television ratings and Eddie Murphy's domination of the movie box office, he argues that their popularity derives from underlying assumptions of white notions regarding Black life: "Television's top Superdad and Hollywood's slickest hipster operate not as cultural purveyors of black American life, but rather as safety valves, generating laughs that mask the conflict between black aspirations and the maintenance of white power" (p. 9).

At first glance, "The Cosby Show" is a successful attempt to break the chokehold of traditional stereotypes. The Huxtable family—close-knit, clean-cut, parentally controlled—seems to undercut white racism even as it serves as an ideal for black viewers: "This is who you are" becomes "this is who we *should* be." And it would be ridiculous to expect anything else from Cosby, whose early comedy routines were founded on a frank refusal to deal with racial differences—a refusal that whites found utterly charming. Black and white children were at base no different, his routines suggested, so black and white adults should be, too.

Likewise, the world on "The Cosby Show" is founded on assumptions of complete racial harmony and total integration. But while the notion of a world without racial strife may have been admirable in the integrationist sixties, on eighties television this idyllic conceit becomes little more than a monstrous blocking mechanism. The characters seem incapable of *imagining* (much less experiencing) racial adversity—even in a comic context. Black identity is reduced to a visual style, a fashion statement. (p. 11)

Race, argues John J. O'Connor (1990), is undergoing radical changes on television, which he calls "The Great Emulation Machine, whose very existence depends on correctly identifying and servicing its audiences" (p. H1). He claims that the ratings success of *The Cosby Show* has encouraged more Black artists to gain control over their products, influencing their images to the public. Furthermore, O'Connor states,

Like all other Americans, black viewers are likely to have difficulty reconciling their television-entertainment images with their everyday lives. "The Cosby Show" isn't, and doesn't pretend to be, any more representative of blacks in general than "Doogie Howser, M.D.," with its teen-age doctor, is of the medical profession. . . . But whatever the omissions and distortions, television indisputably transmits, directly or subliminally, formative social messages about role models, values and attitudes for the population at large.

Using Stuart Hall's encoding/decoding process to discuss ideological connotations regarding *The Cosby Show*, Real claims that the show has recoded
Black ethnicity:

It has had potentially decisive effects in convincing middle Americans that a Black
man and his family can be their most favored weekly guest. Reversing the tradition
of "Amos 'n' Andy" in which Blacks were funny because they were different, and even
inferior linguistically, Cosby establishes very firmly a strong, positive role model for
father, family, education, career, and pride. (1989, p. 121)

Ramifications of *The Cosby Show* by and for Blacks, then, remains a controversial topic, depending on one's perspective.

THE UNIQUENESS OF *THE COSBY SHOW*

A person's attitudes about sense of "realism," humor, relevance, even the
Blackness issue on *The Cosby Show* might perhaps come from the encoding/
decoding process. Or they might derive from ethnographic circumstances of
the television-viewing experience, or even from textual interpretations.

Looking for differing points of view in the television aesthetic, Horace M.
Newcomb decided to analyze "One Night of Prime Time" (1988) to determine
the degree to which television is an open or closed textual system. Arguing
that television has reached the stage of being a central storyteller in our
society, that it is "an extension and elaboration of other popular culture
processes . . . a cultural forum," he wanted to look for cases of text variations
both within and outside of specific episodes. Newcomb chose a Thursday
night in 1985, deliberately bypassing *The Cosby Show* for *Magnum, P.I.*, then
switching to NBC for *Cheers*, *Night Court*, and *Hill Street Blues*. By the end
of the evening, he had come to the following conclusion about the differences:

Suffice it to say that the dialogic, heterological nature of these texts would be altered
even more if I began my night not with "Magnum," but with most American viewers
and the "Cosby Show." To arrive at the conclusion of "Hill Street Blues", having begun
with a story in which a small child and her father learn gentle lessons of social and
personal responsibility, would be to experience a very different text. (p. 100)

Therefore, what we watch, as well as when we watch, where we watch,
what else we have watched, with whom we watch, and how we "read" what
we watch are all factors.

Marjorie Ferguson adds the important observation that, although Clair Huxtable is a lawyer, she is most visible on *The Cosby Show* as a wife and mother:
"The appearance of more women on television with jobs outside the home
also owes something to the economics of network television decline, frag-
mentation in the wake of cable and VCRs, and attempts to woo female viewers

with prime-time sitcoms and night-time soaps" (1990, p. 227). Yet, how many television programs feature both parents as professionals?

In terms of masculinity, *The Cosby Show*, in line with a tradition of other sitcom fathers, breaks from the dominant, authoritative male of traditional television. Cantor (1990, p. 276) compares Cliff Huxtable with the Jim Anderson father character of thirty years ago on *Father Knows Best*, saying that both project "an open, responsive and sensitive image." In many ways, *Cosby* is thought to represent the return to "feel-good" family shows of the 1950s, fulfilling our desire to return to a what is considered a gentler age.

"Undoubtedly," asserts Kellner (1979), "American television plays an important role as an instrument of enculturation and social control. What is not yet clear is *how* television constructs and conveys hegemonic ideology and induces consent to advanced capitalism." Although the dictionary definition of enculturation is "to cause to adapt to the prevailing cultural patterns of one's society,"[8] we as individuals are in a constant state of trying, whether consciously or unconsciously, to coordinate media messages that reflect, reinforce, or restructure our ever-developing personal/sociocultural identities. That so many of us are regular viewers of *The Cosby Show*, that so many survey respondents report wanting to be part of the Huxtable family, makes it clear that many of us seek identity with the show and its personalities.

George Gerbner and his colleagues at the Annenberg School of Communication/University of Pennsylvania have long been concerned about how television is the "mainstream" of our cultural process. Cultivation theory as discussed by Wober and Gunter (1988, p. 4) is based on two basic assumptions: (1) Television's images, regardless of whether they are offered as fact, fiction, or even "faction," are assumed to cultivate stereotyped notions about the social environment, and (2) television viewing is largely nonselective. With regard to the first assumption of cultivation effects, the discussion about *The Cosby Show*'s ramifications by and for Blacks takes on added significance. As to the second, however, it has been largely discovered that viewers of the show hardly are indiscriminate about that interaction: for its fans, ritualized television viewing tends to be a planned, regular, anticipated, and later talked-about event. The "ritual" is there largely as a weekly, scheduled occasion.

An alternative conceptual and operational approach for examining television-viewing behaviors and effects is offered by Chang and Heald in pattern analysis: "A pattern of viewing levels is a distributional shape of absolute viewing levels across various television program types" (1989, p. 8), proposing that persons with different television-viewing patterns will be cultivated differently. Again, it is important to note how many of the survey respondents to *The Cosby Show* questionnaire, especially Americans, commented on how it is their only television show, or the highlight of their week, or "It's the only time the family gets together."

Recognizing the substantial research that has been done on television's impact on viewer attitudes and behaviors, Reep and Dambrot have decided to focus on sex-role stereotypes from both male and female perspectives. Their findings support both high-impact image theory and frequent-viewing effects theory; they conclude that the two processes are not mutually exclusive, but rather interrelated in their explanations of television viewing. They therefore conclude:

A salient image which attracts frequent viewing, such as . . . Cliff Huxtable('s), a black, upper class father, may override the less significant stereotypical portrayals of all other blacks on television. Perhaps television's portrayal of a few, high-impact, nonstereotypical characters is more important for reducing stereotypical perception than sheer numbers of characters which make little or no impact. (1989, p. 556)

Certainly all the excitement and amusement on a single half-hour of *The Cosby Show* must be kept in perspective. No one leads a life that consistently solves problems and at the same time amuses others in twenty-two-minute time blocks. We cannot fall prey to the notion that "TV barrages us with so many seemingly perfect families that we end up feeling depressed about our own."[9]

Miller argues that there are some crucial differences between *The Cosby Show* and earlier prime-time idylls:

1. First of all, "The Cosby Show" is far more popular than any of its predecessors . . . attracting an audience that is not only vast, but often near fanatical in its devotion.

2. Second, and stranger still, this show and its immense success are universally applauded as an exhilarating sign of progress. Newspaper columnists and telejournalists routinely deem "The Cosby Show" a "breakthrough" into an unprecedented *realism* because it uses none of the broad plot devices or rapid-fire gags that define the standard sitcom. Despite its fantastic ambience of calm and plenty, "The Cosby Show" is widely regarded as a rare glimpse of truth.

3. And there is a third difference between this show and its predecessors that may help explain the new show's greater popularity and peculiar reputation for progressivism: Cliff Huxtable and his dependents are not only fabulously comfortable and mild, but also noticeably black. (1986, p. 209)

Truly, *The Cosby Show* is unique. In its day (in 1968), so too was *Julia*, but it was still a case of Black images being created by white hands; twenty years later, we at last have a television program over which the Black star has power and control. Meanwhile, the show's executive producers have become legends in their own time. It could easily be argued that Carsey-Werner took over in the 1980s places held in the 1950s by the MCA-Revue studios, Filmways and Screen Gems in the 1960s, and Norman Lear and MTM in the 1970s. From the look of things in the early 1990s, their influence appears likely to continue.

One predominant aspect of *The Cosby Show* is its device of storytelling. Unique to this program, this device allows not only plot development, but also advancement of the oral history of the Huxtable family. Family, friends, colleagues, and visitors alike relate "stories" about funny and/or telling incidents, typically from Cliff and Clair's past. An integral part of Black conversation, noticeably more so than others' linguistic communication patterns, storytelling captures our attention, gives location and explanation, adds insight into character, and can be enormously entertaining. It is also a powerful tool for interpretation. Cliff's parents often retell stories from his past, even embarrassing ones. An old former teammate might reveal a different ending to an otherwise famous, frequently told family story about an athletic event. Other friends share "stories out of school" with the children, to their delight.

Although Gerbner and his colleagues are fascinated by these stories and this storytelling as part of a wider ritual analysis in which we the audience collectively share acts and symbols about social life, we should note that something else very important is happening here: In *The Cosby Show*, the family gets together and *talks*. They might gather in the living room, sit down to a meal together, and pay attention to one another or to visitors who are talking.

One particular episode will help underscore this storytelling-within-a-story, or meta-storytelling point. Conceived as a showcase for jazz teacher Max Roach of the University of Massachusetts, a good friend of Bill Cosby's, the plot revolved around Denise's decision to be a teacher, albeit via an alternative approach to traditional education. When she goes to stepdaughter Olivia's preschool, she is impressed by the math instructor who teaches addition using rap music. Denise decides to work at the school. "Great, we'd love to have you—but do you have a master's degree, or just a B.A.?" ask the administrators. Having dropped out of college, she has no degree. Denise angrily wonders why one is needed when, in her mind, she would make a wonderful teacher. Besides, she says poutingly, she should be given credit for her "life experiences." When her parents discuss her poor grades from Hillman College, she snaps back, "What is a D? 70%!—which, if you were eating a pie, would be quite a bit." The upshot is that Denise eventually comes around, discussing with her parents success via hard work, paying one's dues, having commitments, and generally buying into the system—or at least playing by its rules, if you want to be part of it.

In a microcosm, this simple and amusing episode becomes symbolic of the simple moral lessons embedded in *The Cosby Show* episodes and the Black situation in the United States today. On the one hand, some would say, are numbers of Blacks with "demands," "outraged" whenever statistics on their numbers in positions of power are unveiled, wanting equal opportunity but wanting to get it "handed to them." On the other hand (and it is too bad to be discussing this as a dichotomy, but it appears to be at the root of a new unearthing of racism in our society), a number of people, even some who consider themselves liberals, are tiring of the rhetoric and are telling people of color to work hard, pay their dues, be committed, buy into the system, and play by its rules. Denise decides to go back to school and to enter Medgar Evers College. It is a good compromise, and it makes a good analogy: She will do what she has to do because she wants to buy into middle-class respectability, but she will do it through a Black institution and she will do it so that she can use alternative teaching methods. But it must be remembered that Denise is married to a man currently stationed at a Rhode Island naval base; the military-media-industrial complex is complete.

In her study of cultivating moderate perspectives on racial integration, Matabane cites *The Cosby Show* as epitomizing

the Afro-American dream of full acceptance and assimilation into U.S. society. Both the series and Bill Cosby as an individual represent successful competitors in network television and in attaining a high status. Although this achievement is certainly not inherently negative, we should consider the role television plays in the cultivation of an overall picture of growing racial equality that conceals unequal social relationships and overestimates of how well blacks are integrating into white society (if at all). The illusion of well-being among the oppressed may lead to reduced political activity and less demand for social justice and equality. (1988, p. 30)

At the end of *The Cosby Show*'s fifth season, *USA Today* (Curry, 1989) polled its readers for attitudes on the number 1 show for the year; it found the "'Cosby' aura fading, still fascinating" (p. 3D), continuing to be tops with women, but losing some of its male viewership. The biggest ratings competition appeared to be from blue-collar sitcom families who showed their caring for one another by wise-cracking, sarcastic one-liners and far-fetched schemes, shows deliberately "anti-Cosby" in their constructions. The 1989–1990 season opened with the return of Lisa Bonet, Denise, coming back from Africa with "something for the whole family"—two new family members: husband Martin (Joseph C. Phillips) and his adorable three-year-old daughter Olivia (Raven-Symone), a perfect Rudy-type counterpart. *Variety* reported it this way: "Supersuccessful NBC series starts gracefully, delivering a satisfying episode that may do little to enhance its reputation but, more importantly, also does nothing to disgrace it." It was to be the last season for garnering high ratings without having to change too much.

The seventh season was something else altogether. In an interview with *TV Guide*'s "Grapevine" reporter Marilyn Beck (April 28–May 4, 1990), Bill Cosby announced that the next season of *The Cosby Show* would have a feminine touch: "We're bringing in more female writers—we already have two on our staff—with experience in life and love," for a stronger female perspective (p. 39). Particular attention was to be given to Theo in terms of his attitude toward girls: "What we are going to try to do with the boy is have him realize his existence in terms of making a commitment to the person he's in love with. There is a playground out there; he's in love but he still wants to play. It is a problem area for a lot of males—and a rich area for us to deal with." The star then added: "It is going to end up making a lot of men feel Theo's a wimp." The unique aspect of this revelation is a continual concern for the image of *The Cosby Show*, especially for its appropriate target markets.

The show's season premiere concerned a belated bachelor party thrown by the Huxtable men for Martin, complete with a stripper; the Huxtable women weren't too happy about it, to say the least. This was only the beginning, literally, of what was to be a very different set of episodes on the show.

Nine new writers were brought in for the seventh season. The three original ones, all men, were off doing other projects, and four of the new writers were women, headed by Janet Leahy. Their influence was evident in the kinds of topics and language that began to predominate. Probably in response to criticisms that there weren't enough "typical" Blacks on the show, seventeen-year-old cousin Pam (Erika Alexander) came from the inner city to live at the household, bringing with her a whole new entourage of *A Different World*–type teen friends. One hour-long episode that aired during the November 1990 sweeps week centered on Pam's being pressured by her boyfriend, Slide, to "go all the way." She has a good heart-to-heart talk with Clair, and she gets some good advice from Cliff when she asks him for a prescription for birth control pills. But the audience may have reacted most to Pam's fast-talking friend, Charmane: "What I got may not be precious to the world, but it's precious to me. What I got ain't no knick-knack. You understand what I mean?" After discussing premarital sex, *The Cosby Show* centered the following week on Rudy getting her first menstrual period. The episode was a cross between loving education and humor. In the Huxtable household, this event is known as "Woman's Day," when mother and daughter, and in this case sisters, too, rally to celebrate. Clair adamantly states, "I will not have my children grow up thinking they shouldn't go to the beach, or they'll be followed by sharks." Other menstrual myths are debunked, like the one about the girl who went to the circus and the animals stopped performing, or the one who said she could stop it if she crossed her eyes. The message was that it's not a situation of "Aunt Flo is visiting," or that it's "the curse," but a very natural biological beginning to womanhood. Obviously this was a script written by women.

Another hour-long special featured the "birds and the bees" when the good doctor has a dream that he, and all the other Huxtable men, as well as 11 million other American men, are pregnant. He ends up giving "birth" to a 9-foot-long hero sandwich and a bottle of orange soda, and at the end of the ordeal states, "Thank God for women." Yet another time Clair comes home from her ob/gyn appointment announcing "I'm healthy. I'm in great shape. And I'm beginning menopause." Clearly, these are not the stuff of the more than 100 previous episodes, when a lesson in the effects of drinking might be considered deviant from a typical plot.

Another factor was at play for the seventh season, although neither the show's actors nor staff would admit it made a difference: the Fox network's decision to pit its wildly successful *Simpsons* in the Thursday night at 8 P.M. slot. The battle began on October 11 and had plenty of media hype. *Advertising Age* (Walley, 1990) reported that "(t)he foundations at NBC shook" when it heard about the head-on confrontation (p. 3). *Adweek* (Battaglio, 1990, p. 17) pointed out that the competition could mean more advertising money from movie companies and retailers, who tend to choose Thursday night prime time as a good way to reach the eighteen to thirty-four year olds who might be at the theaters the next night.

Although taping for *Cosby's* new season had begun on July 19, theoretically before news of the *Simpsons* competition, within a month Bill Cosby was quoted in *Entertainment Weekly* (Appelo, 1990) as saying, "TV should be moving in a direction from the Huxtables *forward*, not backward. The mean-spirited and cruel think this (kind of programming) is 'the edge,' and their excuse is, that's the way people are today. But why should we be entertained by that?" (p. 34). Continuing to say he acts on principle, Cosby actually seemed rejuvenated by the new competition. When asked to comment on audience reaction to the seventh season, NBC Entertainment President Warren Little-field responded that *The Cosby Show* realizes that it appeals most to urban, upscale viewers, and that the star himself wanted to gear the series specifically toward them: "Bill's leading that charge," he told me.[10]

When the last ratings point was counted, *The Cosby Show* won—if by one-tenth of a point! Still, both shows captured a 29 percent audience share that night. The gap between them progressively grew, with the Huxtables attracting a larger audience every Thursday, despite Fox's aggressive marketing of its popular animated show.

An early clue to the eighth season came from a public statement by Bernie Kukoff, executive producer of *The Cosby Show*, made to *Entertainment Weekly* (February 22, 1991): one episode might focus on the impact of these hard times on one of the good doctor's patients, who belongs to "a younger family, where the wife's pregnant and husband's lost his job." Art began (or continued?) to reflect life. Since, for example, a fall 1989 episode on Theo's dyslexia has reportedly become the single most requested videotape for use by public interest groups and schools, a two-parter on the topic was developed toward the end of the seventh season. When Theo later was practice teaching, he was able not only to diagnose a student's learning disability, but he also learned a lesson himself: that you can't always help all the students all the time.

The 1991–1992 season of *The Cosby Show* opened with Vanessa surprising her parents with the announcement of a fiancé. The publicity promo read: "Vanessa engaged, Cliff enraged!" Yet, there are some communication lessons to be learned from the parents' actual responses and rhetoric. Sondra and Elvin have had to move into the crowded brownstone with their four-year-old twins, played by Jessica Vaughn and Gary Gray, while they await getting a place of their own. Theo encounters a single parent on parent-counselor night, Rudy goes to a club for older teens, Cliff runs a "For Men Only" seminar at the community center, more celebrities are showcased, and a finer line seems to be running between riotous and relevant. We still get vignettes like Rudy's bounding into her parents' bedroom and being reprimanded by her father, "How many times have I asked you to knock before entering this bedroom?" "Why?" she wonders out loud, "It's daytime."

What is next for *The Cosby Show*? As this book goes to press, the series has just completed its run. The final episode was taped on March 5, 1992, receiving general press reports as occurring before "a cheering audience."[11] Devoted to Theo's college graduation, the episode was called "And So, We Commence," symbolizing the next step for both Theo and the rest of his family. The only hint Bill Cosby would let drop to the press about this episode was that he wanted this last show to revolve around the running gag of the doorbell that Cliff has continually been trying to fix. "This has been the best," commented Phylicia Rashad about her role on *The Cosby Show*. "Like climbing to the peak of Mount Everest."

What is next for Bill Cosby? Beginning in the fall of 1992, he will host a comeback of the Groucho Marx show, *You Bet Your Life*. But the biggest news is economic; or, as Bill Carter of the *New York Times* tells it, "The biggest network television star of the last decade will soon walk away from network television" (1991, TV 3). Learning a lesson on the sales successes of syndication, from which *The Cosby Show* has reputedly already made more than $1 billion, Cosby plans to remain network-free, selling this new show independently in first-run syndication.

In its restructuring in 1990, Viacom made Dennis Gillespie president of worldwide marketing, domestic features and off-network sales after the resignation of Joseph Zaleski. It continued to run "Cos + Effect" advertisements in the trade publications. Declaring that before syndication of *The Cosby Show* there had been no clear leader among off-network sitcoms, it focused on ratings of 8.9 overall for the show among women ages eighteen to forty-nine for November 1989. Those numbers include Baltimore breakdowns of 10.7 reported in February 1990, 8.8 in St. Louis, 10.6 in Dallas, 12.3 in Charlotte, and 10.9 in New York. *The Cosby Show* is still an incredible, unique story in syndication.

NBC's director of corporate relations and audience services, Vera Wells, tells of continuing audience enthusiasm for *The Cosby Show*. At the end of an episode from 1991, for example, Clair wanted Cliff to cuddle, and decided to entice him by putting on a blues record; the network was besieged with "a ton of calls" asking about the song.

Bill Cosby personally has remained in the news with the release of the first of his *Bill Cosby Jazz Series* albums, put out by Verve/Poly-Gram. Entitled "Where You Lay Your Head," it includes five songs co-written by Cosby and his long-time collaborator, Stu Gardner. Cosby also made news with an early

1990s birthday wish telephone call to a two-year-old AIDS victim in Syracuse, New York. Cosby knows his constituency and stays in touch.

On an economic note, another critical factor regarding the future of *The Cosby Show* also concerns whether or not Carsey-Werner will stay with NBC. CBS, which reportedly made a bid for *The Cosby Show* after its sixth season, is said to be waiting in the wings. Some critics think that the show should quit while it's ahead, a sentiment that has been echoed yearly since it went into syndication. Meanwhile, media watchers stand by to see if this most recent part of *The Cosby Show* phenomenon will also make the record books. The show has proven itself to be unique, and its producers are trying to cash in yet more on that success.

THE COSBY SHOW'S EFFECT ON THE SITCOM GENRE

Back in 1974, Horace Newcomb devoted an entire chapter to problems, families, and fathers in situation and domestic comedies in his book *TV: The Most Popular Art*. Using *I Love Lucy* as the introductory archetype, he discusses the sitcom formula for ordering and defining the world, with its special sense of reality, its special physical world, its special funny "thing" that happens each week to a special set of characters. In addition to the formula, Newcomb argues that two other elements must be added: complication and confusion. Then, at the center, are the characters, "cause and effect, creator and butt of joke, the audience's key to what the formula means" (p. 34), as well as other sets of supporting characters. Action in the sitcom comprises the establishment of the "situation"; the complication, the confusion that ensues; and the alleviation of the complication (p. 39).

The "ritualistic, paradigmatic" sitcom world, Newcomb contends, is the antecedent to that of domestic comedy: "Its [sitcom's] dependence on people, on some sort of family setting, and on human error as the basis of plot structure offer many elements to its more 'homey' counterpart" (p. 42). Differentiated from *Lucy, Bewitched, The Beverly Hillbillies*, or *Gilligan's Island*, domestic sitcoms (which today we might call domesticoms) are, with some restrictions,

more expansive. There is less slapstick, less hysterical laughter. There is more warmth and a deeper sense of humanity. The cast built on the family as group is capable of reducing dependence on a single star, a single style. A richer variety of event, a consequent deepening of character, and a sense of seriousness enable the formula to build on the previous comic outline in significant ways. (p. 43)

Examples are familiar: *Father Knows Best, My Three Sons, The Jimmy Stewart Show*, and the like. Establishing shots focus on setting, rather than on situation; emphasis is on people rather than events. Hence, Newcomb points out, "The world of the domestic comedy is a world that creates, by contrast, the illusion of being lived in rather than acted in, and consequently there is a sense of involvement" (p. 46). Homes are comfortable, there is stability both in possession/ownership and in the family unit, characters are interdependent, and at the center of it all is the father: the kindly if authoritative decision maker, the person in power, the wise leader, the nonjudgmental adviser. Plots are contrived around problems and are offered up as learning experiences. Concepts of "peace, love, and laughter" are central virtues, "grounded in the belief in the family as a supportive group" (p. 55) for mutual support and respect.

The Cosby Show, according to Newcomb's description, would fit in the category of domestic comedy rather than sitcom. Many of his broad statements about the genre still apply, especially about the father as the ultimate control source for the family and the interwoven learning lessons that are contained as subplots. From this perspective, the series reflects the family-comedy tradition, with only a few new elements—racial considerations, and the fact that the wife is also a professional. Sociologically, however, these factors break new ground in the comedy genre's history.

Himmelstein discusses the situation or domestic comedy from a structural point of view:

Television's staple comedic vehicle is simply a 23-minute, two-act playlet with an epilogue. Episodes are generally self-contained. They revolve around a single "umbrella" plot or situation. There is a regular cast of core characters who are generally stereotypical ones and who engage in ritualistic humor through the repetition of action and "running gags"—physical comedy of gestures and one-liners. The main characters' stance toward the world of social relations is generally illogical or irrational. (1984, p. 77)

Are the Huxtable family members stereotypical? If so, stereotypical of what—of "typical" families, "typical" Americans, "typical" Blacks, "typical" middle-class people? Although most survey respondents could identify with one or more of the characters, few found them matching up as "typical" character types. Moreover, most episodes tend to have several running miniplot sequences—borrowing clothes, playing basketball, stealing food, and the like—built around what might be listed in the television guide as the story of the night; seldom is there one simple situation. Instead of repeated action or artificial gags, comedy in *The Cosby Show* tends to come more from a familiar, universal moment we can all relate to: a date for the prom, worrying about grades, preparing for a costume party. And, of course, Cosby's mugging antics are what we laugh at out loud. Furthermore, it could certainly be argued that the Huxtable family hardly has a jaded world-view; if anything marks the advice offered in the show, it is to join that world, to be in the mainstream.

Calling situation comedy "The Unworthy Discourse" in terms of social science research, Paul Attallah points out how typically it is defined in terms of its antecedents (vaudeville, radio, film, theater) or its humor types (Freudian, Bergsonian, etc.). In terms of narrative, he argues, it is necessary that the "situation" remain unchanged:

If the program is to be repeated week after week, the characters and their mode of interaction must not be allowed to evolve. Were they to acquire experience, then evolution would occur and the show could not continue. The ideal situation, therefore, is one that is both open and closed at the same time: open to outsiders or to other discursive hierarchies but closed to experience or to the modification of discursive hierarchies. (1984, p. 239)

As has been noted earlier, the various Huxtable characters have certainly gone against this mold. We have seen Sondra mature as she got married and had children, Denise become less flaky and more direction-oriented, Vanessa more responsible, Rudy a discerning and sensitive preteen, and apparently we are about to see Theo become more committed in his relationships. Only the parents have remained true to character type. Yet, even Cosby's Cliff character has evolved narratively; more frequently of late he has been recalling past incidents in the aforementioned storytelling vein.

Economically and institutionally, David Marc (1984) postulates:

The sitcom is a representational form, and its subject is American culture: It dramatizes national types, styles, customs, issues, and language. Because sitcoms are and have always been under the censor of corporate patronage, the genre has yielded a conservative body of drama that is diachronically retarded by the precautions of mass marketing procedure. (p. 13)

Yes, *The Cosby Show* aims to please the widest possible audience. It appears to have found that magic fine line to please, as we phrase it for media students, "everyone from the teenage Hispanic girl living in the urban East to the elderly, conservative farmer in the midwest—and everyone else in between." Besides, comedies do well in the rerun business—another reason we can expect a plethora of them from now on.

Elsewhere contrasting the sitcom to standup comedy, Marc (1989) labels the sitcom "the technology of the assembly-line brought to art." "Even when live audiences are used, their reactions are 'sweetened' with carefully calculated titters, chortles, and guffaws," he continues.

Large sums of investment capital must be assembled to produce a sitcom; all factors must be controlled by recognized experts. The sitcom has no tank towns to tour, but is always a nationally marketed product whose "effects" are tested on "sample" consumers and refined accordingly. A complex system of checks and balances among advertisers, networks, and production companies continuously negotiates problems of textual dissent while the audience is kept at arm's length. (p. 13).

British sitcoms typically are recorded before live audiences, a process that has not been the norm in the United States.[12] It is a known fact that Bill Cosby is highly dependent on that close interaction, and undoubtedly his style has influenced the other cast members. Since the success of the live audience-show interactions of *The Cosby Show,* several other productions have used the studio audience notion, "sweetening," as it were, by means of editing procedures.

Family, which Attallah (1984) claims to be "probably the dominant metaphor for all North American television" (p. 240), today appears to be children- or parent-ruled according to social class. Elizabeth Stone states:

When the TV family in question is working class, or minority, the heavy-duty moral considerations, when they need to be made, are typically made by the parents. Not infallibly, but reflectively, with hands on. . . . When the parents are middle class or better, they, like Dad in "Growing Pains," seem to lack any real authority within the family at all. (1990, p. H30)

The sole exception she finds is *The Cosby Show,* "where the parents are just as smart as if they were blue collar." "Is this because," Stone wonders, "as upper-middle-class minorities, they can have it both ways?" Important role models are at stake here, and again *The Cosby Show* stands out as defying sitcom genre expectations.

" 'Cosby' has inaugurated what amounts to a third epoch in the history of TV sitcoms," according to Mark Edmundson:

1. It all began in the Imperial Age, when the work-a-daddies reigned. On *Father Knows Best, My Three Sons, Leave It to Beaver,* and a dozen others, papa dispensed humane, homiletic justice from his sanctum in the den. Occasionally he blundered, but acts of wise humility restored his authority by half hour's end. If he "learned from the boys," it was never anything he hadn't known, though he might briefly have forgotten it. The presiding image from those days is of papa seated in the study, at the kitchen table, or at the workbench, deploying such words as good and bad, right and wrong; drawing on experience; laying down the law, when need be.

2. Think of the second period in sitcom history as the Revolt of the Prime Time Proletariat. It began with *All in the Family,* and though its residues are still with us, "The Cosby Show" signals its extinction. (1986, p.71)

Now, instead of Archie Bunker's chair, the center of action for the whole family is the couch, in the living room—which Patricia Leigh Brown assures us is "Where America Feels at Home": "The set [for the show], by the production designer Garvin Eddy and his assistant, Rosaria Sinisi, clearly reflects the taste of two sophisticated people who have thought a lot about their interiors" (1987, p. C1).

A number of people have rushed to duplicate the success of *The Cosby*

Show. As early as 1985 an article in the *Christian Science Monitor* predicted this imitation:

We'll be seeing fewer cop shows and a batch of "Cosby clones" next fall. . . . Bill Cosby's show is extraordinary. It has been dominating the ratings. It's certainly entertaining. It's not preachy. And yet it manages to convey, week after week, more good ideas about parental guidance, family communication, discipline, and education than does a convention full of family counselors. Most of all, it makes clear that parents can enforce constructive discipline and be loving without the least inconsistency.[13]

Socioculturally, sitcoms, focusing as they do on a conflict or problem that is patently resolved in a preconceived time period, can have yet another lulling effect. Douglas Kellner (1979) is particularly concerned that the "conflict/resolution model" of sitcoms suggests that all societal problems can be solved.

For the Black performer, Bogle reminds us, the sitcom has been the most important of all series genres, "mainly because it was and has continued to be the only type of program to acknowledge or comment on black life, no matter how trivial or superficial that acknowledgment or comment might be" (1988, p. 237). In this difficult time for Blacks in the United States, Bill Cosby has decided to use the sitcom as his vehicle for delivering his messages to a wide population.

Andrew Greeley, a Roman Catholic priest who teaches in the Sociology Department at the University of Arizona, calls sitcoms "Today's morality play": " 'Cosby' is No. 1 because it has mastered the art of renewing hope for the family. Your family. . . . [It] provides moral paradigms and displays warm and renewing love" (1987, p. 1).

For a brief while, there were predictions that *The Cosby Show*'s audiences would tire of its simple messages, that it would turn to more acerbic entertainment like that of Fox's *Married . . . with Children*. *Newsweek*, for example, wrote: "For some, no doubt, the squabbling, hypercrude Bundys seem a welcome antidote to the hyperglycemic Huxtables" (Waters, 1990, p. 60). Yet, as has been seen here in an eight-year review of this sitcom, the popularity of *The Cosby Show* has endured.

Viewed historically, economically, psychologically, socioculturally, and/or morally, the sitcom genre has been redefined and redistributed since the advent of *The Cosby Show*. Zhengkang Wu (1990) maintains that television programs, especially sitcoms, should be used in social scientific investigations: "The situation comedy is an equally important artifact as other artistic works for cultural studies, and TV programmings reflect social values and mores, serving as a barometer for discovering changes in such values and mores" (p. 3). As an artifact of Americana, a distinct and identifiable embodiment of our popular culture, *The Cosby Show* deserves our scrutiny.

CONCLUDING REMARKS

As a case study, *The Cosby Show*, both as its own distinct artifact and as analyzed here, serves as a barometer for better understanding our society.

For persons interested in marketing and business, this case study provides invaluable insight into how the notion of *The Cosby Show* was first sold to the networks and then how NBC has engaged in selling its successful *Cosby* image. This case study is replete with information for both current and would-be media marketers about the business of television, providing in-depth explanations on the workings of the ratings game, the role of advertising, constraints and constructions of the television industry, how syndication works, and the overriding concern to attract audiences who not only can be sold to advertisers but who can also be continually encouraged to be consumers. While in this instance the star himself was central to the process, anyone in the know will reiterate the fact that *The Cosby Show*, as the most lucrative program in television history, has changed all the rules.

For those interested in the media, this case study has numerous functions. It makes scholarly usage of a wide range of print media, both popular and academic; it provides an in-depth study of the sitcom genre and the role of spinoffs, clones, and spillovers; it gives us a lesson in ratings—what they are, how they are accumulated and counted, how they compare to shares, and why they are so critical to a show's success; it examines the politics and process of syndication; it discusses television research, particularly audience studies; it dissects media content by means of various interpretations; it explores the role of comedy and humor and how it can have application across cultural parameters; it studies the roles of producers, directors, and writers—as well as, in the case of *The Cosby Show*, a psychological consultant; and overall, it focuses on how to approach study of a media phenomenon.

For those interested in media audiences, this case study discusses program loyalty, program appeal, and how one program has been able to cross boundaries of gender, age, race, occupation, and television-viewing characteristics. Its argument for looking at both demographic and psychographic variables is sustained. Himmelstein has written:

To understand the myth life of our television culture, we must first consider the construction of the television message and the social, political, and economic nature of the processes of construction as they are reflected in the powerful visual and verbal symbols produced and perpetuated by the "diversified entertainment companies" of advanced capitalism—financial institutions masquerading as culture producers. We must then consider the status of the message receiver—the well-trained viewer—in this process. (1984, p. 2)

This case study has done just that.

For those interested in family studies, the Huxtables provide a fascinating

forum for role models. As a multigenerational family unit, they help reconceptualize the notion of family not only for Blacks, but for all viewers. Or,
viewed from another perspective, *The Cosby Show* cast might be seen symbolically to represent our desires to be part of such a supportive network.

For those interested in Black and/or African-American studies, this case
study offers numerous examples of cultural pride and dignity. From a minority
perspective, *The Cosby Show* can be assailed for not fully addressing its critical
role as a new stereotype of and for Blacks—and these issues need to be
brought out into the open. Then, too, specifics like style, language, musical
talent, athletic prowess, sense of humor, even the narrative convention of
storytelling need to be celebrated.

Methodologically, this case study is the result of cross-cultural networking
and cooperation with colleagues around the world. While it lacks similarity
of approach to gathering data from the survey instrument, nevertheless at
least each instance of reportage and each country are discussed in detail.
Even though some administrators used captive audiences and others depended on volunteers, all reported high degrees of respondent participation
and enthusiasm. The questionnaire remained intact, but this researcher cannot account for what changes in meanings might have occurred in various
translations. What is especially critical to this study, as has been pointed out
earlier, are the many extra, idiosyncratic comments made by the numerous
survey participants. In addition to methodology, this case study also includes
discussion of legal roadblocks to conducting social science research that, it
is hoped, will be helpful to other scholars.

For those interested in theoretical perspectives to studying media, this case
study makes an argument for the use of a systemic approach. Although numerous other potential theoretical perspectives are considered, ranging from
semiological to symbolic to psychosociological, it is posited that systems
theory forces us to look at the whole picture, not fragments or biased perspectives on it. It allows us to consider not only the background development
to a media phenomenon, but also its economic, political, sociocultural, and
critical aspects. What is its content? Who is its audience? What is its process?
What is its meaning? The systems theoretical perspective connects many of
the disparate pieces to the Cosby puzzle, suggesting, for example, mutual
interaction effects between the star and the audience, the audience and the
show's various production components, and the wider economic ramifications. In addition, special attention has been given to the role of ritualistic
television viewing, and its fit in the cultivation/enculturation continuum.

For those interested in context, this case study places *The Cosby Show*
within the framework of its time and place today. As such, this case study
then becomes a case study in its own right. It offers many perspectives and
should be useful when meta-analyzed in terms of its own history and historical
role, discussing as it does a media phenomenon for the times in terms of its
large audience, implications for Blacks, the role of the star, comedy, lessons

in parenting, and the television industry at a time when networks are losing their power. Newcomb and Hirsch have written: "A cultural basis for the analysis and criticism of television is, for us, the bridge between a concern for television as a communications medium, central to contemporary society, and television as aesthetic object, the expressive medium that, through its story telling functions, unites and examines a culture" (1984, p. 58).

Contextually, is this truly the "Cosby decade"? How will we look at *The Cosby Show* in retrospect?

Near the end of his comprehensive study of television history, Rick Marschall includes a photograph of Bill Cosby but does not even need to credit the star in his writeup: "Underpinned by excellent situational writing and memorable reaction-lines, 'The Cosby Show' was a success" (1986, p. 195). Other interpretations of *The Cosby Show* phenomenon presented here credit the comedian singlehandedly with creating, sustaining, and planning the future for the show. Although Donald Bogle has written about *The Cosby Show's* role in television history for Blacks, Michael Real its decoding of Blackness, and John D.H. Downing its enabling of positive messages being conveyed to multiple audiences, beyond all that the people have voiced their opinion, and some 60 million of them continued to be loyal fans. Consider all the hundreds of millions of persons around the world who have spent some time sharing the Huxtables' hospitality.

Research for this book began when *The Cosby Show* was in its second season. The original goal was to document it as a quick ratings success story. Once data on audiences came in and all the literature had been digested, however, this study took on a personality of its own. The story of this domestic sitcom had to be told and had to be completely documented. Admittedly, more audiences could be sampled. The last chapter has waited until the final episode has played. But it is important to report on a very timely, popular media happening while it is still fresh. As such, this work should represent the first time an entire television program has been considered so exclusively.

While some persons may want to compare and contrast *The Cosby Show* to popular shows of the 1950s, others might think that it best depicts life in the 1980s. Many people in the current recession are saying that we are going through a justly deserved hangover from the partying of the 1980s. A graphic depiction of the U.S. GNP during the last eight years shows an all-time high in 1985–1986 that almost exactly coincides with the program's popularity. It would appear that as we became ultimate consumers of the material world we also wanted to hold onto the values of consuming interest to us. *Cosby's* comforts are beginning to be more memories than featured plot devices or even background statements, as "reality" themes slowly become the new conventions of television.

This book has attempted to trace that process. As a pioneering academic attempt to study a prime time television phenomenon in depth from a systems-theoretical perspective—including a show's history/background, economics, politics and legalities, production process, domestic and international audiences, kudos and criticisms, and sociocultural implications—this work aims to encourage future research in the area of popular culture.

Epilogue

This book was in the pageproof stage when the final episode of *The Cosby Show* aired on April 30, 1992, and it seemed fitting that we incorporate a few comments about this last episode. Little could we have known how symbolic this exercise would prove.

Prior to the final episode, there was quite a flurry in the press leading up to its airing. The *Boston Sunday Globe*, for example, devoted much of its April 19, 1992 Arts section to a discussion of "Life after 'Cosby.'" The paper's television critic, Ed Siegel, argued that in the "scheme of telethings" the show had altered the face of television and that its parts were greater than its sum, making it safe for network executives to portray African-Americans in a position of power on television. It was a positive factor in how whites look at blacks and how blacks look at themselves; it offered an idealized reality rather than pure fantasy; it emphasized family values; and it broke molds of race, parental sexuality, and control. Siegel concluded: "Perhaps the most fitting epitaph for the program is that, at its best, it showed us what beautiful music a family can make" (1992, p.A6). Mark Muro, in the same paper, said *The Cosby Show* was a "genuine Social Phenomenon," the most-watched sitcom in history (1992, p.A1). He cited radical African-American novelist Ishmael Reed: "You can't deny the Huxtables opened up new possibilities for black people, at least in imagination" (1992, p.A6). He also quoted economist Glenn Loury of Boston University: "It's been a very good thing having these images projected. People object that this comfortable family interferes with keeping our eye on the more disadvantaged, but I say the Huxtables actually opened up alternative identities for black Americans while showing whites there were folks very much like them who happen to be black" (1992, p.A6).

Coretta Scott King wrote a warm farewell to Bill Cosby and his show in

TV Guide, anticipating that its final episode would mark "the end of an era, for no other program of the last decade has had a more lasting and far-reaching impact on television and the nation" (1992, p. 19). In the *New York Times*, Bill Carter added his perspective: "The series was the most-watched show of the last decade, the comedy seen by more people than any other in television history, the show that resurrected the sitcom as television's most popular genre and the first to portray mainstream black middle-class life" (1992, p.H1). Carter discussed in more detail, however, *The Cosby Show*'s role in restoring the television image of parents as loving authority figures, emphasizing education and achievement. There also is a half-page devoted to pre- and post-*Cosby* Black casts.

Many other paens to *The Cosby Show* were written: The *Chicago Tribune*, for example, featured a " 'Cos' to celebrate," with articles by TV critic Rick Kogan, who wrote of his continuing affection for the show (1992, p. 1). Rachal Jones of the *Detroit Free Press* wrote: "In the course of that show's life, perceptions of black people in America have undergone a profound shift. Thanks to the Huxtables, the Spike Lees, the Jesse Jacksons and the Anita Hills of the world, white people have a bigger palette for forming images of black people. No longer do one-dimensional images of us proliferate" (1992, p. 15). William Raspberry of the *Washington Post* offered this perspective: "It has entertained us, of course. But it has also educated us, sensitized us, induced us to introspection and, perhaps, during its eight-year run, even helped bring us together across the divides of race and class. . . . And it taught us as television has rarely managed—and as too few of our leaders even attempt—how much alike we really are, and how little money, class and race have to do with it" (1992). Ellen Goodman focused on the family values gleaned from the show: "The messages that spoke to a new generation of parents and children watching this show together were clear: Parents could wield authority without being authoritarian. They could pass on values without laying on trips. They could raise kids without losing their sense of humor or self-confidence." (1992, p. 19) Bobby Crawford, in the *Los Angeles Times*, wrote of its profound influence, especially regarding "reality-based clowning" that set new standards of parenting, humanizing Black sitcom characters, and encouraging and supporting Black writers (1992). *Entertainment Weekly* devoted a six-page article to the final episode, focusing on how Bill Cosby was not looking back—"He has told every story he wanted to tell about Heathcliff and Clair Huxtable and their five children at 10 Stigwood Avenue, Brooklyn Heights, New York."[1]

The final, hour-long episode of *The Cosby Show*, taped before a live audience of some 300 people, focussed on Theo's graduation from college. Entitled "And So, We Commence," its premise concentrated on a proud father trying to get tickets for all the family. Then, in addition to showing Denise calling from Singapore announcing that she is pregnant, there were flashbacks and highlight clips: Theo's earring, the goldfish funeral, lip-syncing, the prom, news clips on the show's success, a comment about eight years of magic, a Thank You. Finally, there was the long-anticipated ending: Satisfied that the doorbell finally works, Cliff takes Clair in his arms and the two dance through the living room and break down the fourth wall that exists between performer and live audience. The final episode drew a national Nielsen rating of 28 and a 45 share, reaching some 54 million people in all. It was the highest-rated final episode of any NBC program in history,[2] outdrawing ABC, CBS, and Fox combined.[3]

In Los Angeles on the day the final episode was to air, a number of real-life dramas were unfolding. On the day before, a wider racial issue had hit our television screens and our consciences. The word came in in the jury trial of the white police officers who had been captured on videotape brutally beating Rodney King, a Black man—the police had been acquitted. The city erupted, mobbing and marauding in scenes reminiscent of the Watts riots of 1965. Curfews were imposed. Los Angeles declared a state of emergency.

Early in the day on April 30, it was reported that KNBC, the local Los Angeles affiliate, would not be airing the prescheduled final episode of *The Cosby Show*. All day media from around the country were contacting NBC headquarters in New York City, checking not only if the show would be broadcast but also whether Bill Cosby would be making some kind of statement.[4] Finally, Reed Manville, general manager of KNBC, decided that *The Cosby Show* would run after all and that Bill Cosby would indeed make a statement. (Actually, he made two statements, one in case the episode was not aired.) The airing of the finale was announced by Mayor Tom Bradley, who urged his fellow Los Angelenos to stay home and watch *The Cosby Show*.[5] News anchorperson Jess Marlow then introduced it:

For eight years *The Cosby Show* has made us laugh, has made us cry, has made us think. *The Cosby Show* has been a breath of fresh air in a sometimes crazy and chaotic world. Tonight is the final episode of *The Cosby Show*. Their farewell.

Today Mayor Bradley urged us to stay home. . . . Stay off the streets and watch *The Cosby Show*. We believe we need this time . . . a cooling off period . . . some breathing space. A time to remember what our Thursday nights were like before this all began. At KNBC we will use this hour to update the stories and during this hour, if major events dictate, be assured that we will return immediately. We hope you will use this hour to say goodbye and thanks to some very good friends.

At the end of the KNBC telecast came Bill Cosby's statement: "Let us all pray that everyone from the top of the government down to the people in the streets, they would all have good sense, and let us pray for a better tomorrow, which starts today." When asked the next day whether he thought the final episode should in fact have been broadcast, Cosby replied:

Yes. At first, I didn't really feel that this would be a part of what was going on in real life. However, I do recall that when Dr. [Martin Luther] King was shot, when John F. Kennedy was shot, I wanted something to take me away from the horror.

So I was happy they decided to go with [it] because there was a family in the show that for eight years had given people a good feeling about themselves.[6]

Something else *Cosby*-related took place that week: Two researchers from the University of Massachusetts at Amherst, Sut Jhally and Justin Lewis, released results of their study of the show. Called *Enlightened Racism: The Cosby Show, Audiences, and the Myth of the American Dream*, the study had been funded by Bill and Camille Cosby with no strings attached. What they found did not please the Cosbys, however: *The Cosby Show*, the authors contend, has stimulated a trend toward the appearance of more middle- and upper- middle-class Black television characters—a negative factor for race relations, they claim, because it causes white viewers to think racism is no longer a problem in the United States.

Jhally and Lewis, who are both from the United Kingdom, talk about race but say they're concerned about class, then use as a sample episode one they categorize as dealing with sexism. They continually take intuitive leaps without either validity or justification, trying to "prove" negative effects from the show. They got quite a bit of press with this controversial approach, mostly in the print media, but they also appeared on NBC's *The Today Show*, which had been promoting the final episode all week—but they appeared on the show with Dr. Alvin Poussaint. The psychiatrist made the academics' claims look foolish, particularly when he questioned them about whether they had considered other confounding factors in the racism quotient besides *The Cosby Show*. Jhally himself said they felt undone and "used" by the program. Still, he and Lewis had an important article in the *Christian Science Monitor* about television's need to broaden its images of Black experience: "The Cosby/Huxtable persona tells people that there really is room in the United States for minorities to get ahead, without affirmative action, anti-poverty, education, housing, and employment programs."[7]

The previous week, juxtaposed with an editorial on "Verdict and Violence," the *Monitor* ran its farewell to *The Cosby Show*:

The groundbreaking show . . . brought a view of blacks as social and professional equals with whites and inserted blacks into the television mainstream. In so doing, it might have glossed over, for some viewers, the racial inequalities still engrained in American life.

Still, in this era of dysfunctional families and domestic violence, the Huxtables were a model—for all viewers—for a family that loved, laughed a lot, and worked things out.

The editorial closes by saying, "This was a show that deserved to be cared about."[8] *Time* magazine's Lance Morrow also wrote about the symbolism of

Bill Cosby's ending his program by walking off the stage set into "real time": "It seemed perfect that Cosby, America's ideal fantasy father (black) should vanish just at the moment: video metaphysics." (1992, p. 68)

The *New York Times* also included a touching piece some weeks later on its Op-Ed pages by Dympna Ugwu-Oju, a Black English professor. As she tucked her young children into bed on the evening of April 30, after they had shared conflicting images of the riots and *The Cosby Show*, the youngsters began crying. Her six-year-old son wondered what would happen to Olivia, a concern she first brushed off but then considered deeper:

He was right. What will happen to Olivia? As I left the room, I wondered if Clair Huxtable feared for her son's life, especially as he moved into adulthood. I wondered how she would explain to her grandchildren the events on TV that day. I also wondered how she had explained to her own children their blackness. I wish I knew what to tell my children. (1992, p.E17)

Clearly, the fine line between reality and the world of television becomes continually blurred. We are bombarded with "reality" shows, with anecdotes about people being disappointed in their lawyers or doctors or other professionals who don't live up to certain television role models, with children's toys based on children's programming and vice versa, and with any number of instances in which the stories of television are replacing our own oral histories.

While the media is continually blamed for perpetuating its commercialism at any price, it must also be said that these events have at least begun a much-needed dialogue in the press about our neglected racial and economic inequities. When the mainstream media sees the irony between the images of rage and despair caused by the widening gap between rich and poor and the gentle, joyous images of the Huxtable family, perhaps there is hope.

And so, *The Cosby Show* is over, both literally and figuratively, at least on its regular Thursday nights. As some families have videotaped it along the way, many of them the final episode, it is my hope that this book will rest alongside a number of family and library collections. It has been envisioned throughout as a time capsule, describing and dissecting a media phenomenon; hopefully it will help extend our caring for all "families," regardless of complexion.

Appendixes

Appendix 1
Media Coverage of *The Cosby Show*, 1984–1992

about . . . time 1985: Jan
Advertising Age 1986: 5/12, 6/16, 6/30, 10/27, 11/10, 12/29; 1988: 10/10; 1990: 6/4, 11/5
ADWEEK 1989: 1/23, 6/19, 5/15; 1990: 6/4
American Film 1986: Oct; 1988: Sept
American Medical News 1990: 3/16
Billboard 1986: 5/3, 9/13, 10/18
Black Enterprise 1989: Feb
Black Scholar 1985: May–June
Boston Globe 1986: 2/20; 1992: 4/19
Broadcasting 1986: 1/27, 3/10, 10/20, 11/7, 11/10; 1987: 4/27; 1988: 2/1, 5/9, 9/12, 10/10; 1989: 5/29, 8/14, 11/13; 1990: 3/26, 6/25
Business Marketing 1990: Sept
Business Week 1986: 11/10
Channels of Communication 1985: Jan-Feb; 1986: Jan-Feb, June, Sept, Oct, Nov; 1988: Field Guide, April, May, Sept
Chicago Tribune 1992: 4/30
Childhood Education Annual 1989
Christian Science Monitor 1985: 3/8, 5/1, 5/14; 1986: 6/20; 1987: 1/12, 12/15
Current Biography 1986: Oct
Daily News Record 1989: 3/10
Daily Variety 1992: 5/1
Down Beat 1985: Dec; 1986: June; 1988: July
Ebony 1985: April; 1986: Feb, Dec; 1987: Sept; 1988: Oct; 1989: May
English Journal 1988: Oct
Entertainment Weekly 1990: 8/31; 1991: 6/7; 1992: 5/1
Essence 1984: June; 1988: April; 1989: Dec
Family Circle 1985: 11/5; 1990: 10/16
Forbes 1986: 5/5, 10/20
Jet 1985: 8/12; 1986: 4/14, 7/28, 8/4; 1987: 9/28, 10/27
Ladies Home Journal 1985: April
Library Journal 1986: 6/15
Life 1985: June; 1989: Fall
Los Angeles Times 1985: 3/7, 4/24, 5/17, 6/12, 7/31, 9/23, 9/26; 1986: 8/1; 1987: 5/20; 1992: 5/2, 5/11
Macleans's 1986: 6/16; 1989: 5/1
Marketing and Media Decisions 1986: June
McCalls 1985: April
Media & Values 1986: Spring
Nation 1986: 9/6
National Review 1986: 7/18
New England Monthly 1987: Feb
New Republic 1985: 8/5; 1986: 8/25
New York 1984: 11/8, 11/22
New York Times 1984: 8/6, 9/20, 11/18; 1985: 4/28, 5/9, 9/23; 1986: 1/6, 2/17, 6/20,

11/7, 11/10; 1987: 1/7, 9/24, 12/3; 1988: 1/21, 5/7, 5/19, 10/10, 11/10, 11/15; 1989: 2/22, 6/7, 11/8, 11/12, 11/26, 12/19; 1991: 3/10, 3/23, 3/30, 4/9; 1992: 3/5, 4/26, 5/17

Newsweek 1984: 11/5; 1985: 9/12; 1986: 5/19; 1987: 3/23, 9/14; 1988: 1/25

Parents Magazine 1985: Nov

People 1984: 9/24, 12/10; 1985: 12/16; 1986: 2/24; 1987: 10/26, 11/16; 1989: Fall; 1990: 10/29

Philadelphia Enquirer 1985: 11/17

Playboy 1985: Dec

Psychology Today 1986: June

Publishers Weekly 1986: 4/11; 1989: 3/17, 9/8

Reader's Digest 1985: Sept

Redbook 1987: June

Rolling Stone 1986–1987: 12/18–1/1

Saturday Evening Post 1985: April; 1986: April

Savvy Woman 1989: Oct

School Library Journal 1985: April, Oct, Nov; 1986: March, Oct

Television–Radio Age 1986: 10/27; 1987: 2/2, 9/14

Time 1984: 12/3; 1985: 5/6; 1986: 4/28; 1987: 9/28; 1992: 4/25

TV Guide 1984: 10/13–19; 1985: 9/7–13; 1986: 3/22–28, 4/5–11, 4/19–25, 7/26–31, 11/22–28; 1987: 10/10–16; 1988: 4/23–29, 5/7–13, 8/13–19; 1990: 6/30–7/6

US 1985: 10/21

US News & World Report 1985: 8/29, 12/5; 1986: 4/23, 12/23; 1987: 1/23, 8/31; 1988: 8/12

USA Today 1985: 8/29, 12/5; 1986: 4/23, 12/23; 1987: 1/23, 8/31; 1988: 8/12

Variety 1984: 9/26, 10/10, 11/14; 1985: 1/30, 9/4, 12/4, 12/11, 12/18; 1986: 1/15, 1/22, 12/3; 1987: 6/10, 7/22, 9/21; 1988: 1/16, 2/1, 2/10; 1989: 1/11, 7/12, 8/9, 10/4; 1990: 1/10, 5/30

Videography 1986: Fall

Vogue 1985: Jan; 1987: Sept

Wall Street Journal 1984: 11/19; 1985: 8/29, 10/21; 1986: 4/16, 6/24, 7/30, 10/31; 1987: 2/19, 3/13, 7/29; 1988: 5/9, 11/14

Washington Post 1984: 11/15; 1985: 3/7, 5/15; 1986: 5/31; 1987: 4/5

World Tennis 1985: Oct

Appendix 2
Survey Instrument: *The Cosby Show*—A Survey

1.Have you seen THE COSBY SHOW?
__No (skip to #8)   __Yes

2.If yes, how often have you seen the show?
__Only once   __Several times   __Regularly

3.On a scale from 1-10, 1 being the lowest, circle your rating of it.
  Not very good   Excellent
      1   2   3   4   5   6   7   8   9   10

4.Which member(s) of the cast do you identify with/relate to:
  __Dr. Heathcliff ("Cliff") Huxtable--Bill Cosby
  __Clair Huxtable (wife/mother/lawyer)--Phylicia Ayers-Allen
  __Sondra Huxtable (college student)--Sabrina LeBeauf
  __Denise Huxtable (17-year old daughter)--Lisa Bonet
  __Theodore Huxtable (only son, aged 14)--Malcolm-Jamal Warner
  __Vanessa Huxtable (11-year old daughter)--Tempestt Bledsoe
  __Rudy Huxtable (youngest daughter, age 5)--Keshia Knight Pulliam
  __None

5.Which character on THE COSBY SHOW is your favorite?_____

6.Which episode on THE COSBY SHOW was your favorite?_____

7.Circle your opinions on the following issues:

	Agree	No opinion	Disagree
a.The Huxtables are a typical family.	1	2	3
b.They are a typical American family.	1	2	3
c.They are a typical black family.	1	2	3
d.They are a typical wealthy family.	1	2	3
e.I'd like to be in their family.	1	2	3
f.The show is about being black.	1	2	3

Some information about you:
  8.Sex: __Male   __Female
  9.Race:
  10.Age:
  11.Occupation:
  12.How much television do you watch:
          __Less than 1 hour/day   __1-3 hours/day   __3+ hours/day

  Thank you very much. Please feel free to add any comments about
THE COSBY SHOW.

                              Linda K. Fuller, Ph.D.
                              Media Dept/Worcester State College
                              Worcester, MA 01602 USA

Appendix 3
Countries Represented in *The Cosby Show* Survey

Country	Number of Respondents
Austria	—
Australia	35
Bahamas	17
Canada	—
Denmark	—
Finland	18
France	10
Germany	32
Greece	—
Indonesia	—
Ireland	—
Italy	—
Japan	—
Malaysia	—
Malta	—
Mexico	—
The Netherlands	36
Norway	—
Poland	—
Singapore	—
South Africa	49
Spain	231
Sweden	37
Turkey	118
United Kingdom	13
United States	192
West Indies (Barbados, Jamaica, St. Vincent, Trinidad)	21

Subtotals:

United States	192
Other countries	617

Total: 809

Appendix 4
Celebrities on *The Cosby Show* (a partial listing)

Debbie Allen

John Amos

Count Basie

Joe Black

Sonia Braga

Valerie Briscoe-Hooks

Roscoe Lee Browne

Red Buttons

Josh Culbreath

Robert Culp

Sammy Davis, Jr.

Dave DeBusschere, Senator Bill Bradley, Walt Hazzard, and Wali Jones (former professional basketball players)

Placido Domingo

Meg Foster

Dizzy Gillespie

Robin Givens

Moses Gunn

Armand Hammer

Eileen Heckart

Lena Horne

Bill Irwin

Danny Kaye

B. B. King

Sheldon Leonard

Nancy Lieberman (and other women basketball players)

Miriam Makeba

E. G. Marshall

Melba Moore

Rita Moreno

The Muppets

Tony Orlando

Christopher Plummer

Anthony Quinn

Ann Reinking

John Ritter
Frank Robinson
Wallace Shawn
Sandman Sims
Eden Svendahl
Leslie Uggams
Clarence Williams
Joe Williams
Vanessa Williams
Nancy Wilson
Troy Winbush
Stevie Wonder

Appendix 5
Personnel Related to *The Cosby Show* (a partial listing)

Creators: Ed. Weinberger, Michael Leeson, and William Cosby, Jr.

Cast: see chapter 4

Executive Producers: Marcy Carsey and Tom Werner

Co-Executive Producers: John Markus and Earl Pomerantz

Co-Supervising Producer: Gary Kott

Producers: Carmen Finestra (supervising producer), Terri Guarnieri, Steve Kline, Gary Kott, Caryn Sneider Mandalbach, John Markus, and Matt Williams

Directors: Jay Sandrich and Tony Singletary

Writers: Gary Kott (head writer), Elaine Arata, Janet Leahy, Michael Leeson, and Ed. Weinberger

Music Directors: Stu Gardner and Arthur Lisi

Costume Director: Sarah Lemire

Psychological Consultant: Dr. Alvin F. Poussaint

Appendix 6
Bibliography: Alvin F. Poussaint, M.D.

Abrams, Bill. "In Television Today, the Script Doctor Is Apt to Be a Freudian." *Wall Street Journal* (February 19, 1985).

Brooke, Jill. "Cosby Script Doctor Gives Racism the Boot." *New York Post* (March 27, 1986).

————. "The Conscience of the Cosby Show." *Elle* (December 1986).

" 'The Cosby Show' and Poussaint: A Winning Team." *Children's Today*. Boston Children's Hospital (April 1985).

Davidson, Bill. "I Must Be Doing Something Right." *McCall's* (April 1985).

Gaston, Janice. "Psychiatrist Keeps 'Cosby Show' Believable." *Winston-Salem Journal* (November 30, 1987).

Gillespie, Judy. "The Cosby Show's Secret Ingredient." *Family Circle* (November 5, 1985).

Hall, Jane. "Bill Cosby Huffs and Puffs on and off His Hit Sitcom, But His TV Kids Say Father Knows Best." *People Magazine* (December 1984).

Haugh, Brian. "Shrinks Put TV Shows on the Couch." *Star* (March 12, 1985).

Kenneally, Christopher. "Bill Cosby Agrees with This Doctor." *Brookline Citizen* (April 25, 1985).

————. "Boston Psychiatrist's Special Patient: A Television Sitcom." *Boston Herald* (May 12, 1985).

Kiesewetter, John. " 'Cosby' Lets Conscience Be the Guide." *Cincinnati Enquirer* (February 22, 1987).

LeConte, Phil. "The Psychologist as TV Guide." *Psychology Today* (August 1986).

Lindsey, David. "Cosby Is Positively Successful." *Dallas Times Herald* (April 17, 1986).

MacDougall, William, et al. "Black Actors + Hit Shows = Mass Appeal." *U.S. News & World Report* (May 13, 1985).

O'Connell, John. " 'Cosby Show' Draws Praise for Views on Black Family." *Union-News* (January 25, 1989).

Oliver, Kitty. "His Humor Is Based in Reality." *Miami Herald* (February 13, 1986).

Poussaint, Alvin F. "The Huxtables: Fact or Fantasy?" *Ebony* (October 1988).

Raspberry, William. "Cosby Show: Black or White?" *Washington Post* (November 5, 1984).

Rodrigues-Taylor, K. S. "Teaching Cosby a Lesson." *Boston Herald* (January 22, 1987).

Scoon, Valerie G. "Med School Psychiatrist Edits The Cosby Show." *Harvard Crimson* (November 6, 1984).

Sherry, Shirley. "He's Cosby's Consultant . . . and a Good Role Model Himself." *Hanover Sun* (February 28, 1986).

Slate, Libby. "The Psychiatric Treatment: Introducing Hollywood's Newest Breed of Consultant." *Emmy Magazine* (January/February 1987).

Smith, Wendy. "Cosby, TV's Favorite Dad, Sees Humor in Fatherhood: and Consultant Poussaint Adds to Comic's Realism." *Chicago Sun-Times* (June 15, 1986).

Snook, Debbi. "A Conscience for Cosby's Humor." *Albany Times-Union* (March 22, 1986).

Stoneman, Donnell. "The Vanguard of Realism at 'Cosby.' " *Greensboro News and Record* (December 2, 1987).

Terry, Sara. "The Conscience of the Cosby Show." *Christian Science Monitor* (February
    12, 1987).
Vigeland, Carl A. "The Enduring Bill Cosby." *Boston Globe Magazine* (December 28,
    1984).
Waters, Harry F., with Peter McAlevey. "Bill Cosby Comes Home." *Newsweek* (Novem-
    ber 5, 1984).
Woodruff, Cathy. "Cosby Consultant Sees Himself as 'Test Market.' " *Schenectady Ga-
    zette* (March 24, 1986).

Appendix 7
Australian Data on *The Cosby Show* Survey—35 Respondents

1.Have you seen THE COSBY SHOW?
   5 No (skip to #8)   30 Yes

2.If yes, how often have you seen the show?
   2 Only once   11 Several times   17 Regularly

3.On a scale from 1-10, 1 being the lowest, circle your rating of it.
   Not very good   Excellent
      1   2   3   4   5   6   7   8   9   10
     (1)   (1)   (3)   (11)   (9)   (3)   (2)
4.Which member(s) of the cast do you identify with/relate to:
   5 Dr. Heathcliff ("Cliff") Huxtable--Bill Cosby
   4 Clair Huxtable (wife/mother/lawyer)--Phylicia Ayers-Allen
   3 Sondra Huxtable (college student)--Sabrina LeBeauf
   9 Denise Huxtable (17-year old daughter)--Lisa Bonet
   2 Theodore Huxtable (only son, aged 14)--Malcolm-Jamal Warner
   0 Vanessa Huxtable (11-year old daughter)--Tempestt Bledsoe
   4 Rudy Huxtable(youngest daughter, age 5)--Keshia Knight Pulliam
   9 None

5.Which character on THE COSBY SHOW is your favorite? Cliff 18, Clair 3,
   Denise 2, Theo 1, Rudy 4, All 7
6.Which episode on THE COSBY SHOW was your favorite? Rudy in shopping
   center; grandparents' anniversary 2; Rudy brings boyfriend home; camping/
   wilderness store 2; Sondra and new husband
7.Circle your opinions on the following issues:

	Agree	No opinion	Disagree
a.The Huxtables are a typical family.	7	6	17 (57%)
b.They are a typical American family.	5	10	15 (50%)
c.They are a typical black family.	0	8	22 (73%)
d.They are a typical wealthy family.	6	12	12
e.I'd like to be in their family.	14 (47%)	11	5
f.The show is about being black.	0	5	25 (83%)

Some information about you:
   8.Sex: 7 Male   28 Female (80%)
   9.Race: See write-up in text.
  10.Age: 11-20, 21 (60%); 21-35, 11 (31%); 36-50, 3
  11.Occupation: Students
  12.How much television do you watch:
       10 Less than 1 hour/day   15 1-3 hours/day (43%)   10 3+ hours/day

Thank you very much. Please feel free to add any comments about
THE COSBY SHOW.

                                        Linda K. Fuller, Ph.D.
                                        Media Dept/Worcester State College
                                        Worcester, MA 01602 USA

Appendix 8
Bahamian Data on *The Cosby Show* Survey—17 Respondents

1.Have you seen THE COSBY SHOW?
   1 No (skip to #8)   16 Yes

2.If yes, how often have you seen the show?
   1 Only once   9 Several times   6 Regularly

3.On a scale from 1-10, 1 being the lowest, circle your rating of it.
   Not very good   Excellent
       1   2   3   4   5   6   7   8   9   10
                            (1)   (4)   (3)   (3)   (5)
4.Which member(s) of the cast do you identify with/relate to:
   4 Dr. Heathcliff ("Cliff") Huxtable--Bill Cosby
   7 Clair Huxtable (wife/mother/lawyer)--Phylicia Ayers-Allen
   0 Sondra Huxtable (college student)--Sabrina LeBeauf
   0 Denise Huxtable (17-year old daughter)--Lisa Bonet
   4 Theodore Huxtable (only son, aged 14)--Malcolm-Jamal Warner
   2 Vanessa Huxtable (11-year old daughter)--Tempestt Bledsoe
   2 Rudy Huxtable(youngest daughter, age 5)--Keshia Knight Pulliam
   4 None

5.Which character on THE COSBY SHOW is your favorite? Cliff 8, Clair 3,
   Denise 1, Theo 1, Rudy 2
6.Which episode on THE COSBY SHOW was your favorite? Grandparents'
   anniversary (3); Father's Day; Stevie Wonder episode
7.Circle your opinions on the following issues:

	Agree	No opinion	Disagree
a.The Huxtables are a typical family.	3	5	8 (50%)
b.They are a typical American family.	3	8 (50%)	5
c.They are a typical black family.	1	9 (56%)	6
d.They are a typical wealthy family.	3	10 (63%)	3
e.I'd like to be in their family.	6	8 (50%)	2
f.The show is about being black.	2	4	10 (63%)

Some information about you:
   8.Sex: 8 Male   9 Female (53%)
   9.Race: 16 Black; 1 white
  10.Age: 11-20, 1; 21-35, 15 (88%); 36-50, 1
  11.Occupation: social worker, youth officer, secretary, student, administrator
     (2), filing assistant (2), civil servant (2), housekeeper, concilator, psycho-
     therapist, telephone technician, labor inspector, and sales
  12.How much television do you watch:
     6 Less than 1 hour/day   6 1-3 hours/day   4 3+ hours/day

   Thank you very much. Please feel free to add any comments about
THE COSBY SHOW.

                    Linda K. Fuller, Ph.D.
                    Media Dept/Worcester State College
                    Worcester, MA 01602 USA

Appendix 9
Finnish Data on *The Cosby Show* Survey—18 Respondents

1.Have you seen THE COSBY SHOW?
   0 No (skip to #8)   18 Yes

2.If yes, how often have you seen the show?
   0 Only once   17 Several times (94%)   1 Regularly

3.On a scale from 1-10, 1 being the lowest, circle your rating of it.
   Not very good   Excellent
        1   2   3   4   5   6   7   8   9   10
                     (1)   (1)   (1)   (4)   (4)   (3)   (4)

4.Which member(s) of the cast do you identify with/relate to:
   1 Dr. Heathcliff ("Cliff") Huxtable--Bill Cosby
   4 Clair Huxtable (wife/mother/lawyer)--Phylicia Ayers-Allen
   2 Sondra Huxtable (college student)--Sabrina LeBeauf
   0 Denise Huxtable (17-year old daughter)--Lisa Bonet
   1 Theodore Huxtable (only son, aged 14)--Malcolm-Jamal Warner
   0 Vanessa Huxtable (11-year old daughter)--Tempestt Bledsoe
   0 Rudy Huxtable(youngest daughter, age 5)--Keshia Knight Pulliam
   13 None

5.Which character on THE COSBY SHOW is your favorite? Cliff 8, Clair 1,
   Theo 1, Rudy 7
6.Which episode on THE COSBY SHOW was your favorite? Grandparents'
   anniversary (2)
7.Circle your opinions on the following issues:

	Agree	No opinion	Disagree
a.The Huxtables are a typical family.	0	3	15 (83%)
b.They are a typical American family.	1	4	13 (72%)
c.They are a typical black family.	0	2	16 (89%)
d.They are a typical wealthy family.	7	4	7
e.I'd like to be in their family.	5	4	9 (50%)
f.The show is about being black.	0	3	15 (83%)

Some information about you:
   8.Sex: 7 Male   11 Female (61%)
   9.Race: 100% white
  10.Age: 11-20, 5; 21-35, 12 (67%); 36-50, 1
  11.Occupation: students; 2 are translators, one a teacher
  12.How much television do you watch:
        6 Less than 1 hour/day   11 1-3 hours/day (61%)   1 3+ hours/day

Thank you very much. Please feel free to add any comments about
THE COSBY SHOW.

                          Linda K. Fuller, Ph.D.
                          Media Dept/Worcester State College
                          Worcester, MA 01602 USA

Appendix 10
The Cosby Show—Un Sondage (French translation)

1.Avez-vous vu THE COSBY SHOW?
  __Non (passez au #8)   __Oui

2.Si oui, combien de fois?
  __Une seule fois   __Plusieurs fois   __Regulierement

3.Indiquez, de 1 a 10 (1 etant le pire, 10 le mailleur), votre evaluation, en cer-
  clant le chiffre convenable.

Pas tre bon   Excellent
   1   2   3   4   5   6   7   8   9   10

4.Avec quel(s) membre(s) de la distribution identifiez-vous:
  __Dr. Heathcliff ("Cliff") Huxtable--Bill Cosby
  __Clair Huxtable (femme/mere/avocate)--Phylicia Ayers-Allen
  __Sondra Huxtable (etudiante)--Sabrina LeBeauf
  __Denise Huxtable (fille de dix sept ans)--Lisa Bonet
  __Theodore Huxtable (fils unique, 14 ans)--Malcolm-Jamal Warner
  __Vanessa Huxtable (fille de onze ans)--Tempestt Bledsoe
  __Rudy Huxtable (la fille cadette, 5 ans)--Keshia Knight Pulliam
  __Aucun

5.Quel personnage de THE COSBY SHOW est votre favori?_____

6.Quel episode de THE COSBY SHOW etait votre favori?_____

7.Cerclez votre avis sur les questions suivantes:

	D'accord	Pas d'opinion	Non
a.Les Huxtable sont une famille typique.	1	2	3
b.C'est une famille typiquement americaine.	1	2	3
c.C'est une famille typiquement noire.	1	2	3
d.C'est sont une famille typiquement riche.	1	2	3
e.J'aimerais bien etre dans leur famille.	1	2	3
f.Il s'agit d'etre noir.	1	2	3

Quelques renseignements aupres de vous:
  8.Sexe: __Masculin   __Feminin
  9.Race:
10.Age:
11.Metier:
12.Combien d'heures passez-vous en regardant la television?
        __Moins d'une heure/jour   __1-3 heures/jour   __3+ heures/jour

Je vous remercie beaucoup. Veuillez ajouter vos observations et commentaries
au sujet de THE COSBY SHOW a ce sondage.
                     Linda K. Fuller, Ph.D.
                     Media Dept/Worcester State College
                     Worcester, MA 01602 USA

Appendix 11
Familienbande—Eine Umfrage (German translation)

1.Haben Sie THE COSBY SHOW ("Familienbande") gesehen?
___Nein (Fahren Sie mit Frage #8 fort)   ___Ja

2.Wenn ja, wie oft haben Sie die Sendung gesehen?
___Nur einmal   ___Mehrmals   ___Regelmassig

3.Auf einer Skala von 1-10 (1- nicht gut) wie wurden Sie die Sendung einschatzen.
   Nicht gut   Hervorragend
       1   2   3   4   5   6   7   8   9   10

4.Mit welchen Schaupieler Rollen identifizieren Sie sich?:
   ___Dr. Heathcliff ("Cliff") Huxtable--Bill Cosby
   ___Clair Huxtable (frau/mutter/rechtsanwaltin)--Phylicia Ayers-Allen
   ___Sondra Huxtable (student)--Sabrina LeBeauf
   ___Denise Huxtable (17 jahrige Tochter)--Lisa Bonet
   ___Theodore Huxtable (einziger Sohn, 14 Jahre)--Malcolm-Jamal Warner
   ___Vanessa Huxtable (11 jahrige Tochter)--Tempestt Bledsoe
   ___Rudy Huxtable (jungste Tochter, 5 Jahre alt)--Keshia Knight Pulliam
   ___Mit Keiner

5.Wer ist Ihr Lieblingscharakter in THE COSBY SHOW ("Familienbande") ?___

6.Welche Episode der "Familienbande" fanden Sie am besten?_____

7.Kreisen Sie die Buchstaben an die nach Ihrer Meinung mit folgenden Aussagen
   ubereinstimmen:

	Ja	Keine Antwort	Nein
a.Die Huxtables sind eine typische Familie.	1	2	3
b.Sie sind eine typische Amerikanische Familie.	1	2	3
c.Sie sind eine typische schwarze Familie.	1	2	3
d.Sie sind eine typische reiche Familie.	1	2	3
e.Ich mochte der Familie angehoren.	1	2	3
f.Die Sendung handelt sich um die schwarze Rasse.	1	2	3

Angaben zu Ihrer Person:
  8.Geschlecht: ___Mannlich   ___Weiblich
  9.Rasse:
10.Alter:
11.Beruf:
12.Wie oft sitzen Sie vor dem Fernsehapparat am Tag:
     ___weniger als eine studen/tag   ___1-3 studen   ___3+ und mehr studen

Vielen Dank. Wenn Sie etwas uber THE COSBY SHOW ("Familienbande") hinzu-
fugen wollen, benutzen Sie bitte die Ruckseite dieses Frangebogens.
                              Linda K. Fuller, Ph.D.
                              Media Dept/Worcester State College
                              Worcester, MA 01602 USA

Appendix 12
Greek Translation of *The Cosby Show* Survey

" Το σοου του Κοσμπυ"-- Μια ερευνα

I. Εχετε δει το "Σοου του Κοσμπυ "

____ ΟΧΙ (Βλεπε   Νο 8)
____ ΝΑΙ

2. Αν ναι   ποσο συχνα το βλεπετε:
_____Μια φορα
_____Πολλες ωρες
_____Συχνα

3. Σε μια βαθμιδα αποτο ενα μεχρι το 18 ση μειωστε την προτιμιση σας.

    Πολυ χαλο   Θαυμασιο
     1 2   3   4   5   6   7   8   9   10

4. Με πιο μελος απο την οικογενεια βρισκεται   ομοιοτητες :

        Δρ Χαξταμπαλ---Μπιλ Κοσμπυ
        Κλαιρ Χαξταμπαλ ----Φιλλισια Αλλεν
        Σανδρα Χαξταμπαλ---- Σαμπρινα Λε Μπουφ
        Ντεννιςχαξταμπαλ---- Λισα Μπουετ
        Θεωδορ Χαξταμπαλ----Μαλχομ Γουωρνερ
        Βαννεσα Χαξταμπαλ--- Τεμπες Μπεσος
        Ρουντυ Χαξταμπαλ----Χεσια Πουλαμ
        Κανενα

5. Ποιος χαραχτηρας απο το σοου σας αρεσει;_____

6. Ποιο επισοδειο απο το σοου ηταν το πιο αγαπημενο σας :_____

7. Σημειωστε την γνωμη σας στις επομενες προτασεις.

                           Συμφωνω Δεν συμφωνω. : Χωρις γνωμη

   α. Ειναι μια τυπικη οικογενεια   1   2   3
   β. Δεν ειναι τυπικη οικογενεια   1   2   3
   γ. Ειναι μια μαυρη τυπικη οικογενεια 1   2   3
   δ. Ειναι μια πλουσια οικογενεια   1   2   3
   ε. Θα ηθελα να ειμαι στην οικογενεια 1   2   3
   ζ. Το σοου ειναι για μαυρους   1   2   3

        Μερικες πληροφοριες για σας
8. Φυλο Ανδρας_____ Γυναικα_____
9.Φυλη:
10. Ηλικια
11. Εργασια
12. Ποση' τηλεοραση βλεπετε :
_____Πιο λιγο απο μια ωρα την ημερα
_____1-3 ωρες την ημερα
_____3 + ωρες· την ημερα

Appendix 13
Keluarga Huxtable (Indonesian translation)

1.Sudah nonton THE COSBY SHOW ("KELUARGA HUXTABLE")?
　__Tidak (pergi ke #8)　　__Ya

2.Kalau ya, berapa kali sudah nonton itu?
　__Hanya satu kali　　__Berberapa kali　　__Banyak, biasa

3.Dari 1 ke 10, kalau 1 ada lebih kecil, anda senang itu.
　Tidak bagus   Bagus sekali
　　　1　　2　　3　　4　　5　　6　　7　　8　　9　　10

4.Separti siapa di keluarga ada anda:
　__Doktor Heathcliff ("Cliff") Huxtable--Bill Cosby
　__Clair Huxtable (istri/ibu)--Phylicia Ayers-Allen
　__Sondra Huxtable (maha siswa)--Sabrina LeBeauf
　__Denise Huxtable (perempuan, 17)--Lisa Bonet
　__Theodore Huxtable (laki yang hanya, 14)--Malcolm-Jamal Warner
　__Vanessa Huxtable (perempuan, 11)--Tempestt Bledsoe
　__Rudy Huxtable (perempuan paling mudah, 5)--Keshia Knight Pulliam
　__Tidak ada

5.Siapa di "KELUARGA HUXTABLE" yang anda paling senang?_____

6.Apa kali di "KELUARGA HUXTABLE" yang anda paling senang?_____

7.Apa tentang ini bertanya:

	Ada	Tidak tau	Tidak
a.Keluarga Huxtable ada keluarga biasa.	1	2	3
b.Mereka ada keluarga America biasa.	1	2	3
c.Mereka ada keluarga chocolat biasa.	1	2	3
d.Mereka punya banyak uang.	1	2	3
e.Saya senang keluarga ini.	1	2	3
f.Ini tentang orang chocolat.	1	2	3

Sedikit informaci tentang anda:
　8.　__Laki　　__Perempuan
　9.Warna:
　10.Berapa umur:
　11.Busines:
　12.Berapa televisi anda nonton:
　__Lebih kecil 1 jam　__1-3 jam di 1 hari　__3 atau lebih banyak jam di 1 hari

Terima kasih banyak. Kalau anda mau, silhakan tulis lebih banyak tentang THE
COSBY SHOW ("KELUARGA HUXTABLE").
　　　　　　　　　　　　　Linda K. Fuller, Ph.D.
　　　　　　　　　　　　　Media Dept/Worcester State College
　　　　　　　　　　　　　Worcester, MA 01602 USA

Appendix 14
Rivedute del Cosby Show (Italian translation)

1.Avete mai visto il "RIVEDUTE DEL COSBY SHOW"?
____No (*8)   ____Si

2.Se c'havete visto, piu omeno quante volte?
____Une volta sola   ____Piu di une volta   ____O regolarmente

3.Sulla scale da uno a dieci, mette te un circola sul numero che volete.
  Non molto buono   Eccellente
       1   2   3   4   5   6   7   8   9   10

4.Quale persona di questo gruppo nella vostra opinione riconscette una persona
   uquale a voi:
   ____Il dottor Heathcliff ("Cliff") Huxtable--Bill Cosby
   ____Clair Huxtable (mogli/madre/avvocatessa)--Phylicia Ayers-Allen
   ____Sondra Huxtable (una studentessa d'universita)--Sabrina LeBeauf
   ____Denise Huxtable (la figlia di diciasette anni)--Lisa Bonet
   ____Theodore Huxtable (unico figlio, 14)--Malcolm-Jamal Warner
   ____Vanessa Huxtable (la figlia di undici anni)--Tempestt Bledsoe
   ____Rudy Huxtable (la figlia piu giovane di 5)--Keshia Knight Pulliam
   ____Nesuno

5.Quale carattere del "RIVEDUTE DEL COSBY SHOW" e il vostro favorito?_____

6.Quale episodio del "RIVEDUTE DEL COSBY SHOW" era il vostro favorito?_____

7.Fate un circolo per la vostra opinione circa i seguenti soggetti:

	A favore	No opinione	Contrari
a.Huxtables e una famiglia tipica.	1	2	3
b.E una famiglia tipica Americana.	1	2	3
c.E una famiglia tipica di razza nera.	1	2	3
d.E una tipica famiglia ricca.	1	2	3
e.Io vorrei appartenere a questa famiglia.	1	2	3
f.COSBY SHOW e riguarda razza nera.	1	2	3

Qualche informazione circa, voi:
  8.Sesso: ____Uomo   ____Donna
  9.Razza:
10.Eta:
11.Occupazione:
12.Quanto temp de dicate alla televisione?:
     ____Meno di un ora al giorno   ____1-3 ora al giorno   ____3+ ora al giorno

  Grazie infinite. Per favore siate liberidi aggiugere quale si asi commento abbri-
ate cirea il "RIVEDUTE DEL COSBY SHOW."
                              Linda K. Fuller, Ph.D.
                              Media Dept/Worcester State College
                              Worcester, MA 01602 USA

Appendix 15
Dutch Data on *The Cosby Show*—Enquette (36 Respondents)

1.Heeft u THE COSBY SHOW gezien?
   1 Nee (ga door naar #8)   35 Ja

2.Zo ja, hoe vaak heeft u de show gezien?
   1 Slechts a maal   16 Meerdere malen   19 Regelmatig (53%)

3.Op een schaal van 1-10, 1 het laagste, geef uw waardering.
   Niet goed   Uitstekend

1	2	3	4	5	6	7	8	9	10
				(5)	(4)	(6)	(15)	(4)	(1)

4.Tot wie voelt u zich het meeste aangetrokken:
   15 Dr. Heathcliff ("Cliff") Huxtable--Bill Cosby
    7 Clair Huxtable (echtgenote/moeder/advocate)--Phylicia Ayers-Allen
    1 Sondra Huxtable (college studente)--Sabrina LeBeauf
    8 Denise Huxtable (17-jarige dochter)--Lisa Bonet
    4 Theodore Huxtable (enige zoon, 14 jaar)--Malcolm-Jamal Warner
    0 Vanessa Huxtable (11-jarige dochter)--Tempestt Bledsoe
   20 Rudy Huxtable (jongste dochter, 5 jaar)--Keshia Knight Pulliam
    3 Niemand

5.Wie is uw favoriet in THE COSBY SHOW ? Cliff 2, Clair 2, Theo 4, Rudy 17

6.Welke aflevering vond u het leukst van de THE COSBY SHOW? (Translation):
   Rudy playing football, "when they want to fool their Dad," snowball fight,
   grandparents' anniversary

7.Geef uw mening op de volgen de uragen:

	Ja	Geen mening	Nee
a.De Huxtables is een gewone familie.	9	5	21 (60%)
b.Ze zyn een echte Amerikaanse familie.	20 (57%)	5	10
c.Ze zyn een echte zwarte familie.	8	4	23 (66%)
d.Ze zyn een echte ryke familie.	12	14 (40%)	9
e.Ik zou graag in hun familie zyn.	14 (40%)	13	8
f.De show gaat over zwart zyn.	1	3	31 (86%)

Enige informatie over u:
   8.Geslacht: 15 Man   21 Vrouw (58%)
   9.Huidskleur: 100% blank
  10.Leeftyd: 11-20, 11; 21-35, 14 (39%); 36-50, 4; 51-65, 5; 65+, 2
  11.Beroep (translation): student (10), professional (2), retired (2), white
     collar (2), blue/pink collar (6), clerk (3), housewife (8), NA (2)
  12.Hoe vaak kykt u televisie:
     7 Minder dan 1 uur per dag   18 1-3 uur per dag (50%)   11 3+ uur per dag

   Hartelyk dank. Opmerkingen der THE COSBY SHOW.
                              Linda K. Fuller, Ph.D.
                              Media Dept/Worcester State College
                              Worcester, MA 01602 USA

Appendix 16
South African Data on *The Cosby Show* Survey—49 Respondents

1.Have you seen THE COSBY SHOW?
  0 No (skip to #8)   49 Yes

2.If yes, how often have you seen the show?
  1 Only once   12 Several times   36 Regularly (73%)

3.On a scale from 1-10, 1 being the lowest, circle your rating of it.
  Not very good   Excellent
      1   2   3   4   5   6   7   8   9   10
     (2)   (8)   (2)   (9) (12) (16)
4.Which member(s) of the cast do you identify with/relate to:
   18 Dr. Heathcliff ("Cliff") Huxtable--Bill Cosby
   20 Clair Huxtable (wife/mother/lawyer)--Phylicia Ayers-Allen
    2 Sondra Huxtable (college student)--Sabrina LeBeauf
    4 Denise Huxtable (17-year old daughter)--Lisa Bonet
   11 Theodore Huxtable (only son, aged 14)--Malcolm-Jamal Warner
    4 Vanessa Huxtable (11-year old daughter)--Tempestt Bledsoe
    7 Rudy Huxtable(youngest daughter, age 5)--Keshia Knight Pulliam
    8 None

5.Which character on THE COSBY SHOW is your favorite? Cliff 23, Clair 10,
   Theo 11, Rudy 11, All 12, None 2
6.Which episode on THE COSBY SHOW was your favorite? "The one where Rudy
   plays a little old lady with a very posh accent"; Theo had to face the 'Real
   World' (3); Cliff does "do it yourself"; parents sold Theo's room; Cliff explains to Rudy about germs; Stevie Wonder; Theo--drugs; anniversary of
   Cliff's parents; Theo's earring; Monopoly $; fire drill; Denise's first car
7.Circle your opinions on the following issues:

	Agree	No opinion	Disagree
a.The Huxtables are a typical family.	29 (59%)	2	18
b.They are a typical American family.	20 (40%)	15	14
c.They are a typical black family.	17	9	24 (47%)
d.They are a typical wealthy family.	17	11	21
e.I'd like to be in their family.	23 (47%)	11	15
f.The show is about being black.	3	7	39 (50%)

Some information about you:
  8.Sex: 25 Male   24 Female
  9.Race: 86% white, 4 Indian, 3 Black
 10.Age: 11-20, 11; 21-35, 21; 65+, 17
 11.Occupation: retired (7), librarian, receptionist, social worker (2), secretary
    (2), teacher, unemployed, union organizer
 12.How much television do you watch:
    6 Less than 1 hour/day   23 1-3 hours/day   20 3+ hours/day

 Thank you very much. Please feel free to add any comments about
THE COSBY SHOW.

                              Linda K. Fuller, Ph.D.
                              Media Dept/Worcester State College
                              Worcester, MA 01602 USA

Appendix 17
Spanish Data on *El Show de Cosby*—Una Encuesta (183 Respondents)

1.Ha visto alguna vez EL SHOW DE COSBY?
   6 No (pase a la numero 8)   177 Si

2.Cuantas veces ha visto el programa?
   6 Una vez   127 Varias veces (72%)   44 Casi simepre

3.En una escala 1-10, 1 siendo la nota mas baja, puntue al programa:

Pobre								Sobresaliente	
1	2	3	4	5	6	7	8	9	10
(1)	(2)	(5)	(4)	(8)	(16)	(28)	(62)	(30)	(14)

4.Con cuales de los miembros del reparto se siente identificado:
   23 Dr. Heathcliff ("Cliff") Huxtable--Bill Cosby
    9 Clair Huxtable (esposa/madre/abogado)--Phylicia Ayers-Allen
   15 Sondra Huxtable (estudiante universitaria)--Sabrina LeBeauf
   33 Denise Huxtable (hija de 17 anos)--Lisa Bonet
   16 Theodore Huxtable (hijo de 14 anos)--Malcolm-Jamal Warner
    1 Vanessa Huxtable (hija de 11 anos)--Tempestt Bledsoe
   27 Rudy Huxtable (hija de 5 anos)--Keshia Knight Pulliam
   84 Ninguno (46%)

5.Cual es su personaje preferido del programa? Cliff 44, Clair 1, Denise 8,
   Theo 19, Vanessa 1, Rudy 73 (39%), Ninguno 3

6.Que episodio de la serie le ha gustado mas? Stevie Wonder

7.Dibuje un circulo entorno al numero que mejor define sus opiniones acerca
   de la siguientes preguntas:

	Si	No lo se	No
a.Los Huxtables son una familia tipica.	80 (45%)	36	61
b.Son una tipica familia Americana.	77 (44%)	50	50
c.Son una tipica familia negra.	70 (40%)	38	69 (39%)
d.Son una tipica familia rica.	76 (43%)	54	47
e.Me gustaria formar parte de su familia.	64	66	47
f.Le serie trata de lo que es ser negro.	83 (47%)	31	63

Algunos datos acerca de usted:
 8.Sexo: 79 M   98 F (53%)
 9.Raza: -
10.Edad: 21-35, 95 (52%); 36-50, 82 (48%)
11.Ocupacion (translation): nurse (4), architect, unemployed, secretary, teacher,
   journalist, psychologist, Doctor, stylist, economist (2), engineer (2), adminis-
   trative (3)
12.Cuanta television ve:
   52 Menos de 1 hora/dia   115 1-3 horas/dia (63%)   10 3+ horas/dia

Muchas gracias por su colaboracion. Si tiene algun comentario a hacer acerca de
la serie, hagalo detras de este cuestionario

                          Linda K. Fuller, Ph.D.
                          Media Dept/Worcester State College
                          Worcester, MA 01602 USA

Appendix 18
Swedish Data on *The Cosby Show*—Enkat (37 Respondents)

1.Har Du sett COSBY?
   1 Nej (GA TILL #8)   36 Ja

2.(OM JA): Hur ofta brukar Du se pa COSBY?
   3 Har sett det endast en gang
   32 Har sett flera avsnitt (89%)
   4 Har sett praktiskt taget alla avsnitt

3.Pa en skala fran 1 till 10, med 1 lagsta betyget, hur skulle Du betygsatta COSBY:
   Mindre bra   Genialt
   1   2   3   4   5   6   7   8   9   10
         (1)   (1)   (5)   (2)   (4)   (5)   (9)   (5)   (4)
4.Vilken/Vilka i familjen Cosby tycker Du bra om/kanner gemenskap med?
   26 Dr. Heathcliff ("Cliff") Huxtable--Bill Cosby
   18 Clair Huxtable (fru/mor/advokat)--Phylicia Ayers-Allen
   4 Sondra Huxtable (studentska)--Sabrina LeBeauf
   7 Denise Huxtable (17-arig dotter)--Lisa Bonet
   13 Theodore Huxtable (sonen 14 ar)--Malcolm-Jamal Warner
   4 Vanessa Huxtable (11-arig dotter)--Tempestt Bledsoe
   18 Rudy Huxtable ("minstringen," 5 ar)--Keshia Knight Pulliam
   6 Ingen

5.Vilken tycker Du bast om? Cliff 10, Clair 2, Denise 1, Theo 1, Rudy 9

6.Vilket avsnitt gillade Du bast?

7.Ange hur Du staller Dig till foljande pastaendena:
                                               Instammer Ingen asikt Haller inte med
   a.Familjen Huxtable ar en helt vanlig familj.   5   1   30 (83%)
   b.De ar en typisk amerikansk familj.   2   8   26 (72%)
   c.De ar en typisk svart familj.   1   6   29 (81%)
   d.De ar en typisk formogen familj.   17 (47%)   7   12
   e. Jag skulle vilja vara medlem i den familjen.   11   7   18 (50%)
   f.Programmet handlar om dur det ar att vara svart. -   1   35 (97%)

Litet om Dig:
   8.Kon: 16 Man   21 Kvinna (57%)
   9.Ras/harkomst: Vit 100%
   10.Alder: 11-21, 3; 21-35, 27 (73%); 36-50, 6; 51-65, 1
   11.Yrke (translation): teacher (2), student (14), nurse, editor assistant, boss,
      secretary (4), computer operator, receptionist (8), sociologist, researcher (2),
      economist, research assistant
   12.TV-vanor: Tittar Du pa TV:
      21 Mindre an 1 timme om dagen (57%)
      16 1-3 timmar om dagen
      - mer an 3 timmar om dagen

Appendix 19
Cosby Ailesi—Uzerine Anket (Turkish translation)

1.COSBY ailesi filmlerini gordunuz mu?
___Hayir (Cevap hayirsa 8 soruya geciniz)   ___Evet

2.Evetse, filmleri ne kadar siklikla gordunuz?
___Yalniz bir kez   ___Pek cok kez   ___Pevamli clarak

3.1 den 10 a kadar siralayarak, filmi nasil degerlendirirsiniz?
Hic iyi degil   Mukemmel
       1   2   3   4   5   6   7   8   9   10

4.Filmdeki oyuncular arasinda hangisiyle ozdeslesiyorsunuz? Hangisini
   kendinize yakin hissediyorsunuz?
   ___Dr. Heathcliff ("Cliff") Huxtable--Bill Cosby
   ___Clair Huxtable (es/anne/avukat)--Phylicia Ayers-Allen
   ___Sondra Huxtable (universite ogrencisi)--Sabrina LeBeauf
   ___Denise Huxtable (17 yasindaki kizlari)--Lisa Bonet
   ___Theodore Huxtable (tek ogul,14 yasinda)--Malcolm-Jamal Warner
   ___Vanessa Huxtable (11 yasindaki kizlari)--Tempestt Bledsoe
   ___Rudy Huxtable (en kucuk kiz, 5 yasinda)--Keshia Knight Pulliam
   ___Hicbiri

5.COSBY Ailesi filmlerinde hangi karateri tutuyoreanuz?_____

6.COSBY Ailesi filmlerinde oyunlardan hangisini tuttunuz?_____

7.Asagidaki cumelerde yer alan onermeler hakkindaki goruslerinizi daire
   icine aliniz:

	Evet	Fikrim Yok	Hayir
a.Huxtable ailesi tipik bir ailedir.	1	2	3
b.Huxtable ailesi tipik bir Amerikan eilesidir.	1	2	3
c.Huxtable ailesi tipik bir zenci ailesidir.	1	2	3
d.Huxtable ailesi tipik bir zengin ailedir.	1	2	3
e.O aileden olmak isterdim.	1	2	3
f.Show zenciler hakkindadir.	1	2	3

Sizin hakkinizda belgiler:
  8.Cinsiyet: ___Kadin   ___Erkek
  9.Irk:
 10.Yas:
 11.Meslek:
 12.Ne kadar televizyon izlersiniz:
    ___Gunde 1 saatten az   ___Gunde 1-3 saat kadar   ___Gunde 3 saatten fazla

   Tesekkur ederim. Lutfen Cosby Ailesi filmleri hakkindaki dusuncelerinizi
eklemekten cekinmeyiniz.

                              Linda K. Fuller, Ph.D.
                              Media Dept/Worcester State College
                              Worcester, MA 01602 USA

Appendix 20
United Kingdom Data on *The Cosby Show* Survey—13 Black Respondents

1.Have you seen THE COSBY SHOW?
   0 No (skip to #8)   13 Yes

2.If yes, how often have you seen the show?
   0 Only once   7 Several times   6 Regularly

3.On a scale from 1-10, 1 being the lowest, circle your rating of it.
   Not very good   Excellent
        1   2   3   4   5   6   7   8   9   10
                                        (2)   (2)   (3)   (2)   (4)

4.Which member(s) of the cast do you identify with/relate to:
   7 Dr. Heathcliff ("Cliff") Huxtable--Bill Cosby
   3 Clair Huxtable (wife/mother/lawyer)--Phylicia Ayers-Allen
   0 Sondra Huxtable (college student)--Sabrina LeBeauf
   1 Denise Huxtable (17-year old daughter)--Lisa Bonet
   3 Theodore Huxtable (only son, aged 14)--Malcolm-Jamal Warner
   1 Vanessa Huxtable (11-year old daughter)--Tempestt Bledsoe
   4 Rudy Huxtable(youngest daughter, age 5)--Keshia Knight Pulliam
   1 None

5.Which character on THE COSBY SHOW is your favorite? Cliff 6, Theo 2,
   Vanessa 1, Rudy 2
6.Which episode on THE COSBY SHOW was your favorite? Theo's shirt made
   by his sister (2), 25th anniversary, prize awarded to best doctor, car
   purchase
7.Circle your opinions on the following issues:

	Agree	No opinion	Disagree
a.The Huxtables are a typical family.	4	3	6 (46%)
b.They are a typical American family.	3	6 (46%)	4
c.They are a typical black family.	0	8 (62%)	5
d.They are a typical wealthy family.	3	6 (46%)	4
e.I'd like to be in their family.	4	5	4
f.The show is about being black.	2	7 (54%)	4

Some information about you:
   8.Sex: 9 Male (69%)   4 Female
   9.Race: 100% Black
   10.Age: 11-20, 2; 21-35, 10 (77%); 51-66, 1
   11.Occupation: accountant, dress maker, lecturer, researcher, student (3),
      teacher, trainee accountant
   12.How much television do you watch:
        2 Less than 1 hour/day   7 1-3 hours/day   4 3+ hours/day

Thank you very much. Please feel free to add any comments about
THE COSBY SHOW.

                                    Linda K. Fuller, Ph.D.
                                    Media Dept/Worcester State College
                                    Worcester, MA 01602 USA

Appendix 21
United States Data on *The Cosby Show* Survey—116 Sixth Graders

1.Have you seen THE COSBY SHOW?
   1 No (skip to #8)   115 Yes

2.If yes, how often have you seen the show?
   3 Only once   19 Several times   92 Regularly (80%)

3.On a scale from 1-10, 1 being the lowest, circle your rating of it.
   Not very good   Excellent
      1   2   3   4   5   6   7   8   9   10
                                             (3)   (15)   (12)   (14)   (71)
4.Which member(s) of the cast do you identify with/relate to:
   27 Dr. Heathcliff ("Cliff") Huxtable--Bill Cosby
   17 Clair Huxtable (wife/mother/lawyer)--Phylicia Ayers-Allen
   13 Sondra Huxtable (college student)--Sabrina LeBeauf
   33 Denise Huxtable (17-year old daughter)--Lisa Bonet
   46 Theodore Huxtable (only son, aged 14)--Malcolm-Jamal Warner
   44 Vanessa Huxtable (11-year old daughter)--Tempestt Bledsoe
   33 Rudy Huxtable(youngest daughter, age 5)--Keshia Knight Pulliam
    8 None

5.Which character on THE COSBY SHOW is your favorite? Cliff 24, Clair 2,
   Denise 7, Theo 20, Vanessa 4, Rudy 53, All 3, None 3
6.Which episode on THE COSBY SHOW was your favorite? dentist (10), Rudy
   plays football (6), Theo/real world (20), Rudy's birthday party, Hallowe'en
   (9), grandparents' anniversary (7), sleepover (4), teacher for dinner, first
   day of school, Denise deciding college, the first one, Thanksgiving
7.Circle your opinions on the following issues:

	Agree	No opinion	Disagree
a.The Huxtables are a typical family.	72 (62%)	16	26
b.They are a typical American family.	80 (69%)	22	12
c.They are a typical black family.	16	58 (50%)	39
d.They are a typical wealthy family.	40	47	27
e.I'd like to be in their family.	66 (57%)	34	13
f.The show is about being black.	1	8	106 (91%)

Some information about you:
   8.Sex: 46 Male   70 Female (60%)
   9.Race: white 113 (97%), Black 2, Indian 1
  10.Age: 11-20, all
  11.Occupation: students
  12.How much television do you watch:
         14 Less than 1 hour/day   63 1-3 hours/day (54%)   39 3+ hours/day

   Thank you very much. Please feel free to add any comments about
THE COSBY SHOW.

                                    Linda K. Fuller, Ph.D.
                                    Media Dept/Worcester State College
                                    Worcester, MA 01602 USA

Appendix 22
United States Data on *The Cosby Show* Survey—28 Florida Retirees

1.Have you seen THE COSBY SHOW?
   2 No (skip to #8)   26 Yes

2.If yes, how often have you seen the show?
   0 Only once   18 Several times (64%)   8 Regularly

3.On a scale from 1-10, 1 being the lowest, circle your rating of it.
   Not very good   Excellent
   1   2   3   4   5   6   7   8   9   10
                                    (1)   (2)   (6)   (4)   (13)

4.Which member(s) of the cast do you identify with/relate to:
   14 Dr. Heathcliff ("Cliff") Huxtable--Bill Cosby
   12 Clair Huxtable (wife/mother/lawyer)--Phylicia Ayers-Allen
    1 Sondra Huxtable (college student)--Sabrina LeBeauf
    3 Denise Huxtable (17-year old daughter)--Lisa Bonet
    3 Theodore Huxtable (only son, aged 14)--Malcolm-Jamal Warner
    2 Vanessa Huxtable (11-year old daughter)--Tempestt Bledsoe
    2 Rudy Huxtable(youngest daughter, age 5)--Keshia Knight Pulliam
    3 None

5.Which character on THE COSBY SHOW is your favorite? Cliff 17, Clair 4,
   Sondra 1, Theo 1, Rudy 2, All 1
6.Which episode on THE COSBY SHOW was your favorite? card game (2), Theo
   growing mustache, teaching responsibility, Clair broke her foot (2), Rudy
   playing football, grandparents' anniversary (2), Theo--real world, Sondra's
   friend doing research project
7.Circle your opinions on the following issues:

	Agree	No opinion	Disagree
a.The Huxtables are a typical family.	7	3	16 (62%)
b.They are a typical American family.	10	2	14 (54%)
c.They are a typical black family.	2	4	19 (73%)
d.They are a typical wealthy family.	8	4	11 (42%)
e.I'd like to be in their family.	7	8	8
f.The show is about being black.	3	3	18 (69%)

Some information about you:
   8.Sex: 10 Male   18 Female (64%)
   9.Race: white 24 (86%), Black 4
  10.Age: 21-35, 3; 36-50, 6; 51-66, 6; 66+, 13 (46%)
  11.Occupation: professional 2, retired 18 (64%), clerk 6, laborer 2
  12.How much television do you watch:
     4 Less than 1 hour/day   13 1-3 hours/day (54%)   11 3+ hours/day

   Thank you very much. Please feel free to add any comments about
THE COSBY SHOW.

                              Linda K. Fuller, Ph.D.
                              Media Dept/Worcester State College
                              Worcester, MA 01602 USA

Appendix 23
United States Data on *The Cosby Show* Survey—48 Members of California Health Clubs

1.Have you seen THE COSBY SHOW?
   7 No (skip to #8)   41 Yes

2.If yes, how often have you seen the show?
      3 Only once   22 Several times (54%)   16 Regularly

3.On a scale from 1-10, 1 being the lowest, circle your rating of it.
   Not very good   Excellent

1	2	3	4	5	6	7	8	9	10
					(1)	(6)	(13)	(7)	(13)

4.Which member(s) of the cast do you identify with/relate to:
   17 Dr. Heathcliff ("Cliff") Huxtable--Bill Cosby
   14 Clair Huxtable (wife/mother/lawyer)--Phylicia Ayers-Allen
    7 Sondra Huxtable (college student)--Sabrina LeBeauf
    8 Denise Huxtable (17-year old daughter)--Lisa Bonet
   11 Theodore Huxtable (only son, aged 14)--Malcolm-Jamal Warner
    4 Vanessa Huxtable (11-year old daughter)--Tempestt Bledsoe
    7 Rudy Huxtable(youngest daughter, age 5)--Keshia Knight Pulliam
   11 None

5.Which character on THE COSBY SHOW is your favorite? Cliff 17, Clair 4,
   Sondra 1, Theo 1, Rudy 2, All 1
6.Which episode on THE COSBY SHOW was your favorite? Rudy broke Cliff's
   juicer, Theo's math teacher came to dinner, Cosby's father plays the horn,
   grandparents' anniversary (3), Thanksgiving, Theo--real world (2), Cliff
   playing cards vs father, Clair's broken ankle, art gallery, Denise's car
7.Circle your opinions on the following issues:

	Agree	No opinion	Disagree
a.The Huxtables are a typical family.	10	5	25 (52%)
b.They are a typical American family.	8	4	28 (58%)
c.They are a typical black family.	2	9	27 (56%)
d.They are a typical wealthy family.	9	9	20 (42%)
e.I'd like to be in their family.	17 (35%)	10	11
f.The show is about being black.	1	2	38 (79%)

Some information about you:
  8.Sex: 23 Male   25 Female
  9.Race: white 43 (90%), Black 1, Asian 4
10.Age: 11-20, 13; 21-35, 25 (52%); 36-50, 7; 51-66, 3
11.Occupation: student (7), professional (12), white collar, blue collar (7),
   clerk (9)
12.How much television do you watch:
      18 Less than 1 hour/day   28 1-3 hours/day (54%)   2 3+ hours/day

   Thank you very much. Please feel free to add any comments about
THE COSBY SHOW.

                                        Linda K. Fuller, Ph.D.
                                        Media Dept/Worcester State College
                                        Worcester, MA 01602 USA

Appendix 24
West Indian Data on *The Cosby Show* Survey—21 Respondents

1.Have you seen THE COSBY SHOW?
  1 No (skip to #8) 20 Yes

2.If yes, how often have you seen the show?
  0 Only once 10 Several times 11 Regularly

3.On a scale from 1-10, 1 being the lowest, circle your rating of it.
  Not very good   Excellent
    1   2   3   4   5   6   7   8   9   10
            (1) (1)   (2)   (4) (9) (4)
4.Which member(s) of the cast do you identify with/relate to:
  7 Dr. Heathcliff ("Cliff") Huxtable--Bill Cosby
  7 Clair Huxtable (wife/mother/lawyer)--Phylicia Ayers-Allen
  1 Sondra Huxtable (college student)--Sabrina LeBeauf
  2 Denise Huxtable (17-year old daughter)--Lisa Bonet
  5 Theodore Huxtable (only son, aged 14)--Malcolm-Jamal Warner
  2 Vanessa Huxtable (11-year old daughter)--Tempestt Bledsoe
  4 Rudy Huxtable(youngest daughter, age 5)--Keshia Knight Pulliam
  4 None

5.Which character on THE COSBY SHOW is your favorite? Cliff 6, Clair 2,
  Theo 5, Vanessa 3, Rudy 3, All 1
6.Which episode on THE COSBY SHOW was your favorite? grandparents' anniversary (4), "reviews of past" with family", old lady diabetic with pills,
  Rudy's favorite musical instrument, Theo and his bag of gags, when Theo
  tried to hide his pierced ear from his father, Rudy's story
7.Circle your opinions on the following issues:

	Agree	No opinion	Disagree
a.The Huxtables are a typical family.	12 (60%)	2	6
b.They are a typical American family.	6	6	8
c.They are a typical black family.	4	5	11 (55%)
d.They are a typical wealthy family.	3	7	10 (50%)
e.I'd like to be in their family.	7	5	8
f.The show is about being black.	2	3	15 (75%)

Some information about you:
  8.Sex: 7 Male 14 Female (66%)
  9.Race: white 1, Black 20 (95%)
  10.Age: -11, 2; 11-20, 4; 21-35, 9 (43%); 36-50, 5; 51-65, 1
  11.Occupation: student (4), civil servant (3), teacher (2), adminstrator (3),
    nurse, secretary, researcher (2), clerk/typist (2), social worker, sales
  12.How much television do you watch:
    3 Less than 1 hour/day 15 1-3 hours/day (71%) 3 3+ hours/day

  Thank you very much. Please feel free to add any comments about
THE COSBY SHOW.

                                   Linda K. Fuller, Ph.D.
                                   Media Dept/Worcester State College
                                   Worcester, MA 01602 USA

Notes

PREFACE

1. Linda K. Fuller, "Marketing a Star to and Through the Media: The Cosby Case," Paper presented at the Popular Culture Association annual meeting at Atlanta, Georgia, 1986.

2. Andy Rooney, *60 Minutes* (January 24, 1988).

3. Linda K. Fuller, "Audience Appeal of *The Cosby Show*: How It Cuts Across Cultural and Demographic Boundaries," Workshop for Communication, Culture, and Socialism Conference at Carlton University, Ottawa, Canada, 1988.

4. Jack Solomon, *The Signs of Our Times* (Los Angeles: J. P. Tarcher, 1988), cited in a *Los Angeles Times* newswire story written by Connie Koenenn: "Hidden Message Revealed," which appeared in the (Springfield, Massachusetts) *Union-News* on December 24, 1988, p. 16.

5. Also of note is Volume 8 (1987), Number 1, of *Communication Research Trends*, which is devoted entirely to the topic of "Television as Myth and Ritual."

6. Linda K. Fuller, "Research on Ritualistic Television-Viewing: The Loyal Audience of *The Cosby Show* Worldwide," Paper presented at the Audience Measurement Workshop of the International Association of Mass Communication Research (IAMCR) Conference and XVIth General Assembly, Barcelona, Spain, July 1988.

7. Barthes's *Mythologies* was written between 1954 and 1956, and translated into English in 1972.

8. Michael McWilliams, "Cos Celebre," *Rolling Stone* (December 18, 1986–January 1, 1987), p. 130.

9. See William Safire, "People of Color," *New York Times Magazine* (November 20, 1988), p. 18 +.

10. Alvin F. Poussaint, MD, personal correspondence, February 6, 1989.

11. Linda K. Fuller, "Systems-Theoretical Aspects of Popular Culture and Mass Communication," in Ray B. Browne and Marshall W. Fishwick, eds., *Symbiosis: Popular*

Culture and Other Fields (Bowling Green, Ohio: Bowling Green State University Popular Press, 1988), pp. 137–145.

CHAPTER 1: BACKGROUND OF *THE COSBY SHOW* PHENOMENON

1. Interview with Richard Zoglin, "Cosby, Inc.," *Time* (September 28, 1987), p. 59.

2. Monica Collins, "Cover Story: Time Flies While Cosby, 50, Has Fun," *USA Today* (August 31, 1987), p. 2A.

3. Roderick Townley, "Television...Makes Us See One Another," Interview with Ralph Ellison, *TV Guide* (April 23, 1988), p. 4.

4. Brian Winston, "Cosby's New Show: A Hit and a Myth," *Channels of Communication* (January–February 1985), p. 63.

5. See Robert C. Toll, *The Entertainment Machine: American Show Business in the Twentieth Century* (London: Oxford University Press, 1982), pp. 54–55; Gayle Pollard, "From Amos 'n' Andy to Bill Cosby," *Boston Globe* (October 17, 1981); Arnold Shankman, "Black Pride and Protest: The Amos 'n' Andy Crusade," *Journal of Popular Culture* (Fall 1978), pp. 236–52; and Melvin Patrick Ely, *The Adventures of Amos 'n' Andy: A Social History of an American Phenomenon* (New York: Free Press, 1991).

6. Martha Bayles, "The Fall of the House of Huxtable," *Wall Street Journal* (April 18, 1988), p. 22.

7. Quoted in Leslie Bennetts, "Bill Cosby Begins Taping NBC Series," *New York Times* (August 6, 1984), p. C20.

8. Elizabeth Kastor, "They Love Cosby in Washington," *The Morning Union* (September 30, 1987), p. 18.

9. See David Marc, *Comic Visions: Television Comedy and American Culture* (Boston: Unwin Hyman, 1989); Percy H. Tannenbaum, ed., *The Entertainment Functions of Television* (Hillsdale, N.J.: Lawrence Erlbaum Associates, 1980); Hal Himmelstein, *Television Myth and the American Mind* (New York: Praeger, 1984), pp. 75–119.

10. "Marketing," *Wall Street Journal* (February 19, 1988). See also Alan Dodds Frank, "When Smoke Gets in Your Eyes," *Forbes* (May 5, 1986), p. 135, about the cigar industry's using positive role models like Bill Cosby. The quotation is from Ronald Alsop, "In TV Viewers' Favorite 1987 Ads, Offbeat Characters Were the Stars," *Wall Street Journal* (March 3, 1988), p. 19.

11. Werner stated this at a seminar, "*The Cosby Show*: An Inside Look," held on September 20, 1989, at the Museum of Broadcasting.

12. Quoted in Donna Britt-Gibson, "Cover Story: The Cos, Family Man for the '80s," *USA Today* (December 23, 1986), p. 2D.

13. Quoted in Alex Haley, "Talking with Cosby," *Ladies Home Journal* (June 1985), p. 32.

14. Horst Stipp, Director, Social and Development Research, NBC—personal conversation, February 23, 1990.

15. Peter Roth, president of Stephen J. Cannell Productions, Inc., on a panel for the IRTS faculty/industry in New York on program development commented on February 8, 1991, that "8 o'clock has an illusive appeal to children."

16. Muriel Cantor has written in *Prime Time TV: Content and Control* (Beverly Hills, Calif.: Sage, 1980), p. 29, that she considers radio's *Amos 'n' Andy* the first

nationally broadcast drama. She is currently at work on a project comparing domestic series to soap operas, which she discusses in a footnote to her article "The American Family on Television: From Molly Goldberg to Bill Cosby," *Journal of Comparative Family Studies* 32, no. 2 (Summer 1991), p. 205:

Since 1929 when "The Rise of the Goldbergs" first came to NBC radio, there have been two types of family shows which have persisted through the decades: episodic domestic series, the subject of this article, and serials (known as soap operas). These two types of family shows have several qualities in common but usually present diametrically opposed values and ideologies about love, marriage, and sex. Both feature both kinship relationships and family conflicts but the domestic series essentially reflect the traditional values as embodied in the Ten Command- ments while the soap operas present a mixed message. In the soap operas "sinful" acts occur frequently and although acts such as murder, adultery, rape and excessive greed may be punished, they also may be treated benignly or even favorably.

I am grateful to Professor Cantor for sharing a copy of this article with me.

17. "NBC Wins 27 of 30 in Prime Time Final Stats," *Broadcasting* (April 27, 1987), p. 54.

18. Melvin Rothstein, "Brooklyn Finds 'Cosby Show' Good for Business—and Gos- sip," *New York Times* (April 28, 1985), p. 44.

19. Philip H. Dougherty, "Cosby Rerun Ad Time Is Sold for $60 Million," *New York Times* (September 24, 1987), p. C28.

20. Elizabeth Sporkin, "Man's New Uniform: Bold, Bright Knits," *USA Today* (January 23, 1987), p. D–1.

CHAPTER 2: THE ECONOMICS OF *THE COSBY SHOW*

1. Todd Klein, "Bill Cosby: Prime Time's Favorite Father," *Saturday Evening Post* (April 1986), p. 42.

2. See Richard Zoglin, "A Giant Leap to No. 2: Programmer Brandon Tartikoff Leads NBC Out of the Cellar," *Time* (December 3, 1984), p. 74; Bill Carter, "The Man Who Owns Prime Time: NBC's Brandon Tartikoff," *New York Times Magazine* (March 4, 1990), p. 23+.

3. Quoted in Martha Bayles, "Television: The Problem with Post-Racism," *New Republic* (August 5, 1985), p. 25.

4. Vera Wells, director, Corporate Relations and Audience Services, NBC—tele- phone conversation, April 17, 1990.

5. Special thanks to James B. Poteat, manager of Research Services for the Tele- vision Information Center.

6. Special thanks to Kim Palanky of the Media Communications Division of A. C. Nielsen.

7. Lisa Belkin, "First Week of 'People Meters,' " *New York Times* (September 24, 1987), p. C28.

8. Quoted in Andrea Gabor, "Television's Tyranny of Numbers," *US News & World Report* (September 8, 1986), p. 46.

9. Brian Donlon, " 'Cosby,' the Star of NBC's Stellar Year," *USA Today* (April 23, 1986), p. 1D.

10. "Sitcoms in Syndication: Too Much of a Good Thing?" *Broadcasting* (May 29, 1989), p. 49.

11. "Black Viewers Turn to NBC," *Channels of Communication* (November 1987), p. 64. See also Clint C. Wilson II and Felix Gutierrez, *Minorities and Media: Diversity and the End of Mass Communication* (Beverly Hills, Calif.: Sage Publications, 1985), pp. 121–26, on "Advertisers' Courtship of Spanish Gold and the Black Market."

12. "Running the Numbers: Mouth-Eye Coordination," *Channels of Communication* (March 1987), p. 64.

13. Eileen Prescott, "The Networks Fight Back, Finally," *New York Times* (March 5, 1989), p. F4.

14. "Carsey-Werner Wants NBC to Foot Bill for 'Cosby' Show," *Broadcasting* (March 26, 1990), p. 41.

15. Ibid.

16. Thomas P. Vitale, "They Call Themselves 'The Cosby Team,' " *Viacomments* (Fall, 1987).

17. John Flinn, "There's 'Cosby' and 'Boss,' and Then Everybody Else," *Channels of Communication* (Field Guide, 1988), p. 75.

18. John Flinn, "Local Stations: Laughing All the Way to the News," *Channels of Communication* (April 1988), p. 9. The "halo effect" regarding other proximate shows is discussed in Mark N. Vamos, "Cosby Could Stuff $500 Million More in Viacom's Pocket," *Business Week* (November 10, 1986), p. 43.

19. "Viacom Enterprises Announces Plans to Bid the Cosby Barter Minute" (January 27, 1988)—press release.

20. This explanation was given by Scott Kolber, Viacom's director of market strategy, in Vitale, p. 19.

21. Betsy Vorce, vice president of public relations, Viacom International's Entertainment Group—telephone conversation, February 21, 1989.

22. " 'Cosby' Barter Minutes Go to P&G, GF, Group W," *Broadcasting* (May 9, 1988).

23. "Zaleski: Times Are a' Changin': Syndication Is a Whole New Ball Game, Says Viacom Chief," *Television/Radio Age* (September 14, 1987), p. 49.

24. "Viacom, Clients Playing Handball over 'Cosby,' " *Broadcasting* (November 13, 1989), p. 40.

25. Quoted in Richard Behar, "Bill Cosby Versus Bill Cosby," *Forbes* (November 14, 1988), p. 45.

26. Personal interview with Arthur Kananack, president of International Theatrical & Video Sales, Viacom Pictures, Inc., February 8, 1991.

CHAPTER 3: THE POLITICS AND LEGALITIES OF
THE COSBY SHOW

1. Letter from Joella West, Counsel, Law Offices of Stuart I. Glickman, February 8, 1988.

2. Letter from Kim Tinsely, director of public affairs, *The Cosby Show*, March 2, 1987.

3. Quoted in Laura Landro, Paul Duke, Jr., and William Power, "Same Old Story: NBC Wins Suit with Hwesu S. Murray over 'Cosby' idea," *Wall Street Journal* (July 29, 1987), p. 21. See also "Lawsuit over 'Cosby' Idea," *New York Times* (May 20, 1988), p. 22.

4. Kathleen Teltsch, "Blacks' Charities Struggle to Meet Cosby Challenge," *New York*

Times (January 15, 1989), p. 1. See also Penny Pagano, "FBI Enlists Bill Cosby in Search for Missing Kids," *Los Angeles Times* (June 12, 1985), p. V1–1.

5. Larry Kettelkamp, *Bill Cosby: Family Funny Man* (New York: Wanderer Books, 1987), p. 88.

6. Peter W. Barnes, " 'Cosby' Producers File Suit to Protect Profits on Reruns," *Wall Street Journal* (March 13, 1987), p. 7. See also David Crook, " 'Cosby' Producers Seek to Halt Viacom Buyout," *Los Angeles Times* (May 20, 1987), p. 1V–2.

7. "Federal Judge Denies Move to Block Sale of Viacom," *Wall Street Journal* (June 3, 1987), p. 22.

8. Telephone conversation with Hillary Condit of Viacom's Corporate Relations office, March 7, 1989.

CHAPTER 4: PRODUCTION OF *THE COSBY SHOW*

1. "The Huxtable Family" is profiled in M. J. Edrei, ed., *The Cosby Scrapbook: America's Favorite T.V. Family* (Teaneck, N.J.: Sharon Publications, 1986). It is updated in Tim Brooks and Earle Marsh, *The Complete Directory of Prime Time Network TV Shows, 1946–Present*, 4th ed. (New York: Ballantine Books, 1988).

2. Quoted in Wayne Walley, "Carsey-Werner: Cosby's Co-pilots Stay Small and Lean," *Advertising Age* (June 16, 1986), p. 38.

3. Richard W. Stevenson, " 'Cosby' Producers Strike It Rich," *New York Times* (December 23, 1988), p. D1.

4. Walley, "Carsey-Werner," pp. 38–40. There is also a profile of Caryn Mandalbach in Deborah Mason, "The Woman Behind Cosby," *Vogue* (September 1987), p. 206.

5. John W. Ravage, *Television: The Director's Viewpoint* (Boulder, Colo.: Westview Press, 1978), p. 5.

6. "Conversation with Jay Sandrich," *Videography* (Fall 1986), p. 62.

7. Ibid., p. 69.

8. Christopher Kenneally, "Bill Cosby Agrees with This Doctor," *Brookline Citizen* (April 25, 1985), p. 9.

9. Judy Gillespie, "The Cosby Show's Secret Ingredient," *Family Circle* (November 5, 1985), p. 88.

10. Sara Terry, "The Conscience of 'The Cosby Show,' " *Christian Science Monitor* (February 12, 1987), p. 1.

11. " 'The Cosby Show' and Poussaint: A Winning Team," *Children's Today* (Boston: Children's Hospital, April 1985), p. 3.

12. Telephone conversation with Dr. Alvin F. Poussaint, April 7, 1988.

13. Quoted in Larry Kettelkamp, *Bill Cosby: Family Funny Man* (New York: Wanderer Books, 1987), p. 87.

14. Quoted in James McBride, "Cosby: The Secret Passions of TV's Biggest Star," *US* (October 21, 1985), p. 25.

15. Frank Lovece, " 'Cosby' and Black Artists: Is Exposure Enough?" *Channels of Communication* (May 1988), p. 17. The issue here is that, although *Cosby* features work by Black artists, the show has a "no-credit policy" such that the artists' names are not listed.

16. Robert Pekurny, "The Production Process and Environment of NBC's 'Saturday Night Live,' " *Journal of Broadcasting* 24 (Winter 1980), p. 90, mentions this fact, listing only one other study: James E. Lynch, "Seven Days with 'All in the Family,' "

Journal of Broadcasting 17 (Summer 1973), pp. 259–74. I would also add: Michael J. Porter, "A Comparative Analysis of Directing Styles in 'Hill Street Blues,' " *Journal of Broadcasting & Electronic Media* 31 (Summer 1987), pp. 323–34.

CHAPTER 5: AUDIENCES FOR *THE COSBY SHOW*

1. Acknowledgment is given to the following persons and organizations for their participation in *The Cosby Show* survey: John Sinclair, senior lecturer in the Sociology Cultural Studies Unit of Footscray Institute of Technology in Melbourne, *Australia*, who administered the questionnaire to thirty-five of his undergraduate students in October 1988—see Appendix 7; Ms. Cora E. Bain, "With the Compliments of the Women's Affairs Unit, Ministry of Youth, Sports and Community Affairs," for seventeen respondents from the *Bahamas*—see Appendix 8; Markku Henriksson, co-director for North American Studies at the University of Helsinki's Institute for Historical and Documentation in *Finland*, for "some results of a small investigation about the Cosby Show among a group of first and second year college students"—eighteen participants from September 1988 documented in Appendix 9; Frida Navti of Cameroon and French teachers Jennie Celona and Gail Speer for French translations of the survey (see Appendix 10), then responses thanks to Dr. Morton Giersing, chief of Unesco's Division of Communication Development and Free Flow of Information in *France*; from *Germany*: Ursula Rommerskirchen, vice consul of the Generalkonsulat der Bundesrepublik Deutschland, for information that *The Cosby Show* is called Familienbande, and is shown by the Zweites Deutches Fernsehen (ZDF) in Mainz, Dr. Hans Mathias Kepplinger, "universitatprofessor" at the Institut für Publizistik at Johannes Gutenberg-Universitat Mainz, and especially to Professor Dr. Peter Winterhoff-Spurk, Fachrichtung Psychologie at Universitat des Saarlandes, whose thirty-two students' survey responses from spring 1990 are available in Appendix 11; Marieke de Bruyne and her family for data from the *Netherlands*—a neighborhood outside of Amsterdam, including some Belgian respondents (see Appendix 15); from *South Africa*—Keyan Tomaselli, director of the Contemporary Cultural Studies Unit at the University of Natal, Durban, for not only arranging for forty-nine South African respondents (see Appendix 16), but also for proofreading this section on South Africa while he was a guest at my home in October 1989. Also, Dr. D. P. Van Vuuren and Dr. Aliza Duby of the South African Broadcasting Corporation in Johannesburg; Joy Morrison, a white South African studying at the University of Iowa; and Elirei Bornman of the Human Sciences Research Council in Pretoria; from *Spain*: Alex Muns, who got forty-eight people in his Barcelona neighborhood to complete the survey in 1986, and Macu Alvarez of the Facultad de Ciencias de la Informacion, Universidad del Pais Vasco in Bilbao, who administered the questionnaire to 183 of her students (see Appendix 17); Charly Hulten of the Audience and Programme Research Division of Sveriges Radio AB in Stockholm, *Sweden*—who not only supplied data on *The Cosby Show* on Swedish Television, but also put me in touch with Hedvig Ekerwald of the Sociology Department at the University of Uppsala, whose students gathered data from thirty-seven "friends or housemates" (see Appendix 18), as well as Swedish free-lance writer Anna Wahlgren; Professor Dr. Oya Tokgoz, director of the School of Journalism and Broadcasting at Ankara University in *Turkey*, who conducted 118 interviews during November–December 1988 (see Appendix 19); Musa Mohammed, a Nigerian Ph.D. candidate at the University of Leicester in the *United Kingdom*, who arranged for thirteen Blacks in

London, Manchester, and Leicester to participate in the survey (see Appendix 20). In addition, Barrie Gunter, head of Research for Britain's Independent Broadcasting Authority, Shehina Fazal, also of the IBA, and Dr. Graham Mytton, head of International Broadcasting and Audience Research for the BBC, all sent pertinent data on *The Cosby Show* in England. Target markets in the *United States* came through three diverse sources: (1) questionnaires to the sixth grade classes of Barbara Blinn in Longmeadow, Massachusetts, to gather data from 116 affluent schoolchildren in 1986 (see Appendix 21); (2) Miriam Keating, a retired school psychologist now residing at "Leisureville" in Boynton Beach, Florida, distributed the survey among twenty-eight senior citizens (see Appendix 22); and (3) Paige Harrigan obtained responses from forty-eight participants at the Sherman Oaks, California, Health Club (see Appendix 23). Finally, the section on the *West Indies* incorporates survey responses from Barbados (St. Michael, St. George), with thanks to D. O. Kellman, director of the Bureau of Women's Affairs at the Ministry of Employment, Labour Relations and Community Development, St. Michael; Jeanie McDonald, St. Vincent; Dr. Stuart H. Surlin, Department of Communication Studies, University of Windsor, Ontario, Canada; and Joan Williams, director of the Bureau of Women's Affairs, Ministry of Employment, Labour Relations and Community Development, Barbados; Tina M. Spiro of Kingston, Jamaica; and R. Reddock, Institute of Social and Economic Research, University of West Indies, Trinidad— see Appendix 24 for data on the twenty-one West Indian respondents.

2. This point was made in a paper combining data on *The Cosby Show* in the West Indies and the Bahamas, presented as "COSBY in the Caribbean" at the Seventh Annual Intercultural and International Communication Conference in February 1990 in Miami, Florida.

3. Acknowledgment is given to the following persons and organizations for their participation in the overall study of *The Cosby Show:* CTV Television Network, Ltd., in Toronto, *Canada*; Niels-Aage Nielsen, Media Research, Danmarks Radio (*Denmark*); Kostas Valetas, program director of Hellenic Radio-Television in Athens, *Greece*, and Andy Haidis for the translation that appears in Appendix 12; Keith K. Fuller, for a translation of the survey into *Indonesian* (Appendix 13); Robert K. Gahan, assistant director general of Radio Telefis Eireann, Dublin, *Ireland*; Sal Venturini, for a translation of the survey into *Italian*, as well as Rev. Msgr. Pierfranco Pastore, Pontificio Consiglio of the Delle Comunicazioni Sociali at the Vatican; from *Japan*: William May of the Kyoto News Service, Kazuto Kojima of the Institute of Journalism and Communication Studies at the University of Tokyo, and Professor Youichi Ito at the Institute for Communications Research at Keio University, Tokyo; Haji Ilias Haji Zaidi, head of the School of Mass Communication at the Mara Institute of Technology in Selangor, *Malaysia*, as well as Brajesh Bhatia of the Asia-Pacific Institute for Broadcasting Development in Kuala Lumpur; A. J. Ellul, chief executive of the *Malta* Broadcasting Authority; Santiago Cavazos Roel of Monterrey, *Mexico*, and Pablo Casares, general secretary of CONEICC; Ellen M. Almaas of the "Light Entertainment Department, Television," division of Norsky Rikskringkasting, Norwegian Broadcasting Corporation in Oslo, *Norway*; Professor Dr. Walery Pisarek, director of Osrodek Badan Prasoznawczych press research center in Krakow, *Poland*, and Sergiusz Mikulicz, director of Polski Radio I Telewizja in Warsaw; and Lim Heng Tow, head of Public Relations for the *Singapore* Broadcasting Authority.

4. Quoted in Ben Brown and Eric Marsden, "Cosby Cheers S. Africa Family," *USA Today* (August 29, 1985), p. 1.

5. Daan P. Van Vuuren, "Children's Perception of and Identification with the Social Reality of 'The Cosby Show': A Comparison Between the USA and South Africa," Draft paper, p. 3.

6. "The Cosby Sanction," *New Republic* (August 25, 1986), p. 7.

CHAPTER 6: KUDOS AND CRITICISM FOR
THE COSBY SHOW

1. Quoted in Monica Collins, "Cover Story: Time Flies While Cosby, 50, Has Fun," *USA Today* (August 31, 1987), p. 2A.

2. Lynn Norment, "The Cosby Show: The Real-Life Drama Behind Hit TV Show About a Black Family," *Ebony* (April 1985), p. 29.

3. Quoted in Collins, "Cover Story," p. 4D.

4. The reader is directed to David Barker's "Television Production Techniques as Communication," in Horace Newcomb, ed., *Television: The Critical View*, 4th ed. (New York: Oxford University Press, 1987), pp. 179–96.

5. Edward Sorel, "The Noble Cos," *Nation* (September 6, 1986), p. 166.

6. Jeff Danziger, "Advice on Being a Father, Cosby-Style," *Christian Science Monitor* (June 20, 1986), p. 24.

7. Sandra Dickerson—personal correspondence, February 21, 1989.

8. Quoted in "Sitcoms Called Yuppie Paradise," *Variety* (June 10, 1987), p. 35.

CHAPTER 7: THE SOCIOCULTURAL IMPLICATIONS OF
THE COSBY SHOW

1. Quoted in Brad Darrach, "Cosby!" *Life* (June 1985), p. 39.

2. Kevin D. Thompson, "Cosby's $20 Million Gift: A Source of Funds—and Hope," *Black Enterprise* (February 1989), p. 27.

3. Quoted in Harry F. Waters, "Cosby's Fast Track," *Newsweek* (September 2, 1985), p. 54.

4. Walter M. Brasch, *Cartoon Monickers: An Insight into the Animation Industry* (Bowling Green, Ohio: Bowling Green University Popular Press, 1983).

5. Harry F. Waters, "TV's New Racial Hue," *Newsweek* (January 25, 1988), p. 52. See also Roger Simon, "Want a Clue About America? Check Out Our Favorite Shows," *TV Guide* (April 5, 1986), p. 2; and Morry Roth, "Black Inroads on Broadcasting: Dramatic Change in U.S. TV Audience and Viewing," *Variety* (December 18, 1985), p. 33.

6. See, for example, Jack Beatty, "A Cultural Encounter," *Boston Globe Magazine* (November 17, 1985), p. 14 +.

7. Cited in "Racial Stereotypes Persist," *USA Today* (August 1988), p. 12—not the newspaper, but a publication of the Society for the Advancement of Education. See also the editorial "Rescuing Black Males" in the *Christian Science Monitor*, July 24, 1990, p. 20.

8. Linda K. Fuller, "Enculturation: An Axiomatic Theory of Mass Communication," Paper presented to the Fifth International Conference on Culture and Communication, Philadelphia, 1983. I tracked down the dictionary definition to Melville J. Herskovits's book *Man and His Works: The Science of Culture* (1948).

9. Martha Bayles, "Holidays and the Huxtables," *Wall Street Journal* (December 14, 1987), p. 22.

10. Informal Q&A session of the International Radio and Television Society (IRTS) faculty/industry seminar, New York City, February 9, 1991. Note: There is an insightful profile of Warren Littlefield by Bill Carter in the August 11, 1991, edition of the *New York Times*, p. H25.

11. "Cosby Show prepares sign off," *Union-News* (March 6, 1992), p. 2.

12. Paul Taylor, "The Studio Audience for Television Situation Comedies," in Heinz-Dietrich Fischer and Stefan Reinhard Melnik, eds., *Entertainment: A Cross Cultural Examination* (New York: Hastings House, 1979), pp. 22–33.

13. Earl W. Foell, "The Cosby Clones: More Oases in the Vast TV Wasteland," *Christian Science Monitor* (May 14, 1985), p. 4. See also Jack Curry, "The Cloning of 'Cosby,' " *American Film* (October 1986), p. 49.

EPILOGUE

1. Lisa Schwarzbaum, "The Cosby Show's Last Laugh." *Entertainment Weekly* (May 1, 1992), p. 20.

2. Still, it was not *The Cosby Show's* highest-rated program, which was the episode that aired on January 22, 1987: "Say Hello to a Good Buy," featuring comics Sinbad and Gilbert Gottfried. It drew a 41.3/56, 82 million viewers, making it the most-watched episode in television history.

3. Brian Lowry, "Riot-weary L.A. viewers tune to 'Cosby' for relief." *Daily Variety* (May 1, 1992).

4. Telephone interview with Rosemary O'Brien, NBC Media Relations, Entertainment Programs, May 18, 1992. I am indebted to Ms. O'Brien for transcripts of Jess Marlow and Bill Cosby's statements regarding the final episode.

5. Richard Schickel (*Time*, May 11, 1992, p. 33) called the move for an hour of crisis counterprogramming "Tom Bradley's only visibly shrewd move during the Rodney King riots."

6. Rick Du Brow, " 'Cosby' Finale: Not All Drama Was in the Streets." *Los Angeles Times* (May 2, 1992), p. F1 +

7. Justin Lewis and Sut Jhally, "But TV needs to broaden its images of black experience." *Christian Science Monitor* (May 11, 1992), p. 19.

8. "Goodbye, Huxtables," *Christian Science Monitor* (May 4, 1992), p. 20.

References

Adler, Bill. *The Cosby Wit: His Life and Humor*. New York: Corevan Publishers, 1986.

Adler, Richard P., ed. *All in the Family: A Critical Appraisal*. New York: Praeger, 1979.

Alley, Robert S., and Irby B. Brown. *Murphy Brown: Anatomy of a Sit-Com*. New York: Delta, 1990.

Alsop, Ronald. "In TV Viewers' Favorite 1987 Ads, Offbeat Characters Were the Stars." *Wall Street Journal* (March 3, 1988): 19.

Ang, Ien. *Watching Dallas: Soap Opera and the Melodramatic Imagination*. New York: Methuen & Co., Ltd., 1985.

Appelo, Tim. "It's Cosby's Brood vs. the Radical Dude." *Entertainment Weekly* (August 31, 1990): 32–35.

Attallah, Paul. "The Unworthy Discourse: Situation Comedy in Television." In Willard D. Rowland, Jr., and Bruce Watkins, eds., *Interpreting Television: Current Research Perspectives*. Beverly Hills, Calif.: Sage Publications, 1984, pp. 222–49.

Barker, David. "Television Production Techniques as Communication." *Critical Studies in Mass Communication* 2 (1985): 234–46.

Barnes, Peter W. "Viacom Sells Rights to 'Cosby' Reruns in New York Area." *Wall Street Journal* (November 7, 1986): 15.

Barnes, Peter W. " 'Cosby' Producers File Suit to Protect Profits on Reruns." *Wall Street Journal* (March 13, 1987): 7.

Barthes, Roland. *Mythologies*. New York: Hill & Wang, 1972.

Battaglio, Stephen. "Family Feud: 'The Simpsons' vs. 'Cosby.' " *Adweek* (June 4, 1990): 17.

Bayles, Martha. "Television: The Problem with Post-Racism." *New Republic* (August 5, 1985): 25.

Bayles, Martha. "Holidays and the Huxtables." *Wall Street Journal* (December 14, 1987): 22.

Bayles, Martha. "The Fall of the House of Huxtable." *Wall Street Journal* (April 18, 1988): 22.

Beatty, Jack. "A Cultural Encounter." *Boston Globe Magazine* (November 17, 1985): 14.

Behar, Richard. "Bill Cosby Versus Bill Cosby." *Forbes* (November 14, 1988): 45.

Behrens, Steve. "Billion Dollar Bill." *Channels of Communication* (January-February 1986): 13.

Belkin, Lisa. "First Week of 'People Meters.' " *New York Times* (September 24, 1987): C28.

Bennett, W. Lance. "Myth, Ritual, and Political Control." *Journal of Communication* 30, no. 4 (Autumn 1980): 166–79.

Bennetts, Leslie. "Bill Cosby Begins Taping NBC Series." *New York Times* (August 6, 1984): C20.

Berle, Milton. "Talking with Bill Cosby: 'My Wife Helped Me Become a Better Person.' " *Redbook* (June 1987): 72.

Berry, Venise T. "From 'Good Times' to 'The Cosby Show': Perceptions of Changing Televised Images Among Black Fathers and Sons." Paper presented at the Speech Communication Association, 76th annual meeting, Chicago, 1990.

"Bill Cosby: The Doctor Is in." *Saturday Evening Post* (April 1985): 42.

"Bill Cosby's Two Wives." 1. Audrey Edwards, "At Home with Camille Cosby"; 2. Judith Regan, "Phylicia's Romantic New Marriage." *Ladies Home Journal* (April 1985): 32.

Billings, Victoria. "Culture by the Millions: Audience as Innovator." In Sandra J. Ball-Rokeach and Muriel G. Cantor, eds., *Media, Audience, and Social Structure.* Newbury Park, Calif.: Sage Publications, 1986.

"Black Viewers Turn to NBC." *Channels of Communication* (November 1987): 64.

Blair, C.J. "Writing about 'The Cosby Show.' " *English Journal* 77, no. 6 (October 1988): 61.

Blosser, Betsy J., and Donald F. Roberts. "Children's Understanding of Themes in Prosocial TV Shows: A Study of 'Fat Albert and the Cosby Kids.' " Paper presented at International Communication Association annual meeting, May 1986 at Chicago.

Blum, Richard A., and Richard D. Lindhelm. *Primetime: Network Television Programming.* Boston: Focal Press, 1987.

Blumler, Jay. "European-American Differences in Communication Research." In Everett M. Rogers and Francis Balle, eds., *The Media Revolution in America and in Western Europe.* Volume 2 in the Paris-Stanford Series. Norwood, N.J.: Ablex Publishing Corp., 1985, pp. 185–199.

Bogle, Donald. *Blacks in American Films and Television: An Encyclopedia.* New York: Garland Publishing, 1988.

Bogle, Donald. *Toms, Coons, Mulattoes, Mammies & Bucks: An Interpretive History of Blacks in American Films.* New York: Continuum, 1989.

Boyer, Peter J. " 'Cosby' Captioning Sparks Dispute." *New York Times* (January 6, 1986): C16.

Boyer, Peter J. " 'Cosby' Reruns Give Stations an Intimidating Weapon." *New York Times* (July 25, 1988): D8.

Brasch, Walter M. *Cartoon Monickers: An Insight into the Animation Industry.* Bowling Green, Ohio: Bowling Green University Popular Press, 1983.

Breen, Myles, and Farrel Corcoran. "Myth in the Television Discourse." *Communication Monographs* 49 (June 1982): 127–36.

Breen, Myles, and Farrel Corcoran. "Myth, Drama, Fantasy Theme, and Ideology in Mass Media." In Brenda Dervin and Melvin J. Voight, eds., *Progress in Communication Sciences*. VII. Norwood, N.J.: Ablex Publishing Corp., 1986, pp. 195–223.

Britt-Gibson, Donna. "Cover Story: The Cos, Family Man for the '80s." *USA Today* (December 23, 1986): D1.

"Brooklyn finds 'Cosby Show' Good for Business—and Gossip." *New York Times* (April 28, 1985): 1.

Brooks, Tim, and Earle Marsh. *The Complete Directory of Prime Time Network TV Shows, 1946-Present*. 4th ed. New York: Ballantine Books, 1988.

Brothers, Dr. Joyce. "If You Want to Be a Better Parent..." *TV Guide* (March 4–10, 1989): 22–25.

Brown, Barbara M., Erica W. Austin, and Donald F. Roberts. " 'Real Families' Versus 'Television Families': Children's Perceptions of Realism in The Cosby Show." Paper presented at the International Communication Association, New Orleans, La., 1987.

Brown, Ben, and Eric Marsden. "Cosby Cheers S. Africa family." *USA Today* (August 29, 1985): 1.

Brown, Patricia Leigh. "Where America Feels at Home: The Sitcom Living Room." *New York Times* (January 29, 1987): C1.

Buck, Jerry. "NBC Scores Smashing Victory in Nielsen Television Ratings." *Union News* (February 3, 1989): 32.

Cantor, Muriel. *Prime Time TV: Content and Control*. Beverly Hills, Calif.: Sage Publications, 1980.

Cantor, Muriel. *The Hollywood TV Producer: His Work and His Audience*. 2nd ed. New Brunswick, N.J.: Transaction Books, 1988.

Cantor, Muriel. "Prime-time Fathers: A Study in Continuity and Change." *Critical Studies in Mass Communication* 7, no. 3 (September 1990): 275–85.

Cantor, Muriel. "The American Family on Television: From Molly Goldberg to Bill Cosby." *Journal of Comparative Family Studies* 22, no. 2 (Summer 1991): 205–16.

Carey, James W., ed. *Media, Myths, and Narratives: Television and the Press*. Newbury Park, Calif.: Sage Publications, 1988.

"Carsey-Werner Wants NBC to Foot Bill for 'Cosby' Show." *Broadcasting* (March 26, 1990): 41.

Carter, Bill. "The Man Who Owns Prime Time: NBC's Brandon Tartikoff." *New York Times Magazine* (March 4, 1990): 23 + .

Carter, Bill. "In the Huxtable World, Parents Knew Best." *New York Times* (April 26, 1992): H1 + .

Carter, Bill. "Big Stakes for Bill Cosby." *Sunday Republican* (November 3, 1991): TV3.

Carter, R. G. "TV's Black Comfort Zone for Whites." *Television Quarterly* 33 (1988): 29–34.

Chang, Ikchin, and Gary R. Heald. "Pattern Analysis: An Alternative Conceptual and Methodological Approach to Measuring Audience Behaviors and Media Effects." Paper presented at the World Communication Association Conference, Singapore, 1989.

Cherry, Dianne L. "The Effects of Exposure to *The Cosby Show* on Social Attitudes." Paper submitted to the Minorities and Communication Division, Association for Education in Journalism and Mass Communication 1988 annual convention in Portland, Oregon.

Cieply, Michael. "Thursdays Spell Trouble for the Huxtables." *Wall Street Journal* (September 25, 1986): 28.

Citrin, Jack, Donald Philip Green, and David O. Sears. "White Reactions to Black Candidates: When Does Race Matter?" *Public Opinion Quarterly* 54 (Spring 1990): 74–96.

Cohen, Joel H. *Cool Cos: The Story of Bill Cosby.* New York: Scholastic Book Services, 1972.

Collins, Monica. "Cover Story: Time Flies While Cosby, 50, Has Fun." *USA Today* (August 31, 1987): 1.

"Conversation with Jay Sandrich." *Videography* (Fall 1986): 62.

Cosby, William Henry, Jr. "An Integration of the Visual Media via Fat Albert and the Cosby kids into the Elementary School Curriculum, as a Teachers Aid and Vehicle to Achieve Increased Learning." Unpublished dissertation, University of Massachusetts, 1976.

" 'Cosby' Barter Minute Go to P&G, GF, Group W." *Broadcasting* (May 9, 1988).

"Cosby Barter Plan Checklist." Viacom Enterprises.

" 'Cosby': Off-network's Biggest Deal Ever." *Broadcasting* (September 12, 1988): 76.

"The Cosby Factor." Viacom International, 1988.

"The Cosby Facts." Viacom International, 1988.

"The Cosby Sanction." *The New Republic* (August 25, 1986): 7.

"The Cosby Show. Changing the Balance of Power." Viacom International, 1988.

" 'Cosby Show' Wins Award for Showing Human Values." *Jet* (August 12, 1985): 34.

" 'Cosby' Takes $131-Mil to Bank After Sales in Five TV Markets." *Variety* (December 3, 1986): 46.

Crawford, Bobby. " 'The Cosby Show' Was Profound, Influential—and Indispensable." *Los Angeles Times* (May 11, 1992).

Cripps, Thomas. "Stepin Fetchit and the Politics of Performance." In Paul Loukides and Linda K. Fuller, eds., *Beyond the Stars: Stock Characters in American Popular Film.* Bowling Green, Ohio: Popular Press, 1990, pp. 35–98.

Crook, David. " 'Cosby' Producers Seek to Halt Viacom Buyout." *Los Angeles Times* (May 20, 1987): IV–2.

Cummings, Melbourne S. "The Changing Image of the Black Family on Television." *Journal of Popular Culture* 22 (Fall 1988): 75–85.

Cunningham, Kim. "How the Superhackers Stack Up." *World Tennis* (October 1985): 28.

Curry, Jack. "The Cloning of 'Cosby.' " *American Film* (October 1986): 49.

Curry, Jack. "Huxtables Help Keep Viewers Happy." *USA Today* (June 13, 1989): 3D.

Danziger, Jeff. "Advice on Being a Father, Cosby-style." *Christian Science Monitor* (June 20, 1986): 24.

Darrach, Brad. "Cosby!" *Life* (June 1985): 35.

Dates, Jannette L. and William Barlow, eds. *Split Image: African Americans in the Mass Media.* Washington, D.C.: Howard University Press, 1990.

Davidson, Bill. "I Must Be Doing Something Right." *McCall's* (April 1, 1985): 2.

Dempsey, John. "$81.9–Mil Is 'Cos' Enough for Concern." *Variety* (February 10, 1988): 89.

Donlon, Brian. " 'Cosby,' the Star of NBC's Stellar Year." *USA Today* (April 23, 1986): 1D.

Donlon, Brian. " 'Cosby' Producers up the Ante with NBC." *USA Today* (March 22, 1990): 1D.

Doty, William G. *Mythology: The Study of Myths and Rituals.* University: University of Alabama Press, 1986.

Dougherty, Philip H. "Cosby Rerun Ad Time Is Sold for $60 Million." *New York Times* (September 24, 1987): C28.

Downing, John D.H. " 'The Cosby Show' and American Racial Discourse." In Geneva Smitherman-Donaldson and Teun A. van Dijk, eds., *Discourse and Discrimination.* Detroit: Wayne State University Press, 1988, pp. 46–73.

Du Brow, Rick. " 'Cosby' Finale: Not All Drama Was in the Streets." *Los Angeles Times* (May 2, 1992):F1 + .

Dupree, Adolph. "Mirror, Mirror on the Wall: Reflections of *The Cosby Show*." *about . . . time* (January 1985): 8–11.

Dyson, Michael. "Bill Cosby and the Politics of Race." *Z Magazine* (September 1989).

Edmundson, Mark. "Father Still Knows Best." *Channels of Communication* (June 1986): 71.

Edrei, M.J. "The Cosby Scrapbook: America's Favorite T.V. Family." Teaneck, N.J.: Sharon Publications, 1986.

Ehrenstein, David. "The Color of Laughter." *American Film* (September 1988): 8–11.

Eisenach, Allen. "Creating Cosby: The Power of Television." *Media & Values* 35 (Spring 1986): 10–11.

Ellis, John. *Visible Fictions: Cinema, Television, Video.* London: Routledge & Kegan Paul, 1982.

England, David A. "Television and Our Humanity." *English Journal* 74, no. 8 (December 1985): 61–64.

Ephron, Delia. "TV Families: Clinging to the Tried and Untrue." *New York Times* (June 26, 1988): 2–1.

Fazal, S., and M. Wober. *The Cosby Show: Some Black and White Audience Perceptions and Possibilities.* London: Independent Broadcasting Authority, November 1989.

"Federal Judge Denies Move to Block Sale of Viacom." *Wall Street Journal* (June 3, 1987): 22.

Feldman, Gayle. "The Best-Seller Blues: Hard Lessons from a Cosby Book." *New York Times Book Review* (June 10, 1990): 11 + .

Ferguson, Marjorie. "Images of Power and the Feminist Fallacy." *Critical Studies in Mass Communication* 7, no. 7 (September 1990): 215–70.

Fischer, Heinz-Dietrich, and Stefan Reinhard Melnik, eds. *Entertainment: A Cross-Cultural Examination.* New York: Hastings House, 1979.

Fiske, John, and John Hartley. *Reading Television.* London: Methuen & Co., Ltd., 1978.

Flinn, John. "There's 'Cosby' and 'Boss,' and Then Everybody Else." *Channels of Communication* (Field Guide 1988): 75.

Flinn, John. "Local Stations: Laughing All the Way to the News." *Channels of Communication* (April 1988): 9.

Foell, Earl W. "The Cosby Clones: More Oases in the Vast TV Wasteland." *Christian Science Monitor* (May 14, 1985): 4.

Foell, Earl W. "More Communication Needed—for Superpowers as well as Families:

'The Cosby Show' as Model for Family Communication." *Christian Science Monitor* (December 15, 1987): 3.

Frank, Alan Dodds. "When Smoke Gets in Your Eyes." *Forbes* (May 5, 1986): 135.

Fuller, Linda K. "Enculturation: An Axiomatic Theory of Mass Communication." Paper presented at Fifth International Conference on Culture and Communication in Philadelphia, 1983.

Fuller, Linda K. "Marketing a Star to and Through the Media: The Cosby Case." Paper presented at Popular Culture Association annual meeting, April 1986 at Atlanta, Georgia.

Fuller, Linda K. "Audience Appeal of *The Cosby Show*: How It Cuts Across Cultural and Demographic Boundaries." Workshop for Communication, Culture, Socialism Conference, April 1988 at Carlton University, Ottawa, Canada.

Fuller, Linda K. "Research on Ritualistic Television-Viewing: The Loyal Audience of *The Cosby Show* Worldwide." Workshop on Audience Research, IAMCR Conference and XVIth General Assembly, July 1988 at Barcelona, Spain.

Fuller, Linda K. "Systems-Theoretical Aspects of Popular Culture and Mass Communication." In Ray B. Browne and Marshall W. Fishwick, eds., *Symbiosis: Popular Culture and Other Fields*. Bowling Green, Ohio: Bowling Green State University Popular Press, 1988, pp. 137–45.

Fuller, Linda K. "*Cosby* in the Caribbean: Audience Data on *The Cosby Show*." Paper presented at the Seventh Annual Intercultural and International Communication Conference, February 1990 at Miami, Florida.

Fuller, Linda K. "Comedy Across Cultures: A Case Study of *The Cosby Show*." Paper presented at the Tenth International Humor Congress, July 1992 at Paris France.

Fuller, Linda K., and Lilless McPherson Shilling. *Communicating Comfortably: Your Guide to Overcoming Speaking and Writing Anxieties*. Amherst, Mass.: HRD Press, 1990.

Fury, Kathleen. "Witness the Humors of Bill Cosby." *TV Guide* (October 13–19, 1984): 35.

Gabor, Andrea. "Television's Tyranny of Numbers." *US News & World Report* (September 8, 1986): 46.

Gans, Herbert J. "The Famine in American Mass-Communications Research: Comments on Hirsch, Tuchman, and Gecas." *American Journal of Sociology* 77, no. 4 (January 1972): 697–705.

Gates, Henry Louis, Jr. "TV's Black World Turns—But Stays Unreal." *New York Times* (November 12, 1989): H1 +.

Gay, Verne. " 'Cosby' Smashes Upfront Records." *Advertising Age* 57 (June 30, 1986): 1.

Gerard, Jeremy. " 'Cosby' Reruns Fail." *New York Times* (October 10, 1988): 26.

Gerard, Jeremy. "Producers Carsey and Werner: What Have They Done for Us Lately?" *New York Times* (November 25, 1990): 54 +.

Gerbner, George. "Cultural Indicators: The Third Voice." In George Gerbner, Larry P. Gross, and William H. Melody, eds., *Communications Technology and Social Policy: Understanding the New "Cultural Revolution."* New York: John Wiley & Sons, 1973, pp. 555–573.

Gerbner, George. "Telling Stories in the Information Age." In Brent D. Rubin, ed., *Information and Behavior*. New Brunswick, N.J.: Transaction Books, 1987.

Gerbner, George. "Symbolic Functions of Violence and Terror." Keynote address at the Conference on Communication in Terrorist Events, March 1988 at Emerson College.

Gerbner, George, and Kathleen Connolly. "Television as New Religion." *New Catholic World* (March–April 1978): 52–56.

Gerbner, George, Larry Gross, Michael Morgan, and Nancy Signorelli. "Living with Television: The Dynamics of the Cultivation Process." In Jennings Bryant and Dolf Zillman, eds., *Perspectives on Media Effects*. Hillsdale, N.J.: Lawrence Erlbaum Associates, 1986.

Gillespie, Judy. "The Cosby Show's Secret Ingredient." *Family Circle* (November 5, 1985): 88.

Gitlin, Todd. *Inside Prime Time*. New York: Pantheon Books, 1985.

Gitlin, Todd, ed. *Watching Television*. New York: Pantheon Books, 1986.

Goethals, Gregor T. *The TV Ritual: Worship at the Video Altar*. Boston: Beacon Press, 1981.

"Goodbye, Huxtables." *Christian Science Monitor* (May 4, 1992): 20.

Goodgame, Dan, with Bill Cosby. "I Do Believe in Control." *Time* (September 28, 1987): 62–64.

Goodman, Ellen. "Huxtable Family Made Good parenting Look Possible. *Union-News* (May 1, 1992): 19.

Gray, Herman. "Television and the New Black Man: Black Male Images in Prime Time Situation Comedy." *Media, Culture and Society* 8, no. 2 (1986): 223–242.

Greeley, Andrew. "Today's Morality Play: The Sitcom." *New York Times* (May 17, 1987): H1.

Griffin, Cynthia, and George Hill. "Bill Cosby: In Our Living Rooms for 20 Years." *Ebony Images: Black Americans and Television*. Los Angeles, Calif.: Daystar Publications, 1986.

Grossberger, Lewis. "Home Sweet Clone." *Channels of Communication* (September 1986): 55.

Haley, Alex. "Talking with Cosby." *Ladies Home Journal* (June 1985): 30.

Haley, Kathy. "Now COSBY's Campaign." *Channels of Communication* (September 1988): 29.

Hall, Jane. "Bill Cosby Huffs and Puffs on and off His Sitcom, But His TV Kids Say Father Knows Best." *People* (December 10, 1984): 141.

Halverson, Guy. "The 50 Best-Selling Books of the '80s." *Christian Science Monitor* (February 14, 1990): 12.

Hamamoto, Darrell Y. *Nervous Laughter: Television Situation Comedy and Liberal Democratic Ideology*. New York: Praeger, 1989.

Hickey, Neil. "Decade of Change, Decade of Choice." *TV Guide* (December 9, 1989): 29–32.

Higgins, George V. "Charged the Light Brigade (Thursday Night TV Viewing)." *Wall Street Journal* (December 23, 1985): 13.

Hill, Doug. "The 'Cosby' Push Wasn't Going for Laughs: 'We Gotta Confuse 'Em and Scare 'Em.' " *TV Guide* (May 7, 1988): 3.

Himmelstein, Hal. *Television Myth and the American Mind*. New York: Praeger, 1984.

Hobson, Dorothy. *Crossroads: The Drama of a Soap Opera*. London: Methuen, 1982.

Hogart, Simon. "Black Gold." *The Listener* (March 1988): 7.

Horowitz, Susan. "Sitcom Domesticus—A Species Endangered by Social Change." *Channels of Communication* 10 (September/October 1984): 22 + .

Intintoli, Michael James. *Taking Soaps Seriously: The World of "Guiding Light."* New York: Praeger Special Studies, 1984.

Jhally, Sut and Justin Lewis. *Enlightened Racism: The Cosby Show, Audiences, and the Myth of the American Dream.* Boulder, CO: Westview Press, 1992.

Japp, Phyllis M. "Gender and Work in the 1980s: Television's Working Women as Displaced Persons." *Women's Studies in Communication* 14, no. 1 (Spring 1991): 49–74.

Johnson, Robert E. "Why Bill Cosby and Wife Camille Fight for Black Causes." *Jet* (May 31, 1982): 12–14.

Jones, Rachal. " 'Cosby Show' Broke Some Invidious Molds." *Chicago Tribune* (April 30, 1992).

Kalter, Joanmarie. "Yes, There Are More Blacks on TV—But Mostly to Make Viewers Laugh." *TV Guide* (August 13, 1988): 26.

Karras, Alex. "The Real Men on TV—and the Wimps." *TV Guide* (August 11–23, 1985): 6.

Kastor, Elizabeth. "They Love Cosby in Washington." *The Morning Union* (September 30, 1985): 18.

Katz, Elihu. "Can Authentic Cultures Survive New Media?" *Journal of Communications* 27 (1977): 113–21.

Kellner, Douglas. "TV, Ideology, and Emancipatory Popular Culture." *Socialist Review* 45 (May–June 1979).

Kenneally, Christopher. "Bill Cosby Agrees with This Doctor." *Brookline Citizen* (April 25, 1985): 1.

Kettelkamp, Larry. *Bill Cosby: Family Funny Man.* New York: Wanderer Books, 1987.

Kimball, Mary. "Making Up Is Fun to Do for Cosby Show Artists." *The Sunday Republican* (January 4, 1987): D–1.

King, Coretta Scott. "Goodbye, Bill." *TV Guide* (April 25, 1992): 18–21.

Klein, Todd. "Bill Cosby: Prime Time's Favorite Father." *Saturday Evening Post* (April 1986): 42.

Kneale, Dennis. "Viacom Plans to Auction Off Advertising for Reruns of 'Cosby' Get Bad Reviews." *Wall Street Journal* (January 29, 1988): 24.

Knight, Bob. "Year of the Sitcom for TV Nets: 'Cosby' Sets Precedent." *Variety* (December 4, 1985): 1.

Kogan, Rick. "Finale Reminds Us How the Series Provided Honest Laughter While Also Raising the Level of Network TV." *Chicago Tribune* (April 30, 1992).

Landro, Laura, Paul Duke, Jr., and William Power. "Same Old Story: NBC Wins Suit with Hwesu S. Murray over 'Cosby' Idea." *Wall Street Journal* (July 29, 1987): 21.

Latham, Caroline. *Bill Cosby—For Real.* New York: Tor Books, 1985.

"Lawsuit over 'Cosby' Idea." *New York Times* (May 20, 1988): 22.

Leonard, John. "Leave It to Cosby." *New York* (October 22, 1984): 54.

Lerner, David. "Looking at Number One." *Marketing & Media Decisions* (June 1986): 86.

Lewis, Justin and Sut Jhally. "But TV Needs to Broaden its Images of Black Experience." *Christian Science Monitor* (May 11, 1992): 19.

Linderman, Lawrence. "Playboy Interview: Bill Cosby." *Playboy* (December 1985).

Louden-Hanes, Marie. "Theo's Role in *The Cosby Show.*" Working paper.

Lovece, Frank. " 'Cosby' and Black Artists: Is Exposure Enough?" *Channels of Communication* (May 1988): 17.

Lowry, Brian. "Riot-weary L.A. Viewers Tune to "Cosby' for Relief." *Daily Variety* (May 1, 1992).

Lull, James, ed. *World Families Watch Television*. Newbury Park, Calif.: Sage Publications, 1988.

MacDonald, J. Fred. *Blacks and White TV*. Chicago: Nelson-Hall Publishers, 1983.

Marc, David. *Demographic Vistas: Television in American Culture*. Philadelphia: University of Pennsylvania Press, 1984.

Marc, David. *Comic Visions: Television Comedy and American Culture*. Boston: Unwin Hyman, 1989.

Marguiles, Lee. "Tartikoff Leads NBC out of Wilderness." *Los Angeles Times* (April 24, 1985): V1–1.

Marschall, Rick. *The History of Television*. New York: Gallery Books, 1986.

Marsden, Michael T. "Television Viewing as Ritual." In Ray B. Browne, ed., *Rituals and Ceremonies in Popular Culture*. Bowling Green, Ohio: Bowling Green University Popular Press, 1980, pp. 120–24.

Masterman, Len, ed. *Television Mythologies: Stars, Shows & Signs*. London: Comedia Publishing Group, 1984.

Matabane, Paula W. "Television and the Black Audience: Cultivating Moderate Perspectives on Racial Integration." *Journal of Communication* 38, no. 4 (Autumn 1988): 21–31.

McBride, James. "Cosby: The Secret Passions of TV's Biggest Star." *US* (October 21, 1985): 20.

McBride, James. "The Evolution of a Comic Named Cosby." *Philadelphia Enquirer* (November 17, 1985).

McCain, Nina. "The Significance of 'Cosby.' " *Boston Globe* (February 20, 1986): 69.

McConnell, Frank. *Storytelling and Mythmaking Images from Film and Literature*. New York: Oxford University Press, 1979.

McCroban, Donna. *Prime Time/Our Time: America's Life and Times Through the Prism of Television*. Rocklin, Calif.: Prima Publishing and Communications, 1990.

McGuigan, Cathleen. "Papa Cosby Knows Best." *Newsweek* (May 19, 1986): 70.

McQuail, Denis, Jay G. Blumler, and J. R. Brown. "The Television Audience: A Revised Perspective." In Denis McQuail, ed., *Sociology of Mass Communications*. Harmondsworth: Penguin, 1972, pp.135–65.

McWilliams, Michael. "Cos Celebre." *Rolling Stone* (December 18, 1986– January 1, 1987): 125.

Meisler, Andy. "Jay Sandrich: Ace of Pilots." *Channels of Communication* (October 1986): 50.

Merritt, Bishetta D. "Bill Cosby—TV Auteur?" *Journal of Popular Culture* 24, no. 4 (Spring 1991): 89–102.

Miller, Mark Crispin. "Deride and Conquer." In Todd Gitlin, ed., *Watching Television*. New York: Pantheon Books, 1986, pp. 182–228.

Millerson, Gerald. *Effective TV Production*. New York: Focal Press, 1976.

Moran, Brian. "Cosby's Image Pays Dividends." *Advertising Age* (May 12, 1986): 2.

Morley, David. *Family Television: Cultural Power and Domestic Leisure*. London: Comedia Publishing Group, 1986.

Morrison, Joy. "Television in South Africa: Reinforcing Apartheid or Initiating Social Integration?" Paper for the Ph.D. Convention, April 1986.

Morrow, Lance. "Video Warriers in Los Angeles." *Time* (May 11, 1992): 68.

Mufson, Steve. "The 'Cosby Plan' for South Africa." *Wall Street Journal* (July 30, 1986): 17.

Murphy, Brian, and Howard R. Pollio. "I'll Laugh If You Will ..." *Psychology Today* 7, no. 7 (December 1973): 106–110.

Muro, Mark. "Show's Values Gain Respect." *The Boston Sunday Globe* (April 19, 1992) A1+.

"NBC Wins 27 of 30 in Prime Time Final Stats." *Broadcasting* (April 27, 1987): 54.

Neale, Steve, and Frank Krutnick. *Popular Film and Television Comedy.* London: Routledge, 1990.

Newcomb, Horace. *TV: The Most Popular Art.* New York: Doubleday & Company, 1974.

Newcomb, Horace M. "American Television Criticism, 1970–1985." *Critical Studies in Mass Communication* 3 (1986): 217–28.

Newcomb, Horace, ed. *Television: The Critical View.* 4th ed. New York: Oxford University Press, 1987.

Newcomb, Horace M. "One Night of Prime Time: An Analysis of Television's Multiple Voices." In James W. Carey, ed., *Media, Myths, and Narratives: Television and the Press.* Newbury Park, Calif.: Sage Publications, 1988, pp. 88–112.

Newcomb, Horace, and Robert S. Alley. *The Producer's Medium: Conversations with Creators of American TV.* New York: Oxford University Press, 1983.

Newcomb, Horace, and Paul M. Hirsch. "Television as a Cultural Forum: Implications for Research." In Willard D. Rowland, Jr., and Bruce Watkins, eds., *Interpreting Television: Current Research Perspectives.* Beverly Hills, Calif.: Sage Publications, 1984, pp. 58–73.

Nielsen 1988 Report on Television. Northbrook, Ill.: A. C. Nielsen Co., 1988.

Nielsen 1989 Report on Television. Northbrook, Ill.: A. C. Nielsen Co., 1989.

Norment, Lynn. "The Cosby Show: The Real-Life Drama Behind Hit TV Show About a Black Family." *Ebony* (April 1985): 27.

O'Brien, Robert. "FCC: Cosby Application Rejected by Judge." *Channels of Communication* (November 1986): 11.

O'Brien, Shirley J. "You Can Tell Me the Truth about Anything ... I'll Still Love You." *Childhood Education* (Annual theme, 1989): 307–8.

O'Connell, John. " 'Cosby Show' Draws Praise for Views on Black Family." *Union-News* (January 25, 1989): 15.

O'Connor, John E. *American History/American Television: Interpreting the Video Past.* New York: Frederick Ungar, 1983.

O'Connor, John J. "Cosby in NBC Series on a New York Family." *New York Times* (September 20, 1984): C30.

O'Connor, John J. "An Update on 'The Cosby Show.' " *New York Times* (January 21, 1988): C26.

O'Connor, John J. "On TV, Less Separate, More Equal." *New York Times* (April 29, 1990): H1+.

Okrent, Daniel. "Cosby: The Early Years." *New England Monthly* (February 1987): 8.

Oliver, Stephanie Stokes. "A Father's Day Tribute: Bill Cosby Talks about Raising Children." *Essence* (June 1984): 126.

Pagano, Penny. "FBI Enlists Bill Cosby in Search for Missing Kids." *Los Angeles Times* (June 12, 1985): V1–1.

Pekurny, Robert. "The Production Process and Environment of NBC's 'Saturday Night Live.'" *Journal of Broadcasting* 24 (Winter 1980): 91.

Pollak, Kay. "The Cosby Phenomenon." *Aftonbladet* (March 27, 1987).

Pollard, Gayle. "From Amos 'n' Andy to Bill Cosby." *Boston Globe* (October 29, 1981).

Poussaint, Alvin F. "The Huxtables: Fact or Fantasy?" *Ebony* (October 1988): 74.

Prescott, Eileen. "The Networks Fight Back, Finally." *New York Times* (March 5, 1989): F4.

"Programming/Production: Viacom's Barter Play Seen As Wise Move but Poses Dilemma for Syndicators." *Television Radio Age* (February 8, 1988): 81.

"Racial Stereotypes Persist." *USA Today* (August 1988): 12.

Rapping, Elayne. *The Looking Glass World of Nonfiction TV*. Boston: South End Press, 1987.

Rashad, Ahmad, with Peter Bodo. *Rashad: Vikes, Mikes and Something on the Backside*. New York: Penguin, 1988.

Raspberry, William. "Cosby Show: Black or White?" *Washington Post* (November 5, 1984): A27.

Raspberry, William. "Cosby' Showed the World Life isn't Black and White." *Union-News* (April 29, 1992).

Ravage, John W. *Television: The Director's Viewpoint*. Boulder, Colo.: Westview Press, 1978.

Real, Michael R. *Mass-Mediated Culture*. Englewood Cliffs, N.J.: Prentice-Hall, 1977.

Real, Michael R. *Super Media: A Cultural Studies Approach*. Newbury Park, Calif.: Sage Publications, 1989.

Reep, Diana C., and Faye H. Dambrot. "Effects of Frequent Television Viewing on Stereotypes: 'Drip, Drip,' or 'Drench'?" *Journalism Quarterly* 66, no. 3 (Autumn 1989): 542+.

Reep, Diana C., and Faye H. Dambrot. "Lasting Images of TV Parents." *Family Perspective* 24, no. 2 (1990): 121–28.

Reeves, Jimmie L. "Television Stardom: A Ritual of Social Typification and Individualization." In James W. Carey, ed., *Media, Myths, and Narratives: Television and the Press*. Newbury Park, Calif.: Sage Publications, 1988, pp. 146–60.

Richburg, Keith B. "Cosby Show's Values Lauded: Reagan Aide Extols Effect on Black Children." *Washington Post* (May 31, 1986): A6.

Roth, Morry. "Black Inroads on Broadcasting: Dramatic Change in U.S. TV Audience and Viewing." *Variety* (December 18, 1985): 33.

Rothenberg, Fred. "'Cosby Show' Spurs NBC to Ratings Victory." *The Morning Union* (December 13, 1985): 24.

Rothstein, Mervyn. "Brooklyn Finds 'Cosby Show' Good for Business—and Gossip." *New York Times* (April 28, 1985): 44.

Rowland, Willard D., Jr., and Bruce Watkins. *Interpreting Television: Current Research Perspectives*. Beverly Hills, Calif.: Sage Publications, 1984.

"Running the Numbers: Mouth-Eye Coordination." *Channels of Communication* (March 1987): 64.

Safire, William. "On Language: People of Color." *New York Times Magazine* (November 20, 1989): 18.

Schickel, Richard. "How TV Failed to Get the Real Picture." *Time* (Maqy 11, 1992): 33.

Schwarzbaum, Lisa. "The Cosby Show's Last Laugh." *Entertainment Weekly* (May 1, 1992): 20–25.

Shankman, Arnold. "Black Pride and Protest: The Amos 'N' Andy Crusade." *Journal of Popular Culture* (Fall 1978): 236–52.

Sharbutt, Jay. " 'Cosby' Is First Major Victim of Guild strike." *Los Angeles Times* (March 7, 1985): V1–12.

Sherard, R.G., "Fact and Fiction: Viewer Perceptions of *The Cosby Show*." Paper presented to the American Association for Public Opinion Research, 1987.

Shiver, Jube, Jr. " 'Cosby Show' Asking $350,000 and up for Ads." *Los Angeles Times* (July 1, 1986): 1V–2.

Siegel, Ed. "Sitcom Alters Face of TV." *The Boston Sunday Globe* (April 19, 1992) A1 + .

Silverstone, Roger. *The Message of Television: Myth and Narrative in Contemporary Culture*. London: Heinemann Educational Books, 1981.

Silverstone, Roger. "Television Myth and Culture." In James W. Carey, ed., *Media, Myths, and Narratives: Television and the Press*. Newbury Park, Calif.: Sage Publications, 1988, pp. 20–47.

Simon, Roger. "Want a Clue About America? Check Out Our Favorite Shows." *TV Guide* (April 5, 1986): 2.

"Sitcoms Called Yuppie Paradise." *Variety* (June 10, 1987): 35.

"Sitcoms in Syndication: Too Much of a Good Thing?" *Broadcasting* (May 29, 1989): 48–9.

Skill, Thomas, James D. Robinson, and Samuel P. Wallace. "Portrayal of Families on Prime-Time TV: Structure, Type, and Frequency." *Journalism Quarterly* 64 (Summer, Autumn 1987): 360–68.

Smith, Charles C. "A Worthy Cos: Our Funniest Alum Pulls no Punches in His Support of Higher Education." *Massachusetts* (Winter 1990): 8–11.

Smith, Ronald L. *Cosby*. New York: St. Martin's Press, 1986.

Smith, Sally Bedell. "Cosby Puts His Stamp on a TV Hit." *New York Times* (November 18, 1984): B1.

Solomon, Jack. *The Signs of our Times*. Los Angeles, Calif.: JP Tarcher, 1988.

Sorell, Edward. "The Noble Cos." *Nation* (September 6, 1986): 166.

Sporkin, Elizabeth. "Cover Story: Man's New Uniform: Bold, Bright Knits." *USA Today* (January 23, 1987): D1.

Staples, Robert, and Terry Jones. "Culture, Ideology and Black Television Image." *Black Scholar* 16, no. 3 (May–June 1985): 10–20.

Steele, Shelby. *The Content of Our Character: A New Vision of Race in America*. New York: St. Martin's Press, 1990.

Stevenson, Richard W. " 'Cosby' Producers Strike It Rich." *New York Times* (December 23, 1988): D1.

Stewart, Sally Ann. "Cosby: The Undisputed King of TV." *USA Today* (December 5, 1985): 1–D.

Stone, Elizabeth. "In Today's TV Families, Who Knows Best?" *New York Times* (May 13, 1990): H30.

Surlin, Stuart H. "TV Program and Advertising Values: Perceptions by North American and Caribbean Viewers." Paper presented at the Intercultural Conference on Latin America and the Caribbean, February 1988 at Miami, Florida.

Tannenbaum, Percy H., ed. *The Entertainment Functions of Television*. Hillsdale, N.J.: Lawrence Erlbaum Associates, Publishers, 1980.

"Tartikoff Talks Counterprogramming to Critics in L.A." *Broadcasting* (January 15, 1990): 54.

Taylor, Ella. *Prime-Time Families: Television Culture in Postwar America*. Berkeley: University of California Press, 1990.

Taylor, Paul. "The Studio Audience for Television Situation Comedies." In Heinz-Dietrich Fischer and Stefan Reinhard Melnik, eds., *Entertainment: A Cross Cultural Examination*. New York: Hastings House, 1979, pp. 22–33.

Teachout, Terry. "Black, Brown and Beige." *National Review* (July 18, 1986): 59.

"Television as Myth and Ritual." *Communication Research Trends* 8, no. 1 (London: Centre for the Study of Communication and Culture), 1987.

Teltsch, Kathleen. "Blacks' Charities Struggle to Meet Cosby Challenge." *New York Times* (January 15, 1989): 1.

Terry, Sara. "The Conscience of 'The Cosby Show.' " *Christian Science Monitor* (February 12, 1987): 1.

Thompson, Kevin D. "Cosby's $20 Million Gift: A Source of Funds—and Hope." *Black Enterprise* (February 1989): 27.

Thorburn, David. *The Story Machine*. New York: Oxford University Press, 1990.

Toll, Robert C. *The Entertainment Machine: American Show Business in the Twentieth Century*. London: Oxford University Press, 1982.

Tomaselli, Keyan G., and Ruth Tomaselli. "Between Policy and Practice in the SABC, 1976–1981." In *Currents of Power: State Broadcasting in South Africa*. Durban: Richard Lyon, 1986.

Townley, Roderick. "Phylicia Ayers-Allen: She'll Show You the Serenity—But not the Strife." *TV Guide* (September 7–13, 1985): 27.

Townley, Roderick. "Television . . . Makes Us See One Another." Interview with Ralph Ellison. *TV Guide* (April 23, 1988): 3.

Turner, Lynn H. "Defining Family Theme: A Conceptual Approach with an Illustration from 'The Cosby Show' and 'Family Ties.' " Paper presented at the Popular Culture Association annual meeting, March 1987 at Montreal.

Turner, Richard. "Which Are TV's Best Sitcoms—and the Worst?" *TV Guide* (October 10, 1987): 2.

Ugwu-Oju, Dympna. "Black and No Place to Hide." *New York Times* (May 17, 1992): E17.

Ungar, Arthur. "What Makes 'The Cosby Show' TV's Top Situation Comedy?" *Christian Science Monitor* (May 1, 1985): 29.

Vamos, Mark N. "Cosby Could Stuff $500 Million More in Viacom's Pocket." *Business Week* (November 10, 1986): 42.

Van Vuuren, Daan P. "Children's Perception of and Identification with the Social Reality of 'The Cosby Show': A Comparison Between the USA and South Africa." Draft paper.

"Viacom Clients Playing Handball over 'Cosby.' " *Broadcasting* (November 13, 1989): 40.

"Viacom Enterprises Announces Plans to Bid the Cosby Barter Minute." Press release—January 27, 1988.

"Viacom May Rewrite the Book When 'Cosby' Makes Syndie Bow; Has 2 Series Pilots for NATPE." *Variety* (December 18, 1985): 33.

"Viacom Will Auction Spots in 'Cosby' Reruns." *Broadcasting* (February 1, 1988): 39.

Vitale, Thomas P. "They Call Themselves 'The Cosby Team.'" *Viacomments* (Fall 1987): 18–23.

Wahlgren, Anna. "Njut Av Cosby—Och Lar!" (Enjoy Cosby—and Learn.) Copyright pending.

Walley, Wayne. "Carsey-Werner: Cosby's Co-Pilots Stay Small and Lean." *Advertising Age* (June 16, 1986): 38.

Walley, Wayne. "TV Stations Factor in Big 'Cos' Price." *Advertising Age* (October 27, 1986): 2.

Walley, Wayne. "Cowabunga! Bart vs. Cos." *Advertising Age* (June 4, 1990): 3.

Warren, Elaine. "The 10 Most Attractive Men on TV." *TV Guide* (April 19–25, 1986): 4.

Washington, Mary Helen. "Please, Mr. Cosby, Build on Your Success." *TV Guide* (March 22–28, 1986): 4.

Waters, Harry F. "Cosby's Fast Track." *Newsweek* (September 2, 1985): 50–56.

Waters, Harry F. "Son of 'Fatherhood.'" *Newsweek* (September 14, 1987): 78.

Waters, Harry F. "TV's New Racial Hue." *Newsweek* (January 25, 1988): 52.

Waters, Harry F. "Family Feuds." *Newsweek* (April 23, 1990): 58–62.

Whetmore, Edward Jay. *American Electric.* New York: McGraw-Hill, 1992.

Wilson, Clint C. II, and Felix Gutierrez. *Minorities and Media: Diversity and the End of Mass Communication.* Beverly Hills, Calif.: Sage Publications, 1985.

Winston, Brian. "Cosby's New Show: A Hit and a Myth." *Channels of Communication* (January–February 1985): 63.

Wober, J. Mallory, and Barrie Gunter. "Television Audience Research at Britain's Independent Broadcasting Authority, 1974–1984." *Journal of Broadcasting and Electronic Media*, 30, no. 1. (Winter 1986): 15–31.

Wober, J. Mallory, and Barrie Gunter. *Television and Social Control.* New York: St. Martin's Press, 1988.

Woods, Harold, and Geraldine Woods. *Bill Cosby: Making America Laugh and Learn.* Minneapolis, Minn.: Dillon Press, 1983.

Wu, Zhengkang. "A Comparative Study of the Father/Husband Figure in Popular Prime-Time TV Series of the Fifties and the Eighties." Paper presented at the Popular Culture Association conference, Toronto, Canada, 1990.

Zacks, Richard. "'Cosby' Deal with WOR-TV Angers Many Stations." *TV Guide* (November 22–28, 1986): A–1.

"Zaleski: Times Are a' Changin': Syndication Is a Whole New Ball Game, Says Viacom Chief." *Television/Radio Age* (September 14, 1987): 49.

Zaleski, Joseph D. "The Impact of the Cosby Marketing Plan on Syndication." *Broadcast Daily* (February 27, 1988).

Zoglin, Richard. "A Giant Leap to no. 2: Programmer Brandon Tartikoff Leads NBC out of the Cellar." *Time* (December 3, 1984): 74.

Zoglin, Richard. "Prime Time's New First Family." *Time* (May 6, 1985): 88.

Zoglin, Richard. "Cosby, Inc.: He Has a Hot TV Series, a New Book—and a Booming Comedy Empire." *Time* (September 28, 1987): 56–60.

Zuckman, Harvey L. and Martin J. Gaynes. *Mass Communications Law in a Nutshell.* St. Paul, Minn.: West Publishing Co., 1977.

Index

About the Author

LINDA K. FULLER is an Assistant Professor in the Media Department at Worcester State College. She is the author of *Trips & Trivia: A Guide to Western Massachusetts* (1988) and *Chocolate Fads, Folklore, and Fantasies* (1992). Fuller co-edited *Beyond the Stars: Stock Characters in American Popular Film* (1990, with Paul Loukides) and co-authored *Communicating Comfortably: Your Guide to Overcoming Speaking and Writing Anxieties* (1990, with Lilless McPherson Shilling).

**Recent Titles in
Contributions to the Study of Popular Culture**